the **intercultural**

campus

Studies in the
Postmodern Theory of Education

Joe L. Kincheloe and Shirley R. Steinberg
General Editors

Vol. 97

PETER LANG
New York • Washington, D.C./Baltimore • Bern
Frankfurt am Main • Berlin • Brussels • Vienna • Oxford

greg tanaka

the intercultural
campus

transcending culture & power
in american higher education

PETER LANG
New York • Washington, D.C./Baltimore • Bern
Frankfurt am Main • Berlin • Brussels • Vienna • Oxford

Library of Congress Cataloging-in-Publication Data

Tanaka, Gregory Kazuo.
The intercultural campus: transcending culture and power
in American higher education / by Greg Tanaka.
p. cm. — (Counterpoints; vol. 97)
Includes bibliographical references and index.
1. College student development programs—United States.
2. Multicultural education—United States. 3. Multiculturalism—
Study and teaching (Higher)—United States. I. Title.
II. Series: Counterpoints (New York, N.Y.); vol. 97.
LB2343.4. T35   378.1'94—dc21   98-37867
ISBN 0-8204-4150-3
ISSN 1058-1634

Die Deutsche Bibliothek-CIP-Einheitsaufnahme

Tanaka, Greg:
The intercultural campus: transcending culture and power
in American higher education / Greg Tanaka.
–New York; Washington, D.C./Baltimore; Bern;
Frankfurt am Main; Berlin; Brussels; Vienna; Oxford: Lang.
(Counterpoints; Vol. 97)
ISBN 0-8204-4150-3

Cover design by Joni Holst

The paper in this book meets the guidelines for permanence and durability
of the Committee on Production Guidelines for Book Longevity
of the Council of Library Resources.

Printed in the United States of America

FOR MOM

How can the United States both respect diversity and find unity?

Renato Rosaldo

TABLE OF CONTENTS

FOREWORD

By Alexander W. Astin

In this remarkable book Greg Tanaka takes on one of our most difficult and challenging social dilemmas: how to create a cohesive community in a racially diverse society. It is entirely appropriate that he has chosen the college campus as his laboratory for examining this issue: if higher education, with its relatively protected environment and its tradition of openness to new ideas and differing points of view, proves unable to fashion workable solutions to our racial conflicts, then it is difficult to imagine how they can be resolved in the larger society.

Dr. Tanaka's use of "interculturalism"—the notion that there can be learning and sharing across difference in which no one culture dominates—offers a great deal of promise as a conceptual basis for creating community out of racial diversity within an educational framework. His empirical exploration of these possibilities (see chapters 2, 3, and 4) represents a creative blend of the best that social science research has to offer: a clearly defined problem, a rich combination of carefully designed qualitative and quantitative methodologies, and solid theoretical grounding.

Although it is difficult to do justice to his many important results and conclusions in this brief foreword, the one that stands out for me is the finding that some of our well-intentioned efforts to "diversify" our campuses by adding more race and ethnic diversity through our student bodies may prove counterproductive, *unless* they are accompanied by genuine programmatic efforts to emphasize diversity in the curriculum and co-curriculum. In other words, one cannot expect to create an intercultural campus *community* simply by mixing the different races together.

In short, regardless of your particular views on the issues of "diversity" and "multiculturalism," this book is recommended reading.

Alexander W. Astin
Allan M. Carrter Chair in Higher Education and
  Organizational Change, Emeritus
UCLA Graduate School of Education and Information
  Studies
Los Angeles, California

ACKNOWLEDGMENTS

The best stories you will ever hear are from your parents and grandparents. It is to them, and their memories, that I owe my deepest sense of obligation.

No one starts down the road of social change without the support of others who are close to you. To the following individuals I owe my thanks for their constant support and their dreams of a better world: Cindy Cruz, Laila Aaen, Betty Jones, Dorothy Nakama, Parker Johnson, Cheryl Teruya, Roberto Flores, Doug Toma, Bob Nip, Harold Chu, Brent Hinson, Elyse Garlock, Alma Andersson, Jackie Knight, Scott Zimmer, and Sandy Whitford, and Nicolas, Mike, Christine, and others at Peet's on San Vicente.

In addition, I owe special thanks to Alexander Astin, Peter McLaren, Paul Kroskrity, Art Cohen, James Diego Vigil, Mariko Tamanoi, Pat McDonough, Karen Brodkin, Jeannie Oakes, Danny Solorzano, Teshome Gabriel, Linda Sax, Bill Korn, Ann Walters, and Deborah Raupp from my years at UCLA; Steve Barris, Aurora Sanchez, Ruth Brown, Wayne Reeder, Rupert Trujillo, and Kathy Mulholland in the U.S. Teacher Corps in New Mexico; Roy Schotland and Dennis Hutchinson at Georgetown; Jay Light, Joe Bower, Jay Lorsch, and Dean Currie at Harvard; Jeremy Harrison at the University of Hawaii; and Louise Derman-Sparks at Pacific Oaks College for many of the methods and frameworks I used to organize the stories told in this book.

From the following individuals I learned how to use these stories to "see" a better place: Michelle Fine, Luis Alfaro, Reggie Daniel, Renato Rosaldo,

Dorinne Kondo, Edward Said, Ramona, Carlos Lenkersdorf, Wanda Pillow, Wanda Coleman, Christine Gailey, Peggy McIntosh, Norma Mendoza-Denton, Emily Martin, Michael Pavel, Robert Silverman, N. Brian Hu, Norm Denzin, Yvonna Lincoln, William G. Tierney, Michel Foucault, Michel de Certeau, and Mikhail Bakhtin, and in an earlier life, Mrs. Shevell, Mrs. Oliver, Mrs. Vesco, and Miss Tupica. It was Professor Nick Fersen at Williams College, however, who first urged me to write. From his Russian literature classes I learned how important it is for every human being to find connection to past and place.

To the people who worked in the trenches to evoke change at campuses I will call Pico College and Del Rey University we all owe a large debt of gratitude. As will be evident in the pages that follow, the courage of these individuals to test new models for diversity has shown us all it is indeed possible in a "shrinking" global society to transcend differences based on culture and power and move toward relations of interdependence and harmony.

In supporting the research reported in this book, The James Irvine Foundation and The Hewlett Foundation have confirmed once again that external funding can be used to turn hunches into practical frameworks for positive social interaction in an increasingly diverse United States. Special thanks are also due the Higher Education Research Institute at UCLA, the Kellogg Foundation, and the Association of American Colleges and Universities for providing rich venues in which to discuss diversity. Thanks are also due Christopher Myers, Joe Kincheloe, Shirley Steinberg, and Sophie Appel at Peter Lang Publishing who believed in this project from the beginning. Their support is greatly appreciated.

Finally, I continue to be energized by the dreams and passions of students, staff, and faculty at Pacific Oaks College and its Center for Democracy and Social Change where new models for human social behavior are hypothesized, discussed, and probed daily. It is from the combined spirit of the above influences in my life that I ask, "What new models will be hatched tomorrow?"

INTRODUCTION

In this book I argue the United States has not been adequately trained as a nation of people to comprehend and deal with its own internal racial and ethnic diversity—and that one result of this deficiency is the country's inability to know its purpose and place in history in the wake of the 9/11 World Trade Center bombings. To better prepare the U.S. for its future in a global society, I outline below an approach to diversity that departs from multicultural approaches and places U.S. colleges and universities in a lead role in charting a different direction for humanity.

This book presents findings from three studies performed over an eight-year period on race and ethnic diversity in U.S. colleges and universities. Findings reveal there are clear benefits to making diversity part of the college-going experience, particularly for white students. At the same time, results indicate that today's "multicultural" approaches can lead to increased conflict between ethnic groups and leave white members feeling alienated. To reclaim the original impetus of the nation's multicultural project, this book presents a framework for diversity that builds on the strengths of multiculturalism and promotes learning and sharing *across* difference where no culture dominates.

Written primarily for students and campus leaders at diverse campuses, the following chapters will also examine some of the theoretical assumptions underlying the social movements of "the Sixties." In challenging hierarchies linked to racism and sexism, these progressive strategies were not in all cases modified to take into account the influx of millions of new citizens from Latin America, Asia, and Africa and resulting nationwide "racial demographic shift."

I will argue that while some conservative think tanks addressed this demographic shift in ways that heightened fear among some white Americans, progressive strategies continued to focus on the same "categories of difference" that had rationalized legislative gains beginning with the Civil Rights Act of 1965 and including their progeny, affirmative action, ethnic studies, and bilingual education. While inserting the histories of people of color and other marginalized groups into the national discourse, these category-based approaches neglected to help members of "dominant" groups develop new and meaningful identities not based on superiority. In critiquing *structures* of culture and power, progressives in higher education arguably failed to move into a phase of individual human development and model building to create safe spaces where members of "dominant" groups can acquire identities and skills to participate as equals in a diverse world. If unintentional, it was an oversight conservatives would nonetheless mine with great success and growing ramifications today.

A second macro event should also be considered when reconstituting U.S. higher education for today's global, "transnational" context. While the 1960s based social change projects were introducing into American education the stories of people of color, women, and lesbian, gay, bisexual, and transgendered individuals, to name a few, the same sub-group of conservatives that associated diversity with uncertainty and fear was quietly changing the underlying structure of the democracy. One goal of this book is to trigger fresh thinking about how progressives might reposition future work in social change to collaboratively plan—in concert with a new strategy for diversity—a different democracy that is more "participatory" and prepares the U.S. for greater interdependence with other nations in a diverse global society.

In chapter 1, I begin with a storytelling to demonstrate how current approaches to diversity may be dependent on practices that unintentionally pit one group against another—African Americans against Whites, women against men, heterosexuals against lesbian, gay, bisexual, transgendered ("LGBT") individuals, etc. Arguably, until Americans can let go of a tendency to see the world in binary "us-against-them" terms, the benefits of diversity programs will never be fully realized. Following 9/11, the need for non-oppositional approaches to human social interaction seems all the more urgent.

To examine racial fragmentation in a particular context, chapter 2 presents a case study of the first U.S. college to respond to growing ethnic and racial diversity in its surrounding metropolitan region by making itself multicultural in all its major functions—student affairs, the core curriculum, faculty hiring, and other key areas. While a major step in the evolution of diversity efforts, it also became clear that this first "multicultural model" had its limitations. This study shows that while multicultural approaches can successfully incorporate the stories of historically silenced groups like African Americans, Latinos, women, and lesbians and gays, they can also: (1) magnify the fragmentation of a campus community, (2) overlook the needs of white students, and (3) reproduce the very relations of "oppressor" and "oppressed" they decry.

Does this mean all formal efforts to teach diversity should now be removed from the college-going experience? The answer to this question should be a resounding "No!" Reporting findings from a nationwide quantitative study of 25,000 students attending 159 U.S. colleges and universities, chapter 3 will show that when white college students participate in cross-cultural academic and social experiences on their campuses, they experience gains in important measures, *including overall satisfaction with college.* Given America's current climate of fear and uncertainty linked to race, global capitalism, and anti-U.S. sentiment, I present these findings in some detail, as they lend a degree of hope for humankind in general and the U.S. in particular.

But how would a college or university "teach diversity" if current approaches can magnify the racial fragmentation of a campus? Stated differently, what should a campus do once it admits a diverse entering class? These questions are particularly timely in light of recent U.S. Supreme Court decisions upholding the use of affirmative action to admit diverse classes (*Grutter v. Bollinger*, 2003) when not tied to rigid categories or quotas *(Gratz v. Bollinger*, 2003). Chapter 4 presents findings from a four-year action research project to turn a racially fragmented and diverse campus into the first *inter*cultural university campus in the United States. Experimenting with new approaches to learning and teaching across difference, curriculum development, student leadership, staff training, and faculty hiring, this project generated surprising gains in cross-cultural skills, feeling of control over one's life on campus and overall sense of community, while reducing racial tension. Leaders seeking to promote harmony on their campuses will want to closely examine the methods and findings of this study.

In chapter 5, I will suggest how the intercultural approaches tested at one university campus can prove helpful to a U.S. society still feeling its way to a peaceful co-existence with other nations in a shrinking world. Here I explain why category-based concepts like "culture," "power," and "resistance" may already be *passé* and offer a new framework for diversity. Emphasizing a form of individual agency called "subjectivity," the new framework poses: (1) changing the focus of diversity work from essentialized categories like race and culture to the individual as an agent or *subject*; (2) promoting the idea that each person's development can be linked to helping others also to grow, or *complementarity*; (3) shifting the rationale for egalitarian social change *away from resistance and binary oppositionality* to interconnectiveness and soul creation; (4) *alternative storytelling* as a means of engaging individuals in positive social change; and (5) *schools as parallel spaces* where energy need not be wasted fighting entrenched hierarchies.

This raises a final theme of this book. In the intercultural resides a tangible alternative to the global race conflict and "homeland insecurity" that weigh upon the U.S. psyche during this period of apparent systemic collapse. My belief after writing this book is that the creation of intercultural spaces on college and university campuses will not only have the positive result of reducing racial fragmentation in an increasingly diverse U.S. society, it will teach future citizens and leaders how to interact in peace and harmony with other nations and populations in a shared global society. It is perhaps fitting that the transition to a new U.S. begins with story.

CHAPTER ONE

Why Current Approaches Don't Work: Three Studies of Diversity

On the day before final exams in 1991, African American first-year law students at the University of California at Berkeley's Boalt School of Law found letters in their campus mailboxes accusing them of being admitted to satisfy affirmative action requirements—even though black law graduates as a group had recently outperformed white classmates on state bar exams. Further south, students at the UCLA Graduate School of Education received an email message demanding that professors interested in multiculturalism leave the school because, *"We prefer white professors who have had similar life experiences to ours."*

These were among the experiences I encountered as I began my graduate studies and they helped me see the larger challenge to diversity efforts may rest in its inability to see past binary constructions that place groups in an "us-against-them" relation to each other. I also learned from these early years that there are many ways to tell a story. In this book I will be presenting different stories—of pain, of structural analysis of power, of rebirth. To access these stories I will employ different storytelling forms based in personal narrative, the case method, quantitative analysis, ethnography, and action research.

Whiteness and Binary Oppositionality

In August of 1991, I came upon a handsome, three-story red brick building that seemed to rise above all others. It was the week before classes were to begin in my first year of doctoral studies at UCLA and I had come to visit my faculty advisor whom I had not seen since he gave me advice for my application. When I conveyed to him a sense of excitement over readings I had recently come across about multiculturalism, I was shocked to hear him say he had "no interest in multiculturalism" and that I should find a new advisor. Since the faculty advisor is the key to the life of a graduate student, this came as a real blow and colored my feelings about the school—long before I set foot in my first class. When this professor said he did not think multiculturalism was important, I could not help but feel that *my* culture wasn't important. Without his having intended it, I was registering a strong feeling as a Japanese American living in a diverse city like Los Angeles that *I* didn't count.

I never learned why this professor said these things. I had left a career in law to return to graduate school and learn the research skills necessary to help bring a racially fragmented U.S. society back together and so this tiny experience seemed all the more painful. Looking back on this event, I realized that from the professor's perspective, the idea of multiculturalism might have felt like an attack on him—an affront to his own sense of culture, history, and identity. Feeling his pain, I came upon another hunch that this middle-aged white man might also be seeing his academic world in binary terms. For him it was either *my* multicultur-alism or *his* Western civilization. Faced with that choice, he picked "his culture." At the same time, I wondered if this professor's pain and my own pain might in some strange way be interconnected. We had both been impacted by the onrush of race diversity into Los Angeles and the growing diversity of the UCLA student body. It was also clear that we shared an inability to enjoy a deeper sense of human interaction *across* difference.

Misconception #1: America Has Only Two Choices When It Comes to Increased Race Diversity—Western Civilization or Multiculturalism

In my early years as a graduate student, I began a mini-study of a California university dance department as it was attempting to shift its aesthetic sensibility from a Western one based on ballet and modern dance to a global aesthetic based on Asian, African, Central American, and indigenous American dance forms. From daily observations over a three-month period at this diverse campus, eleven interviews, five participant observations, and several document reviews, I discovered I was watching the erosion of the basis for meaning and identity for white professors and white students (Tanaka, 1996). In effect, I was watching a "dismantling" of social relations in which a Eurocentric discourse, faculty culture, and academic reward system were all being *displaced* by a more global, cross-cultural aesthetic.

The most shocking finding for me, however, was the negative impact of this new aesthetic on sense of belonging for the department's white students, a development that ultimately defined the path of research presented in this book. At this dance department, all entering students were asked to tell a story about the countries where their families came from and how that shaped their identities. But in addressing this assignment, many white students found they could not trace their roots to any specific countries of origin in Europe. Even if they could name specific countries, they found those places held little meaning for them. While storytelling would exert a powerful influence in constructing new meaning, in this case it was framed in a way that often marginalized white students.

Cut off, deracinated, lacking a direct line of history to a specific place in Europe, many of these students felt they had *no* ethnic identities and, as a result, could not "connect with" classmates who were present in such large numbers and could trace roots to specific places in Mexico or Guatemala or China—most often through parents or grandparents who were immigrants. In effect, the presence of so many students of color who knew their direct line to ethnic histories and places made raw the absence of meaning for these white students.

In casting off the primacy of Western tradition, this dance department was unwittingly leading many of its white students to feel culturally *dis*oriented. Finding over half their classmates were of color, these white students were learning much about other ethnic cultures and traditions, but little about an ethnic identity (or identities) they could call their own. At the same time, these white students could no longer hold on to the idea of being "white" because they were learning in class that "whiteness" was a social identifier historically associated with a sense of superiority over people who were not white—a value system considered unacceptable in this international arts program. Nor was it ultimately meaningful for these white students to claim to be "an American" because their classmates of color, who were ethnically Korean American or Mexican American, were *also* American. In this racialized, fast shifting and ethnically complex university space, the mechanisms defining social relations were in some ways "flipped." While it was the student of color who felt alienated and lacked a sense of belonging in the wider U.S. society, it was the other way around here at this dance department where it was the white student who felt out of place.

The irony was that this department was seeking to create a more "egalitarian" space for performed and visual art and had attempted to achieve this by moving away from a dominating Western aesthetic. Through its "multicultural" thrust, however, the department was stripping away the one source of identity for its own white students. There was another irony. While this department was casting off a dominating Eurocentric aesthetic, its students of color continued to be negatively impacted by the "white culture" that prevailed in the larger society and much of the rest of the campus. Without intending it, this department had in effect failed twice. While inclusion of previously silenced cultural voices and histories (reflecting an early form of "multiculturalism") had been necessary to "decenter" the primacy of Western Eurocentrism, this dance department was by virtue of its rejection of Eurocentrism: (1) unable to provide a safe place for its white students to nurture new identity formation *and* (2) unable to grant full release to its students of color from the larger victim status imposed on them by society at large. It was a situation that fairly cried out for a new framework.

This pilot study also surfaced for the first time in my experience the limitations of "culture" and "cultural identity" as tools for analysis in the fast shifting, heterogeneous, "transnational" social spaces of an urban U.S. campus. If members of the so-called dominant group—young, adult male white students—were unable to trace shared meaning to countries of origin in Europe, then how could the word "culture" continue to have *any* meaning?

This was also one dance department at one university. What would happen if an entire campus seeks to make itself "multicultural?" *Chapter 2 will present findings from an eighteen-month study conducted at a small liberal arts college as it sought to become the first campus in the U.S. to transform itself from a white institution to a multicultural one in all its chief functions.* The prevailing questions at Pico College would be familiar: can white students come to find a sense of belonging in an increasingly diverse space and will there only be two frameworks for shared meaning, Western civilization and multiculturalism?

Resistance Back

When I entered UCLA in 1991, I encountered a period of resurgent campus activism. One of the most engaging causes was that of Chicana/o students and faculty who were demanding department status for their Chicana/o Studies program and its associated privileges of fixed professorships and internal control over tenure and curriculum content. In short, the people whose ethnic group comprised nearly a third of the population of Los Angeles wanted to research and share their own histories—and have this work granted the same status in the university as Western European and European American histories.

Finding stiff opposition from senior white professors, Chicana/o students and faculty staged a demonstration in front of stately Royce Hall and its twin towers. While the administration supported the demands of Chicana/o students, the university's Academic Senate continued to oppose the idea of granting full department status. The harder Chicana/o students pushed, the more resolute the white faculty as a group became. Underlying the faculty arguments were assertions of a zero-sum game—that if you award department status to Chicana/o Studies, you would have to close down departments like Slavic Languages. There were even claims by some white professors that "since Chicanos don't have a real culture," the study of their history could never truly be "scholarly."

Like a tug-of-war, each antagonist in this contest became dependent on the other, with the energy exerted by one side resulting in a proportionately greater response from the other. When Chicana/o students resisted, the white faculty "resisted back." Here the scholarly notion of "resistance" seemed to be too dichotomous and antagonistic as a doctrinal thrust to enable either party to find a way out of the intense conflict. In this oppositional dynamic, race tensions only seemed to heighten at each turn. When students from different racial backgrounds—white, Asian, Latino and African American—finally staged a "sit-in" at the sacred space of the upscale Faculty Center, the result was broken glass, defaced works of art, and calls by professors for the administration to bring in the infamous Los Angeles Police Department (see e.g., Tanaka, 1993).

Following the arrest and overnight detention of eighty racially diverse students in the local hoosegow, other students pitched tents on the lawn directly in front of the administration building. A hunger strike was born. When doctors ultimately declared that students were risking permanent harm to their bodies, the administration relented and agreed to a compromise that would grant the Chicana/o Studies program the power to select and nominate for tenure their own faculty—but not the department status they had been seeking to ensure full membership in the academic community. One argument made by white professors and staff throughout this ordeal was that white students did not want to learn about Chicana/o people and culture. Some were even asking if there were *any* redeeming qualities in multiculturalism for white students.

Misconception #2: White Americans Do Not Want to Learn About Cultures Different from Their Own

Chapter 3 will present data from a nationwide study of 25,000 white students at 159 institutions showing that *"overall satisfaction with college" increases for white students when they participate in cross-cultural academic and social activities while in college.* Simply put, white students across the country are concluding that in today's multiethnic society there is great value to learning about cultures different from your own. It is one of the reasons to go to college. At the same time, the findings reveal that increased cultural contact plays out differently in relation to faculty of color and this suggests that differences in power will lead to differential racial impacts on student-faculty relations at such campuses. Apparently, one cannot examine the challenges that come from greater race diversity without also examining and redefining uses of power.

The Need for A Re-Unifying Framework

April and May of 1992 was the time of the L.A. Rebellion—an event some call "the Rodney King Riots." It is difficult to describe how it felt to be living in a town so torn apart by racial strife, where firemen were shot at by snipers on roof-tops, police squad cars screamed by in groups of ten or twenty, where plumes of smoke darkened the skyline and helicopters constantly drummed overhead in wide, sweeping circles. It was during this time that I was hoping in my first year of graduate study to uncover new ways to build race harmony. The bitterness and uncertainty of the times pressed in on me and the resulting irony squeezed my chest all the more tightly. It was while attempting to escape the psychological wounds of these riots that I came upon a volume at a UCLA book sale interpreting public riots in early modern France. In presenting a rationale for those riots, this book offered a possible explanation for the riots in Los Angeles following the Simi Valley acquittal of the police officers who beat African American motorist Rodney King. The parallels were too uncanny to ignore.

In *Society and Culture in Early Modern France,* Natalie Zemon Davis (1965: 154–187) describes how the masses in mid-sixteenth century France rose up and rioted over decisions by the government and church to limit food distribution and punish violators with torture, execution, and other atrocities. That crowd behaved as if its actions were legitimate—acting in a collective spirit to correct a perceived breakdown of justice. Of particular note, the French public's rampage exactly mimicked the violence visited upon them by their government. Not at all unlike the L.A. crowd's beating of truck driver Denny—arguably recapitulating the earlier beating of King by four Los Angeles police officers—the acts of the crowd in early France seemed almost predictable:

> We may see their violence, however cruel, not as random and limitless but as aimed
> at defined targets. (In such circumstances) official acts of torture…anticipate some
> of the acts performed by riotous crowds. (ibid at 154, 162)

Arguably prefiguring a violent L.A. crowd's response to the Simi Valley acquittals of police officers Koon, Powell, Wind, and Briscenio, the widespread public sentiment in France had developed because of the public's impression that judicial verdicts had become either too severe or too lenient. In France, the masses reached a conclusion that political authorities had failed in their duties—a feeling that some Angelenos had evidently come to share in 1992 when the Rodney King beating case was removed by a chief judge to a courtroom in the "white flight" town of Simi Valley, where a jury impaneled from this small pro-police community subsequently acquitted the defendant police officers. What compounded the amplitude of the conflict in Los Angeles was the somewhat under-discussed overlay of this "racialization" upon a pre-existing economic condition that came to leave many Angeleno families jobless and hungry. In

France, the sixteenth-century crowds had believed as a result of their perceptions and widespread public food shortage that they were acting *in place of* their government (id at 161–169).

In such contexts, Davis, a Princeton University scholar, advances an interesting rationale for public violence: the actions of the crowd in effect become "rites of purification" to root out the evil *in the same way* the evil had defiled the local community. At the same time, she notes, the crowd initiates through its violence a *rebuilding of community* by affirming who they are (id at 159, 186). Elaborating, Davis suggests that, "(Riots) remind us that if we try to increase safety and trust within a community...then we must think less about pacifying 'deviants' and more about changing the central values" (id at 187).

While no one should ever want to condone violence, I found this latter point most instructive. In the L.A. riots, one might trace how in the same desperate way a more recent U.S. urban public found violence necessary to root out the evil of an unjust court system and the rising inequities of global capitalism that had stripped Los Angeles of thousands of jobs and left many hungry and without proper education and health services. Still missing in Los Angeles, however, was a clear notion of how to go about "rebuilding community."

Misconception #3: It Will Never Be Possible to Build Community in the United States out of Multiple Ethnic Cultures

It is perhaps fitting that one solution to the growing racial fragmentation in the U.S. would later come out of the LA riots. While serving as a member of the education committee for the "Cultural Explainers Project" initiated by ADOBE LA and the Social and Public Art Resource Center (SPARC) in Venice, California, I watched designers, architects and artists from different ethnic and racial backgrounds come together and create new ways—through public art—of binding together a city that had been ripped apart by riots. Following two years of multiethnic community-based research spearheaded by ADOBE LA, this group came up with a plan to design and build three monuments that would each represent a sub-community impacted by the riots—Pico Union (Latino), South Central Los Angeles (African American), and Koreatown. Later, the monuments were to be "shared" by rotating them to the other sub-communities with each unveiling accompanied by performances and poetry (see e.g., Tanaka, 1994).

While funding was still being sought to complete the construction of this ambitious "public art" project, its re-unifying design had already won my heart. From my participation on this committee, I knew firsthand that members of different ethnic or racial groups could work together to produce expressions of their own ethnic histories and achieve an overarching human quality of interconnectiveness *across* cultures. This was more than a celebration of one's own culture—multiculturalism—it was the evocation of a common bond across difference (see also Sacco, 1999; Alfaro, 1999).

Seeing hope for harmony in the arts, I wondered if similar spaces could be constructed in colleges and universities through dialogue, art, or joint activities where understanding and power might be shared across difference in racial and ethnic groups, and social unity and cultural difference would come to coexist. Stated differently, if a framework of social unity and cultural difference could be acted out in the arts, how might it be implemented in a university setting?

Chapter 4 presents results from one attempt to do just that, revealing *what works and doesn't work when a university sets out to make the entire campus "intercultural."* Would an experiment like this succeed in building community where others had failed? If the answer can one day be "yes," then professor Davis's concern for community might ultimately be answered as it would be "the university" that leads a diverse society to cultivate new "central values."

A Transnational Racial Demographic Shift

In the chapters that follow, I hope to address the three misconceptions noted above so they will no longer stand in the way of progress toward race harmony and sense of community on college and university campuses. I will also venture the view that a proliferation of writers funded by such conservative "free market" think tanks as the John M. Olin Foundation (Bloom, 1987; Kimball, 1990; D'Souza, 1991; W. J. Bennett, 1992), American Enterprise Institute (D'Souza, 1991; Herrnstein & Murray, 1994), and Heritage Foundation (Bennett, 1992) played a key role in sowing confusion over these misconceptions; in the very least, their assertions of *dis*unity from race diversity distracted the public while they inserted free market economics into America's democracy and governance. Often without use of research data, these writers fanned the flames of race fear and uncertainty in America by assigning negative meaning to words like "immigration," "diversity," and "affirmative action" while failing to advance new and re-unifying frameworks for a diverse America.

More importantly, what the three studies in this book will show is that while these conservative think tanks associated people of color in the U.S. with notions of uncertainty and fragmentation, their protestations only worsened race fears when a more positive approach to human interaction in a diverse society had been possible all along. At the same time, while the tactics of these free market proponents succeeded in directing the public gaze away from a growing concentration of wealth among the very people who funded those think tanks—a development that demands separate study—I will suggest that progressives played their own part by responding in ways that were self-limiting in that they were only answering the attacks rather than creating their own new models. With progressive energies spent on stemming the bleeding from racial tensions magnified by these think tanks, the tactics of the free market conservatives essentially prevented educators from authoring new and *re*-uniting approaches to human development and belonging for an increasingly diverse United States.

Table 1A

Percent by Race (White/Of Color) of Students in U.S. Higher Education

Race	1976	1988	1994	1999
White	84.3	81.1	75.4	73.0
Of Color	15.7	18.9	24.6	27.0

Source: National Center for Educational Statistics; B. Hu (2000)

As indicated above, a massive racial demographic shift has begun to impact U.S. colleges and universities and arguably made the larger society "transnational." As shown, the percentage of students of color in U.S. colleges and universities in effect doubled in the last quarter century. In one of the largest states, California, the onrush of ethnic and race diversity reached the point several years ago where students of color attending public institutions surpassed fifty percent:

Table 1B

Percent by Race of Students in California Higher Education Institutions

Race	Fall, 1979	Fall, 1985	Fall, 1990	Fall, 1995	Fall, 1999
White	59.7	57.6	55.7	47.6	–
Of Color	21.5	27.1	32.9	41.6	51 (public)
Other	18.8	15.3	11.4	10.8	–

Source: California Postsecondary Education Commission; N. B. Hu, 2000

With these trends, leading researchers in higher education have concluded that "diversity" is something educators can no longer afford to ignore:

> As student diversity increases, understanding the experience of college and its various impacts will undoubtedly become more complex. Research approaches that try to isolate the influence of a few variables for all students will simply miss the point and probably provide little in the way of useful, practice- or policy-relevant evidence.
>
> (Pascarella and Terenzini, 1998: 155)

In other words, as more and more students of color enter U.S. colleges and universities, it is imperative that educators correct the misconceptions created in part by conservative think tanks and view race diversity in more constructive and less oppositional terms. Stated differently, colleges and universities will want to teach their students the skills to be successful citizens in increasingly multiethnic U.S. and global societies—and this means having new constructs.

The Need for New Tools and Concepts

In the chapters that follow, I will be critiquing key terms employed as "mediating tropes" in our current thinking about difference. *Culture* will be defined initially as "shared meaning" sustained by the beliefs, traditions, and practices of a particular group and can be applied to ethnicity, race, gender, class, sexual orientation, or other social identifier (Tanaka, 1996). *Race* will be initially used to refer to a socially constructed sub-category of culture created by attaching pre-judged values to genetically determined physical characteristics. *Ethnicity* will be seen as another category of culture defined through traditions, beliefs, and behaviors linked to one's family and country of origin. The terms *power* and *resistance* are particularly troublesome and so I will be presenting them as precursors for what will likely become new tools in the forthcoming wave of transnational U.S. education research.

Later in this book I will outline one way to shift from traditional uses of "culture" and "power" to new formulations of human development and social interaction that focus on the individual as a *"subject"* (that is, the individual's capacity to have voice, history, and agency, and be rooted in time and place). I will also suggest that each such individual can possess multiple, shifting *"subjectivities"* (or evolving meanings attached to one's social location based in ethnicity, race, gender, sexual orientation, class, religion and other social identifiers). In a democratic society, an *"intercultural"* framework would represent an approach to learning and sharing across cultures where no culture dominates. This society would be *"intersubjective"* if it accords each person the "subject" status to tell one's stories with respect to all her or his "subjectivities"—and achieves that state of agency without turning other individuals present into "objects" of that individual's storytelling.

While it is also possible to pose an intercultural theory of college student development based in subjectivity and intersubjectivity (e.g., Tanaka, 2002a), in this book I will be emphasizing the more practical steps (and pitfalls) institutional leaders will want to consider as they go about devising their own non-binary strategies for organizational change and employ diversity as a binding mechanism rather than one that drives wedges between groups.

I have traveled a long way since the moment my first Ph.D. advisor refused to join me in a scholarly journey into the world of multiculturalism, where professors at UCLA denied creation of a Chicana/o Studies department, and the spirit of the city I lived in became incinerated under a justice system a diverse public found wanting. Where I have arrived for the moment is a new place—a question really—asking how the United States as a diverse nation might create spaces that accord value and a sense of belonging to all its people. Far beyond a 1990s preoccupation with abstract categories, binary oppositions, and resistance, this place insists that steps be taken to construct actual social change through storytelling, dreaming, and model building—and hints at a new sentiment where hate mail in student mailboxes has faded to a distant past.

CHAPTER TWO

The Problem with Multiculturalism

This case study investigates how one small college sought to turn diversity into a strength by becoming "the first multicultural college" in the U.S. The study also reveals how the institutions's well laid plans turned sour when the project failed to take into account the needs of white students, faculty, staff, and alumni.

In an attempt to present the perspectives of participants in this bold change effort in one written text, I experimented by writing the study in the form of a "polyphonic novelistic ethnography," as called for earlier by Clifford (1986: 15) and others (Tyler, 1986: 127; Bakhtin, 1984/1929: 21; see also Tanaka & Cruz, 1998: 144). In this polyphonic text, which I present below, the gains and shortcomings of this groundbreaking multicultural effort are seen through the eyes of different contributors to the project. It is this experimental writing that opened my own eyes to the possibilities in posing a polyphonic, non-binary approach to diversity *after* multiculturalism.

The Multicultural Model

Noting the massive influx of Latinos and Asians into California in the 1980s, the leaders of Pico College (fictitious name) set out to turn that diversity into an advantage: they led a movement to re-make their institution into the first multicultural college in the United States. The trustees hired a distinguished African American to be the college president. Large numbers of students of color were recruited into the next entering classes. The curriculum was changed to require courses in American Cultures for all entering students. And in perhaps the most important of indicia of positive change, the percentage of faculty of color was raised from 2½ percent in 1982 to 20 percent by 1992. In many ways, Pico College had become a model institution for others to emulate. One particularly impressive measure of the overall success of this multicultural project was that Pico's students were going on to graduate school and medical school in record numbers.

At the same time, it was evident that the multicultural experiment at Pico College was beginning to stall and the financial condition of the institution was falling into serious crisis. What went wrong with the experiment at Pico and what might be learned about how to better construct diversity programs in the future? This chapter will investigate how the project succeeded in major ways but also failed in the final analysis. In addition, it will highlight "best practices" that campus leaders will want to consider when designing diversity programs at their own institutions.

The site selected for this 1993–1995 study was a small, private liberal arts college at the edge of an urban sprawl in California. Since the study was limited in scope, I employed a "triangulation" of three research methods: interviews, observations, and a document review. Interviews were conducted over a year and a half period with the aim of reaching a wide variety of people in age, gender, race, and job status. In addition, I made twelve observations on campus encompassing a student orientation and lunch periods at two student unions, attended three classes, and studied the buildings, student posters, snack bar, president's office, and student and staff activity at the Cultural Resource Center. The documents I reviewed included a five-year strategic plan, the speeches of the college president, several issues of the student newspaper, tables from the Institutional Research Office, syllabi from courses on American Cultures and Gender and Science, student multicultural training materials, an issue of the alumni magazine, the college catalog, and various brochures and reports.

From this data I constructed an experimental ethnographic text that has two parallel columns consisting of storytelling (in the left column) and analysis (in the right column). To facilitate a reading of this unusual text, readers may wish to read the left column first and then go back and examine the column on the right. A discussion of the implications of the findings from this study will follow.

Pico College

Story	Sidenotes

A middle-aged man of medium height looked down from his second-story office and saw a pink rose garden lining a long walkway just as lights at an airport might line a night runway, guiding planes home to safety or directing them to a faraway place. **(1)** From his window in the pristine white building at the top of the hill, he could see young men and women moving with purpose under the bright sunshine, some hailing others as they walked, others stopping to talk in animated voices. They must be animated voices. That was what this business was all about, wasn't it? Voices. And passion.

A long row of California oaks ran along the walkway. Gnarled and thinned, they bravely withstood the smog at the edge of the city and gave shade to those in need. And there, at the very bottom of the hill, a spectacular fountain with flying shiny steel arcs reached frantically in all directions for something unstated. For what, an emotion? An understanding beyond the reach of calculated certainty? Some say the foun-

1. Theoretical Framework. The theoretical basis of this narrative is Mikhail M. Bakhtin's critique of Fyodor Dostoyevsky's "polyphonic" novel, found in *Problems of Dostoevsky's Poetics* (1984/1929). A polyphonic style rejects the author's authority to make all characters and events contribute to a plot that is prefixed in the author's mind. Under a polyphonic approach, narration is no longer "subordinated to the hegemony of a single, unified consciousness" (Gardiner, 1992: 26) and no "single point of view dominates all the presented material" (Fanger, 1965: 95–96). Instead, each character is given the authority to speak for her or himself. What matters is "the hero's discourse about himself and his world" – not a character type or "objectified image of the hero" (Bakhtin, 1984/1929: 53).

Refusing to see life as finished entity, the writer is free to represent reality "as developing idea" (Emerson in Bakhtin, 1984/1929:

tain served tribute to the liberating joy of space-age technology; others saw the imperceptible waning of human spirit.

The man of medium height had a broad nose and big bushy eyebrows. When he smiled, crow's-feet spread from the corners of narrow, sensitive eyes, highlighting the warmth and intelligence of his gaze. His mustache was prematurely thinned and grayed, and his hands were too large for his body.

The man seemed more like a soft spoken traveling salesman than the leader of a highly prestigious institution. But he was nonetheless a man who met challenge with wisdom and gentle words. His aura was that of a person who thought carefully about both people and ideas before making a decision.

Gazing out the window, the dark man with graying close-cropped hair and smiling eyes knew the bucolic peacefulness was deceiving.

xxxix). It is this emphasis on "unfinalizability" (Bakhtin, 1994/1929: 53) that gives a writer the power to see *relationships*. Characters are no longer objects in the author's eye but subjects who can be autonomous (Bakhtin, 1984/1929: 5), contradict themselves (p. 18), act fully in the present (p. 29), and experience the multiple ambiguities of human existence (p. 30). (Ong, 1987: 216, notes the study of cultural change in Malay society is "incomplete, fraught with ambiguity and shifting perceptions.") Under polyphony, characters and plots can be seen in musical terms as "modulations and counter-positions" (Bakhtin, 1984/1929: 40), traits that give an author the ability to represent *interaction*.

In this maelstrom, Dostoyevsky avoids closure and thus reaches a vantage point from which to appreciate "subtle shifts of meaning . . . the smaller shapes: voice zones, shifts in speakers, the overlapping boundaries between various characters' fields of vision" (Emerson in Bakhtin, 1984/1929: xxxviii). Here, contradictions and ambiguities do not merge but stand alongside each other in "an eternal harmony of unmerged voices" (Bakhtin, 1984/1929: 30). It is this coexistence of different voices with harmony that makes Bakhtin's critique of Dostoyevsky so fecund in today's world of social science research, where it seems that difference has shattered all unity.

In the basement of the same building a tall, thin man with sandy brown hair stood and stretched as high as his six-foot-two frame would take him. He let out a long, slow whispered breath. It was not very long ago that students from the Black Students Alliance had engaged in a pitched battle with white students from Sigma Alpha Epsilon. The melee had not lasted long, but it would remain etched forever in the memory of the institution. **(2)**

Why? he asked himself. It started when a white student used racial slurs to say that blacks would not be welcome at a fraternity party. So what happens next? A group of black students attack two fraternity members standing nearby. Well, that was it. Free for all. In one crazed, unthinking, destructive moment, our grand experiment was about to end. Everything we had worked for, ready to go down the drain! Hey, *we* were

2. The Debate. The onset of racial and ethnic fragmentation has become increasingly worrisome at U.S. colleges and universities. Of their own volition, students of color are sitting at segregated tables in student unions across the country. White students have been caught yelling "Water buffaloes!" at large black women students. At the University of Massachusetts at Amherst, there was a violent fight between whites and blacks following a World Series baseball game which some saw as a confrontation between a predominantly black team and a predominantly white team.

Similar hate speech and fights have broken out over issues of sexual identity, class difference, and gender. This meanness of spirit is clearly occurring at a time when many campuses are experiencing large influxes of students of color

the ones who brought all these different races together in one place. Wasn't it our fault?

No, that can't be right! We meant for this to work out right. If some students came with preconceived notions about minorities that were bound to cause trouble, would that be our fault? A deep furrow formed on his forehead. The spark in his eyes flickered and for one moment longer he willed the ideals not to die.

We were always about positive change here, he heard himself say. The road was bumpy but we were willing to take our problems head on. The tall, thin man wanted to tell himself that this was also about who he was, too, and why his life would make a difference.

Taking a seat, Dean Wilder clasped his hands behind his head and closed his eyes. Some students were yelling outside his window. Students were always getting excited about the slightest thing when spring arrived. And the BSU-fraternity riot? It will become a distant memory. Then we will start over. Right?

Opening his eyes, the tallish, sandy-haired man shook his head as if to clear it. His office was neat and his round "dialogue table" was spotless. He was dressed in a long sleeve

and there is rising ethnic pride among many identities.

Against this backdrop, many universities seem caught in a double bind of monocultural past and fragmenting cultural future. Some commentators bemoan the loss of simpler times (Bloom, 1987; W.J. Bennett, 1988, 1992; Cheney, 1989; Kimball, 1990; D'Souza, 1991; Schlesinger, 1991; and Hughes, 1993). But that nostalgia for a Western—based view of what counts as knowledge conjures only a superficial reassurance: white students can see with their own eyes that they are associating with large numbers of students of color and they find it impossible to reconcile what their eyes see with that one culture tradition.

The attempt to sustain a Western world view also gives students and faculty of color no real purchase in the university. Perhaps worst of all, by leaving out large numbers of the campus population, university policy makers leave themselves with no real opportunity to build a new sense of community. By the same token, tribalistic tendencies have proven equally divisive as they promote one ethnic passion over all others (e.g.,

pastel cotton dress shirt, opened at the top. No tie. His thin eyebrows twitched and he knew this day would bring something unexpected.

"Well, it was five years ago that we planned how to multiculturalize this campus," he was saying to himself. "And I was in on the planning. So where are we now, five years later? And what will we tell the trustees? That change doesn't move in a straight line?"

The tall dean stood and went over to the window. He had kind, intelligent eyes. A few strands of light brown hair fell down over his forehead. He remembered how it had been in the beginning, when things were so promising. "We were going to achieve something no other college in the United States had achieved."

"We were going to be a test case. (3) Pico would be the first college to bring diversity into the curriculum. It was in 1978 that we voted *as a faculty* to establish a core program with two world cultures courses, two European cultures courses, *and two American minority cultures courses* required of all entering students. That put us ahead of Stanford and U.C. Berkeley, too!

Deloria championing Native Americans, 1988, and Jeffries on Afrocentrism). This can lead to a cacophony of "separate" cultures.

The two views of Western retrenchment and ethnic separatism seem worlds apart yet share the same debilitating effect on policy makers by providing no clear way out of the dilemma (see e.g., West, 1993; Gates, 1992; McLaren, 1993; cf. Myrdal, 1944). This forces people to choose artificially between a unity that is available only to whites and the multicultural worship of difference at the expense of unity.

3. Research Questions. Following this debate over how to end the social fragmentation on our campuses, one question is *whether a polyphonic novelistic style lends itself to the representation of swirling cultural stories and competing racial agendas.* Here I am testing Bakhtin's belief that a writing which moves away from the author's controlling, authorial voice

But there was one thing none of us anticipated. It wasn't enough for us just to change the curriculum. We had to change the professors, students, and administrative staff. There had to be an *interconnectedness*.

That's it. Our vote to have cultural diversity in the curriculum was not enough. We forgot to allow for retraining, of everyone!

Well, I was right in there with everyone else who thought the new president would give us the impetus we needed. Impressive record. In 1987, he promised right up front to make race diversity a major thrust in student admissions. And he did.

But did he move too fast? That was another step, a good step, to change the face of the student body from historically white to 50 percent of color. But was the decline in number of white students too sudden? Would this come back to haunt?

Well, the student body has a new face. We have a visionary for a president. What more could we ask for? He heard people yelling outside and paused.

There is this little feeling inside me, it's true. I can't deny it. A voice is telling me the younger professors, who never went through the sixties and lets each character have his or her own voice will be *more* able to represent the feelings and ideas of those characters. For example, will a polyphonic orientation let us see the person from his or her own point of view and give voice to that person's own cultural tensions and identities?

How about where one event is perceived differently by different people? Or where there is a serious inconsistency between the statements of two characters, or between two statements by the same person? This study explores whether a polyphonic approach is *better* than a more authoritative style at showing the highly layered, multiplexed, nuanced, shifting, contradictory and often ambiguous findings that current campus conditions reflect.

This inquiry raises a follow-up question. Assuming for the moment that a new social arrangement might be possible, the second issue is *whether a polyphonic novelistic approach will give social scientists a new capability for studying how social unity and cultural difference might come to coexist in a society which is becoming increasingly heterogeneous*. This is where:

and only know material wealth, are forming a faction with very senior white faculty. Will they try to repeal our efforts to multiculturalize the campus?

The dean of students knew then that he was no longer a "young buck" hell-bent on changing the system. Cruelly, he had become suspended somewhere in between an idealistic youth and the tempered period of generativity yet to come. In this in-between space of productivity and achievement, he had begun to harbor a tiny suspicion. Have I *become* the establishment?

We thought it would be easy, he heard himself saying. I helped lead the charge. But then came the sacrifices. Were we ready to change *ourselves*? I mean "us," the faculty? Were we willing to examine who *we* were?

Institutional research says we are getting better. In 1982, we had only six professors of color out of a faculty of 150. By 1992, that number had reached 29. That's 20 percent!

Are the trustees still behind us? Anders Fine has been leading the way and I will continue to support him. But maybe we should have been working to add more pieces. I just wish we had more women and peo-

Unity =   positive sentiment
                that comes from
                interrelating, and
Difference = an appreciation
                of distinct cultural
                identities centering
                on race or ethnicity,
                gender, sexuality,
                class, age, etc.

The question of whether and how unity and difference might coexist is not new (Hwang, 1994; Daniel, 1992; Burbeles & Rice, 1991; Rosaldo, 1989; Tyler, 1987; Trinh, 1987; Bakhtin, 1984/1924; Sandoval, 1982; Lorde, 1979). In his later writings, Bakhtin expanded his discussion of the novel to encompass the idea of multiple languages, the end of reliance upon valorized temporal categories, and a new zone of "maximal contact with the present" (Bakhtin, 1981/1930: 11). In doing this, he may have foreshadowed the emergence of the United States as a multicultural society, stating it was not coincidence that the new novel should appear in Russia at a time of rupture in the history of European civilization, its emergence from a socially isolated and culturally deaf semi-patriarchal society, and its

ple of color on that board. It all takes time. Time. And now what is all that racket outside? At the window, the tall professor looked out to see what the commotion was and immediately saw the large group of students milling about.

entrance into international and interlingual contacts, global trade, and multiple religions.

Michael Holquist (1981) describes Bakhtin's ability to contemplate the dual existence of difference and unity as a "Manichean sense of opposition and struggle...a ceaseless battle between centrifugal forces that seek to keep things apart, and centripetal forces that strive to make things cohere" (p. xviii). Bakhtin had earlier described these opposites in a context of hope:

> This disintegration (of the epic wholeness of an individual) combines in the novel with the necessary preparatory steps toward a new, complex wholeness on a higher level of human development.
>
> (Bakhtin, 1981/1930: 37–38)

Wholeness. I can think of no better way to describe the hope I have for humanity when I contemplate the possible co-existence of social unity and cultural difference. But the question of *how* unity and difference might come to coexist at a campus that has long championed one cultural history is an issue of first impression.

My hunch is that Bakhtin's celebration of Dostoyevsky's writing *mirrors* G. Reginald Daniel's (1992) projection of a third place beyond the extreme poles of ethnic tribalism and Western retrenchment. What Daniel and Bakhtin hold in common is a fundamental view that one must never stop affirming the autonomy of the person, especially when people from different positions of power and different ethnic cultures are interacting with each other.

I did encounter one particular problem here in crafting. While it might appear to the reader that all the characters were interviewed on the same day, in fact, these interviews were spread out over a period of many months. The timing of the stories in this text is therefore accelerated for the purpose of bringing them together under one expression.

This raises the question of whether polyphonic writing can ever truly be adapted to social science research, where interviews of so many different informants are typically conducted separately and over a long period of time. Is it possible to tie this all together in might be an "essential, irreducible multicenteredness, or 'polyphony,' of human life" (Booth in Bakhtin, 1984/1929: xx), without resorting to time–space compression? And if expressing the "super real" now becomes possible for my research, then at what cost?

From high atop the hill, the middle-aged man with large hands could see the cracked plaster and chipped paint on the exterior walls of the buildings that rimmed the long walkway below. **(4)** The brown patches of sun-dried grass and hard dirt appeared more obvious now. Like sentinels, the delicate pink roses stood as if in defiance of the encroaching decay around them. There were no other plants in the quad. Instead, red-tiled roofs drooped over tired buildings. It was then that Marcel Godot recalled when he was first hired to lead Pico College.

To his surprise, first one then another member of the search committee had expressed a desire to make Pico the first highly ranked liberal arts college to "multiculturalize" itself. They did not want a token minority applicant. They wanted a leader of color to take them to a new place.

One member of the faculty, a tall man with sandy brown hair, added

4. The Novelistic Writing of Fieldnotes. Novelistic writing of fieldnotes is not new. Zora Neale Hurston (1935), who studied under Boas, wrote authentically if not poetically in *Mules and Men:*

> Lemme tell you 'bout John and dis frog: It was night and Ole Massa sent John, his favorite slave, down to the spring to get him a cool drink of water. He called John to him. "John!"
>
> "What you want, Massa?"
>
> (Hurston, 1935: 9)

While some might be shocked by her vernacular style, Hurston's storytelling about a southern black community was storytelling, and in a Bakhtinian sense, it was among the first narratives to give the authority to speak to "ordinary" people (see Hernandez, 1995).

In *Under the Mountain Wall*, Peter Matthieson (1962) took the

that Pico needed a leader who could help make the campus reflect the community of the urban sprawl to the south. Walter Wilder would become one of his staunchest allies on the faculty.

Another man, aging and feisty, said that the city was fast becoming cosmopolitan with almost half the population from non-Western cultures. This man said that Pico would become a model for how to build a sense of community among diverse cultures. Anders Fine would become his best supporter on Pico's board of trustees.

But that was then. Today, the dark-complected Marcel Godot wondered how much longer they all would support him.

He watched the students below moving with spirit and chatting excitedly. Many were walking up the hill, toward the administration building. So why am I doing this? he asked himself. Has this idea already become bigger than me, or am I the idea?

I know exactly what it was then, what we all wanted. It was supposed to be about something bigger than the things that separate us. If there is no core that holds people together, and we are only a collection of dif-

art of storytelling one step further by effectively merging art with the formality of ethnographic detail. The problem was that Matthieson too obviously read his own world view into the writing:

> The food in the valley forests was plentiful, and he had brought with him, or there came soon after, the sweet potato, dog, and pig. The jungle and mountain, the wall of clouds, the centuries, secured him from the navigators and explorers who touched the coasts and went away again; he remained in his stone culture. In the last corners of the valley, he remains there still, under the mountain wall.
>
> (Matthieson, 1962: 5)

This passage demonstrates an exoticism about the people of New Guinea and an all-too-frequent Western penchant for wanting to discover "the last aboriginal culture." Still, there is no denying Matthieson's mastery of the art of writing nonfiction as literature (see e.g., Zinsser, 1988: 53ff). He gives me confidence to proceed with this project.

More recently, John Langston Gwaltney (1993) published *Drylongso,* which expresses in narrative style the fieldwork he had completed in the 1970s. In this

ferent identities, then there is no community.

Tortoiseshell glasses framed Godot's soft, doleful eyes, making him seem like the favorite grandfather or uncle of your youth. With his heavy eyebrows and slow manner, he was the epitome of deliberation and reflection. But there was much more to this president than his calm demeanor. The outward appearance hid an inner history of swirling emotions.

At a small school like Pico, he thought, it should be possible for every student to interact with every other student at some point during the four years, and with every faculty member and even me. This is a college where it is possible to communicate, to establish values and principles and discuss them and abide by those that make sense.

So maybe it doesn't matter if I have become the idea or not. It's too late to worry about that. What I do know is this: my stomach is telling me there's something going on. I know I should listen. I know I should listen.

writing, Gwaltney gives his informants real voice by naming them and representing their narratives verbatim:

> Hannah Nelson: I am a colored woman sixty-one years of age. I was born in Boston and grew up right here. I came to Harlem when I was about six or seven....My maiden name is Nelson and I married a man named Nelson, too. Anyone who would see me would say, "There goes a colored woman in her early sixties who could afford to lose a few pounds."
>
> (Gwaltney, 1993: 3–4)

But while Gwaltney achieved the goal of giving each character his or her own authority to speak, he did not *combine* their voices into a unified, novelistic experience. With each story standing on its own, the total expression was not polyphonic in a Bakhtinian sense.

James Clifford (1986) was one of the first to urge ethnographers to write a polyphonic text that could account for multiple perspectives (Park, 1993), and in 1988 he lauded the rich novelistic detail expressed by some earlier ethnographers (e.g., Michel Leiris in 1946 and Barbara Tedlock in 1984).

Then, in 1994, Kamala Visweswaran published *Fictions of Feminist Ethnography*. A powerful and well-researched piece about the use of narrative in qualitative research, this work successfully wove together theory with an autobiographical storytelling:

> Somehow, during the course of that first year in India, I accumulated a lot of saris ... old ones, new ones, cotton ones, and silk; torn, but still lovely ones; others in colors so gaudy I dared not wear them. The logic was, if I looked Indian, surely in a sari, I must be Indian.... I soon discovered, however, that the wearing of saris was coded by factors such as age and class.
>
> (Visweswaran, 1994: 166)

Effective at deconstructing the power and gender relations imbricated in a storytelling, Visweswaran's piece nonetheless remains authorial. Visweswaran arguably sacrifices contradiction, nuance, and multiplicity in order to reaffirm the authority of her own voice but falls short of attaining a truly polyphonic novelistic expression.

What is new in the present paper is its attempt to make a novelistic writing of field notes "polyphonic" and, secondly, to engage that narrative in a dialogue with (what I shall call) "sidenotes" that allow for ratiocination and critique.

In attempting to represent findings through story, I draw further courage from Patricia J. Williams's *Alchemy of Race and Rights (1991),* Michael Taussig's "Montage" (1987), Renato Rosaldo's "Grief and A Headhunter's Rage" (1989), James Clifford's "Identity in Mashpee" (1988), Simon Schama's *Dead Certainties (1991),* Dorinne Kondo's *Crafting Selves (1990),* and Anna Lowenhaupt Tsing's *In the Realm of the Diamond Queen (1993).* I am especially encouraged by the work of Kirin Narayan (1993) who urges ethnographers to continue to combine both narrative and analysis in one text, and Ruth Behar and Deborah Gordon (1995), whose edited volume uses fiction, memoir, plays, and other non-traditional forms to redefine the contours of ethnographic writing.

On the outskirts of campus, a young man sat in a dark room composing his thoughts. **(5)** Dressed in a dark coat and tie, he was short with straight dark brown hair and appeared to the researcher to be a

5. The Setting. Pico College (fictitious name) is a small, highly ranked private liberal arts college on the West Coast. The setting was picked for this pilot study because it is undergoing rapid racial demo-

southern European. After exchanging pleasantries, the young man realized he would soon be saying things in this secluded second-floor library of the Multicultural Center that he never thought he would tell anyone.

"I am assistant director of Student Affairs," Mark Marjorian heard himself saying. **(6)** "But in a few weeks I will be moving from the West Coast to take a job in the Midwest."

When the researcher said he was studying race harmony at Pico, Mark stiffened before speaking again. "Well, there was a very successful student retreat last year. We also have a very strong Peer Mentor Program."

He was finding it difficult to choose between his strong feelings of loyalty for Pico and the opposing need to get some things off his chest.

"Okay, we do need more programming on multiculturalism," he heard himself saying. **(7)** "The problem is, it seems people are either 100 percent for it or dead set against it.

graphic change. With a student body that had been predominantly white since its founding in 1887, the entering freshmen class had by 1994 become 50 percent of color. I picked the name "Pico" in honor of Pio Pico who was the first governor of California, dating all the way back to its settlement by Spanish explorers. Many are unaware that Pio Pico was part black.

6. Access. Access to Pico College was obtained initially through an inside administrator who had been a classmate in my Ph.D. program. Her contacts subsequently opened more doors for me, like this one. How much does fieldwork depend on a lucky tip? In this case, a great deal, since this informant was about to leave town and felt he could speak freely with me, well, almost.

7. Unit of Analysis. The unit of analysis in this study is the process of transition from a monocultural campus to a campus defined by cultural difference. In applying a

Some see us as flag bearers for positive change, but others see us as 'diversity police.'

"We also need to see the professional staffs on this campus go through the same training our students are going through. **(8)** But there is resistance to that idea."

As he sat in the dark room, Mark realized he was no longer in control of his own story. It was all coming out now, taking on a life of its own. In the curriculum, people were only making changes at the edges. Many professors agreed that multiculturalism was important but then failed to actually *do* it. English and Comparative Lit only offered a few special courses and that was it. This forces black students to choose between courses about themselves and courses about Shakespeare and *then* justify how they decide to their peers.

unit of analysis of this kind (and part way through the process), I found I had to focus on such varied tropes as multiple voices, power, resistance back, and privilege, all within a shifting context of disputed, fragmented, and contested cultural terrain.

8. Method and Techniques. I wanted to study the feelings and conflicts of the people who were change agents, resisting change, or apathetic about the decision to multiculturalize the campus. The data came from sixteen interviews, eleven observations, and multiple document reviews taken in a pilot study conducted over an eighteen-month period. Triangulation was helpful in view of the limited number of interviews conducted. Wherever possible, I adopted the style of letting the interviewee tell his or her own story, and this led to particularly rich emotions and impressions: on many occasions there was conflicting data, with stories of different informants at odds with each other.

The documents included the college five-year strategic plan, student newspapers, college program brochures, student diversity and leadership training workshop guides, the college catalog, and the president's speeches.

The data was placed into a "data dump" from which I culled out ten recurring themes: conflict, power, resistance to power, resistance back, whether multiculturalism includes or excludes Whites, Western vs. non-Western racial identities, the need for a new social unifier, white alienation or fear, moving toward an alternative regime or sentiment, and community.

"But it shouldn't have to be that way," he said, and this time he could hear the strain in his voice. **(9)** "Take the Religion Department. Guy comes in and teaches East Asian Religion. Students love it. Then the new prof leaves. The shot of energy is not institutionalized, so it's lost." Sensing he had the full attention of the researcher now, he added for effect, "And this is happening *all over campus*."

9. The Sampling Strategy was to interview administrators and professors who were most active in the move to multiculturalize the campus. This strategy was later amended when an administrator insisted that I interview several student leaders who gave me surprising information about race relations and especially about white students. The interview sample consisted of an even sampling of women and men and people of different ages and ethnicities. Observations were random.

Watching the researcher's eyes get big, he knew he would tell the researcher about the backlash. **(10)**

10. Resistance Back. The outgoing student affairs administrator believed that tension from Whites

How the president of Pico had articulated his vision so well, but that no one had thought out the possibility of a white backlash against multiculturalism.

Ah, this researcher is thirsty for tidbits like this last one, ones that tell him where the tensions really are at Pico. The soon-to-depart junior administrator knew he would be telling this researcher about the extent to which Godot had underestimated white resistance to multiculturalism, and this is *from his own high level staff!* And no one had even thought to prepare the *alumni* for what was coming.

Now he would finally tell someone that the first seven appointments Godot made without searches were all white males. **(11)** *All seven.* He would tell this researcher the story about the one senior white professor who stood up one day and announced that he would resign as a faculty member if one more white male was appointed to a top administrative post, and then not long after

who were feeling threatened by multiculturalism was being applied to the president, a thought confirmed by the dean of students, who strongly urged me to interview the president about this. An interview with the president yielded the opposite claim, namely, that the college and its trustees were still fully committed to the mission of multiculturalizing the campus. My own impression was that the president was telling me the company line and that inside, he was trying to cope with swirling emotions and tensions about the constantly changing levels of support he was receiving from faculty, trustees, staff, and students. Here at Pico, multiculturalism meant different things to different people, and these meanings were transforming.

11. Culture. I am still using "culture" to refer to "shared meaning" (e.g. Lett, 1987; Geertz, 1973). What's different is that I am going beyond ethnic derivations to include meanings based on race, class, gender, sexuality and age (see Park, 1993). This extends Rosaldo's (1989) critique of static definitions of culture, but I feel it is the only definition that makes sense at Pico,

that, accepted an offer to be next dean of students!

Would words ever be enough to describe all his emotions about Pico? How can you explain to an outsider how hard it is to work here? That it's in your face every day? That it enters into room rates, where the single-room dorms are all white because it's the whites who have the money to pay for more expensive rooms.

It hits you in the stomach when you read the first page of the student newspaper and find that the U.S. Office of Civil Rights has found Pico College guilty of sexual harassment. That two other people in the counseling office are suing for race discrimination. That two more employees are suing for age discrimination. All this in one week's issue of the paper!

where there are so many identities rubbing up against and overlapping so many others.

Thus, the idea of having one fixed ethnic history reside in one geographical locale now seems archaic. To have continued meaning, the term "culture" must now operate as a broader rubric that accounts for identities formed around such disparate categories (themselves far from monolithic) as race, ethnicity, gender, class, sexual orientation, immigrant status, age, religion, and physical capability. These meanings change over time, and in most cases an individual will have more than one basis for culture. Under this broader definition, the shared meanings of lesbians of color, for example, might constitute a "culture." Or, culture might derive from gender by itself. Being "a white male" could encompass shared meaning. This is not inconsistent with Rosaldo, who emphasized the importance of "process" and "layers" rather than seeing culture as one fixed structure or ordering mechanism. At Pico College, I definitely found process more meaningful than structure because social relations were changing so rapidly. Even such stratifications as "race" and "gender" were being reshaped, recombined, and recontextualized as the campus shifted from one dominant world view to multiple ones.

Mark was in his late twenties. As he sat staring straight ahead, he let his shoulders drop. His eyes were focusing on a spot between his body and the far wall, as if imagining an object hanging before his face. In a steady, droning voice, he told the researcher a recent story about the alumni office. Citing the alarm a proposed article might have caused within the ranks of a conservative white alumni base, **(12)** the director pulled an article from the forthcoming issue of the alumni magazine. Students were up in arms.

The article had been about "Reggae and Rastafarians" and it described the success of a new, charismatic professor of psychology. The professor, who was from the West Indies, taught that every culture should have a voice. Tall and wiry with fine, smooth facial skin, this professor wore dreadlocks down to his shoulders. His bearing was one of deep intelligence. The intensity and meter of his voice had a mesmerizing effect on students, who

12. Is Multiculturalism A Temporary Way Station? At Pico, patterns of change could be traced to different periods of time corresponding to shifting understandings of multiculturalism. As a result, there was no one campuswide understanding of the transformations necessary to accommodate that change, and some members of the community were holding on to meanings that others had long ago abandoned. Here, the alumni base was believed by some administrators to equate multiculturalism with race intrusion. Recall also the resistance to multiculturalism demonstrated by some professors in their late twenties and early thirties that came as a surprise to professors in their forties who had experienced the liberalism of the sixties and saw in multiculturalism a promising way to reorganize the campus community in the wake of the social upheaval of those times.

Was there an alliance forming between the youngest (white) fac-

were flocking to his classes as if drawn to a magnet.

With all the lawsuits, and the reggae story left out, was there any hope?

But then, I want to explain to this researcher that I will dearly miss this place, too. Do I dare tell him that I think the students here are truly great because they question everything? That the president is a truly superb human being?

As he paused, the young man saw what was really going on in this interview. But he realized it did not matter and sighed. Yes, this researcher is a sly one. He tricks me into telling him everything that peeves me. He knows I am a sucker for unloading all my frustration on him. He knows I am leaving. But I am a willing participant in this charade, am I not? And, of course, this is when the researcher asks, "What about the white students?"

So now I will have to tell him how white students often feel they are owed something because they are reaching out to help students of color and then get rejected.

I will tell him that many white students don't realize this is a life-long process and that you're not in it if you think you are owed something

ulty members and some older professors who had come out of Western tradition? If so, would it change the pace and trajectory of the movement to "multiculturalize" the institution? In contrast to what the president of Pico was claiming, this development implied a new and unanticipated "resistance back" by a potentially growing number of white professors.

While more fieldwork is necessary to confirm these developments, one indication is that there is now a need for a new space *after* multiculturalism that will give people from the "dominant" group, white males, a new and positive role in the new campus culture. This was one setting where a polyphonic novelistic approach worked well, by allowing for surprise and contradiction, and by including the voices of white professors and students who had been somewhat alienated by the relatively sudden transition to multiculturalism.

right away.

It has taken me some time to admit it **(13)**, but now I know you have to be in it for yourself in the sense that you have to risk something personally when you learn about other cultures; you have to be willing to change *yourself.*

At the same time, I will have to say that this thing of multiculturalism is not about you personally. If you are raised in the dominant group and then some Latino student comes along and tells you there are two kinds of whites, racists and paternalizing liberals, you know it's not about you personally but about one Latino student who's had certain experiences and is still trying to work through his perceptions.

What have I learned? I have learned the self-doubts white students are feeling are what students of color have to go through every day. I have learned that the feeling that you always have to prove yourself is not the normal experience for white students. And also...

13. Positionality. As a person of color, I have experienced the sharp sting of cultural domination in the academy, often by people I believed were acting in my best interests. One professor told me to take my interest in multiculturalism and study somewhere else. Another angrily told me his division had not hired a single white male professor in five years because of "overemphasis" on diversity. In fact, his division had not hired *anybody* in five years and his colleagues remained *all white!*

When another professor asked how I could be a third-generation American and in the United States longer than his family had, I could only conclude from his shocked look that as a second-generation Irish American he believed he had more of a right to be in the United States than I did.

At the same time, my position in the field defined the power I held as researcher. I found the two positions often merged, my power as researcher and the emotions that came from prior life experiences. This shaped the way I perceived, recorded, and now represent events: initially, this caused me to be looking for or receptive to certain pieces of data others might not consider important or might miss (like pain or hopelessness). Later it caused me to want to write up only what I felt was important.

Nonetheless, the conflicts are represented as undiluted and multi-layered as I found them. Here, I think it was crucial for me to convey the tensions as action, as unresolved experience, that is, in Bakhtin's sense, in the form of *unfinalized* event. I think this urge to convey the unfinalizability of events will compensate in some immeasurable way for the bias contained in my high authority and pain.

The president of Pico College was finally forced to chuckle. **(14)** His second-floor office also afforded an unobstructed view of the Old Student Union building farther down the hill, and large, garish, multicolored posters were hanging from the false balconies of that aging, off-color Spanish-style building. This week, there were more than usual:

Planned Parenthood. May 10th!
Amandla/New Governance/
  New South Africa!

14. Historicizing and Recontextualizing. In a sense, Pico College seemed to be acting out a flipped application of power and resistance, where people of color now held control (the president, multicultural program administrators and professors, and some students of color) and Whites were on the defensive. But at the same time, some senior white professors, trustees, and alumni also retained much power by virtue of their seniority and numbers, in the sense that

Suburban Alphabet/Art Week
Ancient Celtic Witchcraft. May 23
Zeta Tau Communis
Women's Forum-Discuss
   with/about Black Women.
   May 26
Porn Panel! May 24
AIDS & College Campuses.
   May 24
Asian American Heritage Week.
   May 16-20!

The festive atmosphere of the student marquee always gave him hope. The emotions that emanated from the students every year in the spring were always rejuvenating for him, too. Seeing these banners, the serious man realized that he cherished moments like this and let himself feel emboldened. It's almost like the students are telling me, "You're on the right track, you're on the right track, keep it up!"

Godot now let his emotion turn into a fleeting sense of elation. It had taken five hard years to make this campus into a place where difference could be engaged openly and discussed with good humor.

But was this all an illusion, he asked himself? You keep going back to the board of trustees and each time you leave feeling that you have their support. But don't fool your-

"power" means control over others and over one's own life. The latter had the wherewithal to stall, hold back, even sabotage efforts to add more gender, race, and class perspectives to the campus.

What I am here calling "resistance back" by white males ironically mirrors the resistance one finds in classical studies of resistance *against* the West written about colonized peoples or by women around the world (e.g., Martin, 1987; Ong, 1987; Chatterjee, 1989; Kondo, 1990a; J. W. Scott, 1991; Stoler, 1991; J. C. Scott, 1992; Nordstrom & Martin, 1992; and Tsing, 1993).

What could unite this campus? As a monocultural world view gives way partially to a multicultural one, will new social unifiers supersede a totalizing Western way of knowing? With no new organizing framework, there was confusion about what should constitute truth or *be valued*. As one informant indicated, the decentering forced students to choose artificially between traditional knowledge (as presented in a course on Shakespeare) and a new and as yet unsettled view of "multiple" perspectives.

On the other hand, at least one

self. The leading trustee committees are manned by white males. Sooner or later they will get fed up with all this controversy and demand someone's head. And my fine, cultured head is black!

informant (the associate dean of students) observes that if there is going to be a new sense of community at Pico, it will be a "process" of working to learn about one's own differences and seeing the link between that pain and the pain experienced by others. This means that if there is going to be new unity, it might very well be a *process* or *sentiment* and not a new structure at all.

Was this a case where multiculturalism was moving so quickly that it left out European American stories, or at least failed to rearticulate those stories within the new, shifting context? One result was that some white supporters, alumni, faculty, and administrators had begun to experience a kind of fear, or *anomie*. If so, I do not attribute this to a failure of proponents of multiculturalism at Pico College to plan for it, so much as the newness of multiculturalism as an epistemological thrust and the inability of that movement to break entirely free of its initial need to distinguish itself from and gain freedom from a rooted, totalizing Western epistemology.

At the same time, the alienation of whites at Pico might be a direct result of their own inability to let go of unexamined positions of privilege, a mind-set which could deprive them of future ability to know pain, construct new identities, and attain connections to others (community) not based on superiority.

In the basement of the Old Student Union, a tall, well-built student sat alone at a table in the snack bar. **(15)** White picnic-like tables ran down the length of the room. Loud noises were coming from two places at once, from diners who were sitting to his left and from a young woman cashier who stood behind the counter to his right screaming something through a cubbyhole at the cook in back.

Antonio sat up stiffly as he came to a sudden thought. "Class difference matters a lot around here," he blurted out with a force that caught him by surprise. A light-complected Latino, Antonio had a large, square head with very short brown-black hair. He was broad-shouldered and had the appearance of a high school football player. He wondered how he would explain to the others how he had reached this conclusion.

He would tell Minerva and Liz to check it out for themselves: the

15. Interculturalism. One of the things surfaced by this pilot study is the need for a new cultural mapping that neutralizes the hurtfulness of vertical social or racial hierarchies. One of the most promising is "interculturalism" (e.g., Marranca & Dasgupta, 1991) which promotes exchange *across* cultures. An intercultural approach differs from the "bazaar of ethnic cultures" where one can buy this culture or that culture "straight off the rack," as Mike Davis (1992: 80) once described the L.A. Art Festival's early approach to implementing multiculturalism.

In an intercultural approach, the different identities (ethnic, racial, gendered, etc.) are not arrayed like cans of soup on a supermarket shelf. Instead, they are seen in *interaction* with each other, in all the splendor and disorder one might imagine where there are competing interests, overlappings in identity,

upper-middle-class students sit in the *old* cafeteria and the lower-class students sit in the *new* cafeteria.

Funny, isn't it? It's the old cafeteria that the upper-class students eat in. The long rows of tables are crammed too closely together, so these students eat together like sardines packed neatly in a can. Then there's the new cafeteria, where students from working-class families eat. Loads of space. Go figure. In fact, with all the space, why is it that the ten tables there are bunched tightly together in the middle of the room? It's almost like this is to protect the diners from a large predator.

Will Minerva and Liz listen to me?

Back at the Multicultural Center, a young woman with amber skin and hazel eyes was shaking her head in a heated debate with another woman. "We need to remind ourselves that the Peer Mentor Program *is working*."

A tall, stocky young black male stopped by and whispered something in Elizabeth's ear, but before she could respond the man stood,

and multiple plays of power. (Compare Burbeles & Rice, 1991, regarding the hopefulness in dialogue across difference.)

Interculturalism is not unlike the "cross-culturalism" discussed by Lucy Lippard (1990) and Partricia Hill Collins (1986) in visual art and sociology, respectively. Here, art or discourse is centered within the person and then compared across ethnic or gender groups. Interculturalism also shares a kindred spirit with the "border crossing" metaphor of Anzaldua (1987), which refers to movements of racial or ethnic groups across geographic terrain in the manner exemplified by Mexicans crossing the U.S. border. (See also Rosaldo, 1989; Gomez-Pena, 1990; Giroux, 1992; McLaren, 1994a; and Giroux & McLaren, 1994.)

In border crossings, some cultural patterns are lost, others are retained, and still others are merged in a kind of "mestizaje." One could now ask, might "border crossing" aptly describe the experience of the European American student who comes to Pico College from a homogeneous (white) middle-class suburb?

In a similar tracking of move-

laughed, and moved away. Elizabeth's hair was both blond and kinky. She smiled then, and her whole face lit up.

"Wait, Elizabeth," Minerva said. "Don't you think we should be telling people what needs to be done to *improve* the program, too?

"I mean, okay, a few weeks ago we had Value Diversity Week. Then last semester we did Sexuality and Political Thought. But it's not all roses. I mean, is our work *only* for students of color and women and gays and lesbians?"

ment, Clifford (1992) analyzes how cultural groups come into contact with each other as "traveling cultures."

The most intriguing cultural mapping of all, however, may be "transculturalism" (Ortiz, 1947/1940; Daniel, 1992), which moves away from a dominant-minority or binary view of acts of interrelating and instead focuses on the mutual process of change that occurs when multiple cultures come into contact with each other. G. Reginald Daniel (1992) in particular stresses the need to move beyond the limits of vertical social arrangements and toward an arrangement that is more "horizontal."

In this instance, I am using interculturalism to encompass not only the way in which distinct identities interact but also the way in which this richness of perspective defines a new wholeness in human experience, what Bakhtin once called "an eternal harmony of unmerged voices" (1984/1929: 30).

The fact that Pico College does not yet reflect that wholeness is not what is important. What is important is that *some* people at one private liberal arts college (its president, dean of students, key faculty, student leaders, and others) feel a strong emotional need to carve out something new, something like harmony, while keeping the development of separate identities alive. I think it is not inaccurate to conclude that this campus is struggling to identify a feeling or sentiment that would exemplify Bakhtin's full sense of polyphony.

"Yeah," Elizabeth said after pausing for a split-second, "yeah, okay, Whites. **(16)** We know our white classmates are feeling left out of all this, but what will our friends say if we tell them about this?" Her voice was straining. "Will they listen to us?"

Minerva had dark brown skin and long black hair. She thought for a moment before making a face. "Well, it's true. A lot of whites just want the food and the dance, the nice ethnic stuff. So they are a little behind the times. They need to learn there's more to us than that.

"But to tell you the truth, I see my job as MECHA chair to help Latino students first. The whole system is still set up to support whites. So why should we give them *our* help?"

16. Bias. In an ironic twist, I now find Western crisis and dissolution fascinating. As a third generation Japanese American, I came into this study with scars from having grown up in a dominant culture not always friendly to my family's ethnic history (a total stranger once yelled to me it was "my people" who bombed Pearl Harbor, when in fact my father was U.S. born and a junior at UCLA when that war broke out). As a result, I have a tendency to look for or expect racial tension. In this study, I had a recurring tendency to consider the "dismantling" of Western (or white male) domination an important trope. I *looked* for evidence of it.

At the same time, I have another bias that comes from my own ethnic history, which demands "undy-

At the Old Student Union, Antonio was almost finished with his sandwich when he came to a second realization. "I am going to have to tell Minerva and Liz about this, too. I have to remind them we have a financial crisis at Pico. We're *losing money*. We're dipping into our endowment at the rate of 5 percent a year for operating expenses. Even two years of this would really hurt our endowment fund.

"We have to remind other students that our overall student retention rate is only 70 percent, not good for a school with our reputation. Students are leaving this place in droves! It shouldn't be like that for a small private residential college like us. Minerva and Liz will have to listen to this. They have to. It affects us all."

At the Multicultural Center, Elizabeth and Minerva were giving each other' knowing looks. When they address the student rally, they will have to emphasize the *positive* things, too.

ing optimism." I think it is the *combination* of fascination with breakdown and wanting to find hope that led me to represent what I in fact represented in this write-up. In doing this, I may have missed seeing some information or left out others I had seen (for example, the college president's belief that "excellence" would cut across cultural difference and thereby create unity). Very conceivably, I read in a significance for either disintegration or renewal that was partly of my own making.

With a concern for ethics in naturalistic fieldwork (e.g., Clandinin & Connelly, 1994), I conclude that there are several pitfalls in this study I had to watch out for in particular: (1) a tendency to look for dramatic problems and dive into the first earth-shattering story I encountered; (2) a tendency to romanticize the subject or unit of analysis; (3) a need to become emotionally involved in events; and (4) an inclination to either defer to power or actively resist it.

Here, for example, I was captured by the aura of power to transform held by the president of Pico College. While I tried not to defer too much to that power (or critique it too severely), it was also

A large polished wooden desk stood at one end of the Pico College president's office. On one side of the desk there was a personal computer. A large framed painting of a tiger hung on the wall directly behind the desk. The walls were of dark oak and the rug dark brown. A soft couch ran along the bay window facing due west. At the south end of the room, nearest the door, there was an oval-shaped hardwood table with four wooden chairs.

Alone in his thoughts, Godot was fully aware of the resistance to multiculturalism at Pico. White students were frustrated. Alumni were unhappy. The forty-member board of trustees maintained a wide range of enthusiasm about multiculturalism. Some will up and decide that we have gone far enough and seek a return to a Western Civilization emphasis.

Still, he believed that excellence did not have a color tag. Multiculturalism should not be anti-white or anti-community. It was *enabling*.

Did we send out a signal to Whites that they don't count? **(17)** Well, they *do* count. And this is what's missing from multiculturalism so far. Now we have to bend back the other way to make Whites clear I could do only so much to control my emotions and hunches. One of the advantages to presenting data in a polyphonic novelistic way was to counter those tendencies by including points of view that were not my own, even when I did not like them.

17. The End of Social Theory? In observing the beginning of the end of a one-culture view of history and knowledge at Pico College, I could not help but conclude that all the recent movements (poststructuralism, deconstruction, feminist theory, multiculturalism, queer theory, new history, postmodern art and architecture,

feel they can belong here, too.

Take the catalog. Last year it had a cover photo showing a black, a Latina, and an Asian student talking with a Chicano professor. Boy, did that get the white alumni all hot and bothered! The thing is, the same people who say we should have included Whites in the cover photo would not have been surprised if the picture had contained *only* Whites. To calm the waters, we are revising the catalog by not making multiculturalism so blatant.

But what I want to tell everyone is that we are about something larger than all this, that there is more than just all this difference. But how? I need to tell the students and the trustees that there will be no "community" if we are nothing but a loose collection of differences.

There's a reason I took this job. It had to do with my being black in America. It had to do with my being lucky enough to have opportunities and wanting to make sure others had the same kinds of chances in life. But have things now changed?

Are we now beyond that original purpose? Don't we need a new arrangement, where Whites aren't at the center but they aren't excluded either?

subaltern studies, postcolonial studies, and even critical theory) are fueled by the same sentiment, which is the driving question of whether and how to dismantle a mono racial, male-centered hierarchy of knowledge born of Western colonialism. Implicit in this inquiry is the question of where Whites will now fit in.

Pico College could not of course address overnight all the questions raised by all the dismantling thrusts in social theory. The fact that it had decided to move in a *con*structive direction was admirable.

But toward what end? Why do this?

If C. Wright Mills (1959) was right about locating the need for new social theory at that place where social theory cannot explain a problem that is important and personal to the researcher, then we are perhaps at a turning point. Isn't it here, at a place like Pico where dissolution and re-creation seem to co-reside, that new theory must be born? If so, I had a feeling social theory would not come back as a way of structuring knowledge, not *that* kind of theory. At Pico, theory would become a way of taking into account both process *and* feeling.

My role? I was hired to make this place multicultural, and now I'm trying to make this place better for Whites!

Well, it's paying off. I can't complain. Our fund-raising efforts netted $1.6 million in one month alone. We are up in both percent of alumni donors and total dollars raised for the year.

Godot sucked in his breath and let it out slowly. Well, we are not taking a straight path, but we are making progress. Wait, what are all those students doing down there?

Bakhtin was himself quite taken by the idea of death and renewal. To him, the whole reason for writing about crisis and catastrophe was to discover a new way of social relating which would be life affirming, that is, to find a "place for working out...a new mode of inter-relationships between individuals, counterposed to the all-powerful socio-hierarchical relationships of noncarnival life" (Bakhtin, 1984/1929: 122–127).

And this brings me to my own passion: when existing social theory cannot explain why race, gender, sexual orientation, power, and class differences continue to confound citizens and their social institutions in a "democratic" society, then perhaps theory has become "un-hinged" from its social context. The need for new theory is implicit.

Two rows of lab counters ran down the length of a twenty by sixty foot room at east campus. **(18)** The counters were loaded with scientific equipment. Flasks. Burners. Measuring tools. Copper wires. Several students sat hunched over their work. Except for the sound of their tinkering, and the soft music from a radio, the room was still.

18. Significance/Contribution to the Field. This writing is an experimental attempt at applying Bakhtin's concept of polyphony to the reporting of social science research. Despite several methodological problems that I encountered, this early effort suggests that Bakhtin's approach can make two immediate contributions to

An Asian woman, a Latino male, a white woman, and an Asian male were all fingering their equipment in the biochemistry lab. At one end of the two rows a white woman in her thirties sat reading a manual.

Watching all this from the doorway, Professor Stevens recalled how hard it had been when she first started out here. It had been brutal to be a research scientist, do cutting-edge work, teach eager students, and raise a family, all at the same time.

We did do well in the sciences during my tenure here. What was it? In the last ten years, 192 of our students went to medical school. Another 79 went on to do graduate work in the sciences. Still another 127 had gone on to professional schools.

But getting approval for the new course on "Gender and Science" was what hurt the most. I have kept this inside me all these years. It hasn't been easy, but I'm still here. Stevens looked gaunt from all the wear.

What do you do when the senior professors in biology, physics, geology, and physiological psychology are all white men? It's the subtle forms of discrimination that are the real killers, like not getting guidelines or helpful critiques from senior

research:

1. *First, it appears that a polyphonic novelistic writing allows the researcher to represent the multiple voices and emotions of a heterogeneous population in a more nuanced fashion than traditional reporting.* I could show, for example, that some students saw the fiscal crisis at Pico as truly devastating, while the president saw it as another operating problem that required him to project an image of control for an institution that was receiving "record alumni contributions."

Writing in a novelistic form thus allowed me to discover and express the complexity, conflicts, and surprises of the people I studied by empowering them with their own voices and authority, something that is not easily developed in the traditional reporting form which is linear and requires reducing findings to fixed categories.

A polyphonic novelistic style can be superior to traditional forms when writing about issues of race, gender, and power differences, since the traditional writer's own position as author never gets discussed and is left, as a result, to influence the write-up without ex-

professors along the way.

Professor Stevens shook her head slowly. Someone had to be in the vanguard. Someone had to take the "hits" on the forehead.

But why do they resist us, she asked herself finally. The amazing thing is to watch them. Many of these professors feel terribly threatened by diversity. My own husband is tenure track here, and he can't deal with it!

Then there's Larsen, who feels as a white male there is no longer a place for him, and *he's* one of the ones who's trying! But most of them just shut up. They won't even confront diversity, even if it's in front of their own eyes. Well, except for Tenille, who says, "Why change if it's been so successful?" You see, they only want to teach what's worked for them.

Gathering her notes for the next class, Professor Stevens wondered whether anyone even cared about her travails.

amination.

I also think a polyphonic novelistic writing is particularly effective in times of high cultural fragmentation and change, conditions which are only awkwardly or reductionistically navigated by traditional modes of representation. I find it offers flexibility where there are issues of power and resistance, where people have multiple or conflicting loyalties, or where the story is one of joy or other deep human emotion.

At Pico, for example, two students of color empathized with the alienation felt by classmates who were white and not included in the movement to multiculturalize the campus. In contrast, at least one entrenched professor continued to frustrate attempts by a female professor to teach gender in the sciences. A polyphonic rendition captures this multiplicity of emotions without having to comment on it.

In addition, the polyphonic concept of "unfinalizability" seemed very powerful to me in the sense that I did not ever feel forced to reduce the findings to final resolution or clarity or steer them into fixed categories. Except for the data dump, which I completed as a

Two floors below the president's office, Drew Lockerby was preparing a speech on sexual harassment, race, and ethnicity, what it means to be a woman and a man, what it means to be gay and bisexual, and what it means to be disabled, or Jewish.

With long thin bones and sinewy arms and legs, Drew had a youthful appearance. His face was angular and alive. In a few minutes, he had a scheduled meeting with the organizers of "Faces in the Crowd." As associate dean of students, he knew he played a big role in its continued existence. In fact, he could scarcely contain his energy when it came to this project.

Who could guess that "Faces in the Crowd would be such a smashing success? We take ten or twelve returning students and get them to look into themselves by confronting their diversity, then let them act out their stories on orientation day to entering freshmen. Now in the spring, they were putting the finishing touches on their pieces for next August.

Has this year been *too* successful? Was "too much" pain dripping off of these students' stories? Drew did not want next year's entering

matter of form more than anything else, I did not feel that I had to conform findings to any preexisting vocabulary. What mattered more was the dialogue *between* characters and, in some cases, between two sides to one person. I think this focus on multiplicity and incompleteness allowed me to capture the surprise, contradiction, and incompleteness of events at Pico College.

Finally, as a researcher of color, I find that writing in a polyphonic style lets me see that there are multiple identities within me. This was not possible in my earlier writing, where I had to either write in the authoritarian manner of the dominant culture or express myself in a very fragmented and unsatisfying way. Here, the characters of a polyphonic writing each touch a different part of me and this multiplicity creates a feeling of release for the parts that have been repressed. It creates a euphoria. It is a new way of seeing humanity.

2. *The second contribution that Bakhtinian polyphonic novelistic writing makes to social science research is a new capability, an ability to track and report the progress that a racially heterogeneous community makes toward a*

students to become frightened of Pico before setting foot in their first classes.

A tall white man leaned his head into the open doorway and smiled broadly. He seemed to take pride in interrupting Drew's thoughts. "We're ready," said Trent McWilliams, a junior.

Drew remembered how upset Trent had been when other students in "Faces" started fighting and crying earlier in the year. All it took was someone saying "Gesundheit" and then an atheist yelling at the well-wisher not to make a religious statement! Others then complained about the "overemphasis" on homosexuality and about race being left out.

But Drew knew that for Trent the greatest moment of release and suffering was yet to come. He was "coming out" in front of the entire freshman class next fall. The returning students at Pico did not know that he was gay.

It's all about taking risks and being very vulnerable, Drew concluded. Some of the stories will be negative. But there is always the hope that freshmen will embrace the diversity and pain, and that this will make their own adjustment to college

social arrangement of "unity and difference." Is one reason why we can't break the deadlock between Western retrenchment (monocultural unity) and early multiculturalism (difference at the expense of unity) the fact that we write and know in the mode of a Cartesian "either/or" dichotomy? (e.g., Daniel, 1992). Polyphonic novelistic writing might offer a way out of this impasse by freeing the writer from always having to reduce findings to one fixed result or synthesis that freezes out the possibility of multiple perspectives.

At Pico College, I had hoped to find harmony but instead encountered multiple levels of conflict. Unity and difference did not yet coexist at this campus setting. Ironically, the European American identity seemed for the moment the most marginalized from the move to multiculturalize the campus. It was clear to me, however, that there would be no social unity until the European American student was "re-included."

This is not to say that unity and difference will never coexist, and I tend to think that places like Pico College will be among the first to arrive there. But is the celebration

a little easier.

Drew reluctantly reached another conclusion: not everyone would see that antisemitism was related to "classism," which was related to racism, and sexism, and "ablism."

Well, just knowing you have permission to examine all this, to feel human, to have a safe place to do this, isn't that what we're all about? It's all about –

Process. It's all about *process!* Trent was bending his head into the open doorway one more time, this time finishing Drew's sentence for him. And, just as suddenly, the smiling Trent had whipped his head away and was gone from view.

We're movin' in the right direction, Drew consoled himself. But we live in a capitalistic society which says there must be somebody on the bottom in order for there to be somebody at the top. There has to be oppression, right? Otherwise, capitalism falls apart.

And the European American? He's struggling with "I am a bad person because we've oppressed so many people of color." So, what can be done for them?

Well, *the first step is to validate their fear*. It's wrong to assume their pain is any less than the pain of stu-

of difference, and resulting dislocation of the centrality of European Americans, the necessary precursor to unity and difference at some later date? Or instead, will the acknowledgment of cultural difference forever preclude new unity, as it had done so far for some European American students who wished to participate?

But just when oppressed groups are beginning to articulate their identities and histories free from the totalizing voice of Western knowledge, who will dare ask them for unity across groups? Even if cultural differences could be nurtured to clarity, can these differences be made to exist over a sustained period of time in dynamic tension with unity?

The question of whether social unity and cultural difference might coexist adumbrates the larger question of what happens to human beings when institutions change radically the rules by which value is accorded, worth is felt, and meaning is constructed.

And here I have to ask: if Whiteness has been excluded from efforts to multiculturalize, here and elsewhere, then why so far have social scientists overlooked this?

dents of color or of women, or lesbians and gays and bisexuals. We know what it feels like to have pain and we need to validate how they feel when they are giving up a little bit of their control.

Step two is to move from that pain to recognizing that other people have pain, too. If we all begin to do that, it means I can take my happy black behind to...*Drew could not finish the thought because this time Trent came in and playfully bit him on the back of the neck. Time to go.*

Are some white social scientists blind to examining their own shifting positionalities? These are questions that demand attention over time. It is a call that beckons.

3. *A comment needs to be made here about "carnival," which refers to Bakhtin's vision of how a utopian social order might come to be.* It would require a separate paper to do justice to this concept, but there is in the data here a hint of the "carnivalesque," here at Pico College.

Bakhtin (1984/1929: 122) refers to carnival as a "pageant without footlights" where "everyone is an active participant, everyone communes" and where "the laws, prohibitions and restrictions that determine the structure and order of ordinary, that is, noncarnival, life are suspended." In a carnivalesque moment, everything that buttresses the existing social hierarchy, its "forms of terror, reverence, piety, and etiquette," is discarded. In place of official order, there is a new way of interrelating characterized by the profane: by "free and familiar contact" with others, by parodies or debasings of the sacred text, by laughter, and by a mocking or de-crowning of the person who

The dark oak walls of the president's office echoed the somber mood of the carpet. At the bay window, one could stare for long hours, envisioning another time and place.

Exiting his office, the middle-aged man with large hands stopped and looked at a white-haired Mrs. Knorr. Her smile held a strange mix of hope and despair. There's something you need to know. There are lots of students gathering in the foyer. Seems they are protesting our catalog for next year. Saying we have taken the word "multiculturalism" out of it, that this means we are backing away from multiculturalism. Oh, yes, and Dean Wilder is on the phone.

Oh, my, was all he said, and he reversed course, heading back into his office.

occupies the top of the social hierarchy (in rural Russia, that would be the mayor of the town).

While Bakhtin's wish for the carnivalesque might seem too utopian or dated for us, arising as it did from an almost nostalgic fixation on rural Russia of the late 1800s, it is impossible, I feel, to ignore the at times crazed mood of "carnival" that struck me with all the updendings of social order I encountered here in my research.

I tried to imagine what it felt like to see fraternity brothers in a pitched battle with students from the Black Students Alliance. I wondered how it felt to be a student on this campus when the campus paper reported in one issue that the college had been found guilty of sexual harassment *and* that several more lawsuits were on the way based on age discrimination and race discrimination.

What was happening here, in this place where multiculturalism was supposed to be embraced and everyone's culture was going to be valued?

Was there a profaning of life at Pico College? Had Pico embarked on a course where a social structure based on a Western, male view of what counts was being tipped over? If so, then perhaps the "mayor" here is not a person at all but rather Westernism. In this tilting, some might feel threatened, like those who blocked efforts to include gender issues in the hard sciences and those who prevented an Asian religion professor from being rehired. Recall how alumni affairs had withdrawn an article about reggae and rastafarians from the alumni magazine, in order not to alarm a conservative alumni base?

But the most graphic example of this mood of departing from the existing rules of social hierarchy is the one provided by "Faces in the Crowd," where returning students present entering freshmen with their stories of pain and arrival, the coming out of lesbians and gays, the difficulties with being Jewish, the feelings by some whites that they don't have a culture.

Whether the end of one social hierarchy will lead to a rebirth at Pico College of lived life, community, and human interrelating (Bakhtin, 1984/1929: 166–169) remains to be seen. I have to say that I sometimes wondered if all the introspection here was initiating a healthy process of renewal or merely a painful and drawn out process of social fragmentation. One hopes (and I believe) it is the former.

4. There is a fourth issue. It is the question of *what is lost by the representation of ethnographic findings in a polyphonic novelistic form?* As in Dostoyevsky's writing, there are limitations to the application of polyphonic novelistic writing to social science research. First, I think the idea that a writer can take his or her voice out of the narrative is illusory: I still found myself putting in what I wanted to put in and leaving out what I wanted to leave out.

In this chapter, for example, I could repeat almost verbatim the Pico College president's words about his commitment to multiculturalism coming from his own experience as a black man growing up in America, but I had to read emotions into the "shiny steel arcs" of the fountain based on my take on his personality. This bias can to some extent be compensated for by giving each informant his or her own voice. But I think it is important to do more than that, to actually admit personal biases as part of the write-up, that is, to make the admission of relevant bias *de ri-*

gueur.

Second, the Bakhtinian emphasis on interaction between characters and on the "uninfinalizability" of events and ideas flies in the face of the categorizing that we as Western researchers are taught to do. I find that the emphasis on incompleteness and multiple perspectives makes it difficult to have the narrative itself engage in a dialogue with prior research, which is written in a different key. I miss that direct exchange.

Third, it was impossible to put linear, compartmentalized analysis into the text of the narrative (and indeed, this is not allowed under Bakhtinian polyphonic novelistic writing). The result was that the analysis got crammed into the sidenotes, and my own voice and authority constantly wandered into the story. The "dialogue" between narrative and sidenotes therefore became increasingly strained: the more I sought to make each writing pure (either polyphonic or analytical), the harder it was to relate one to the other. As a result, I think both writings suffered.

Fourth, it was truly a trying task to create a "plot" out of the data I had gathered. As it turned out, the college itself provided a momentary denouement when over hundred students occupied the administration building for three days and demanded a written promise from the institution that it would not back down from its commitment to multiculturalism. The fear among many students of color was that the college was going too far in its recent attempts to reach out to white applicants and wealthy alumni, and that this was signaling the end of the era of multiculturalism on this model campus. But in this ironic flip in power relations, it becomes appropriate to ask: Don't people of color have to be willing to change, too? Don't they have a responsibility to reach out to Whites? Unfinalizability, indeed.

Even with all the difficulties I encountered in writing this experimental text, there is one point that makes it all worthwhile. Somewhat mischievously, I find the polyphonic novelistic style "subversive" in that it almost renders monological expression small.

(Originally published in Tierney, W.G. & Lincoln, Y.S., ed. 1997. *Representation and the Text*. Albany, NY: SUNY Press.)

Finding Limits to Multiculturalism

This study surfaced a number of larger generalizations about the effectiveness of multiculturalism as a framework for social interaction on college campuses and provided a sense of direction for the studies I present in chapters 3 and 4. At the outset, I want to emphasize that the work at Pico College to create "multicultural" course content and student activities teaching students about race, ethnic, gender, and sexual diversity was truly groundbreaking and courageous. At the time, there was no other applied framework available to break the hold of Western Eurocentrism over the life of a college or university campus (see e.g., McCarthy & Apple, 1988; Smith, 1989; Sleeter, 1991; Altbach & Lomotey, 1991; Shohat & Stam, 1994). This alone made the attempt to create "the first multicultural college campus" a valuable first step in carving out constructive approaches to diversity in an increasingly diverse United States. At the same time, this study showed that the earliest forms of multiculturalism could also lead to new problems that other institutions will want to avoid.

First, it was clear that *the kind of multiculturalism at Pico College did indeed overlook the needs of white students, staff, and faculty.* While not the intended result, this development may have derived from a belief that white members on campus were already well taken care of in a white dominant U.S. society, as indicated by the words of the Pico College president. But there was a second factor. While multiculturalism purported to embrace all cultures, in reality it had focused foremost on the cultures of people of color (and at this campus, the "shared meanings" of women and gays and lesbians), in other words, people whose voices had been left out of the mainstream curriculum.

In other words, this study revealed that *multiculturalism was in "binary opposition" to Western Eurocentrism because it had to be.* Fighting to break free from the monolithic perspective of Western civilization and history that by its nature excluded diversity, the Latinos and African Americans and Asian Americans on this campus found that in order to insert their histories they needed to unseat the "naturalizing" quality of a Western colonialist history that defined a Eurocentric perspective as normal and all others as alien. They had to "resist" the monolithic impetus and they did this by telling their stories.

But when they were confronted with these stories, some white members on campus felt a need to defend *their* history, by re-valorizing Western Eurocentrism through hyperbolized versions of the original form or restating that history in a "sanitized" version that allowed in other voices but kept its own stories central. In other words, the more conservative members of the campus community "resisted back." With both sides unbending, each action and reaction further fanned the flames of opposition between two firm positions that seemed mutually reinforcing, perhaps manifesting a true relation of "binary oppositionality."

Third, *the onset of a formal multiculturalism unintentionally exacerbated the ongoing social fragmentation at this site.* For some white members of the campus, any positive feelings deriving from their membership in an advancing Western civilization was instantly diminished and that process of advancement was recast in negative terms as "colonialism." For people of color, the cumulative pain from a long history of oppression in the country was "made raw" by fresh demands by some white members of the campus for a return to Western Eurocentric history. In this context, multiculturalism had the effect of heightening and formalizing the binary quality of an inegalitarian and oppositional set of relations that was already in place.

We know in retrospect that when leaders at Pico College decided to admit a racially diverse student body during the 1980s, they did not anticipate they would trigger the behavior Gordon Allport (1954) encountered in the South in the early 1950s, where mixing together of people from different racial backgrounds, even with the aim of promoting racial harmony, could ironically lead to greater race conflict. At the same time, the multiculturalists at Pico College had a point. With Western knowledge installing its history and whiteness at the center, it was Western Eurocentrism that had created and maintained this "binary oppositionality" in the first place. The problem for Pico College was that the solution of creating a multicultural response could not both "decenter" Eurocentrism and at the same time offer its white members a new, non-binary basis for belonging to a multiethnic campus.

In other words, there was a fourth generalization, that in attempting to dismantle a system that placed European Americans (and heterosexuals and men) at the top of the campus social pyramid, *the nascent framework of multiculturalism could not then articulate a new community that would be inclusive of all groups*. Under multiculturalism, the white student, faculty member, or staff person could not enjoy a redefined role that would feel positive to her or him—as long as the work of deconstructing an oppressive Eurocentric history was still underway. Absent clear guidance about how they might participate as full members, these white students and staff and faculty felt a deeper sense of awkwardness best symbolized by the creation of a "White Student Union" that signals, if nothing else, a wish for a new way of belonging.

Fifth, it was surprising in light of this context of uncertainty, resistance and resistance back that *members of this college campus still wanted to achieve harmony*. They wanted to have a sense of unity across all these forms of difference, and this was perhaps the greatest testimony to this courageous multicultural project.

What Do White Students Want?

Some might conclude from the Pico College experiment that multiculturalism is destructive and a complete mistake. Nothing, however, could be further from the truth. That conclusion would be unfair to those who showed the courage to experiment with early approaches to diversity in U.S. higher education. In fact, a deeper analysis will show it is not *the addition* of stories of people of color and women and lesbians and gays into the curriculum that made for increased tensions on this campus but rather the "dichotomous" way in which these early multicultural efforts located those stories "in opposition to" the dominant stories that were Western and Eurocentric, male and heterosexual.

As reported here, the leaders at Pico College were surprised to discover several years into their project that a large group of their own students was feeling left out. Simply put, the multicultural movement was not addressing the needs of the college's white students. In what was intended to be a "safe" atmosphere for learning about difference, a number of ugly incidents arose. As noted in the polyphonic text, a brawl took place between students from a white fraternity and students from the Black Student Alliance. Soon after that, several students started their "White Student Union." At about this time, the school newspaper reported—in the same issue—two race discrimination suits filed by staff, two filed for age discrimination, and a finding of sexual harassment by the U.S. Office of Civil Rights. What these events suggested was that the bold initiative to introduce social justice into one college by favoring and valuing a multicultural perspective had the result of alienating many white students, staff, and faculty on campus.

One very large implication from this study was therefore that *future diversity efforts would need to treat difference in other than binary terms that always position one group against another and instead establish a system that will enable members of "formerly dominant" classes (white, male, heterosexist, etc.) to co-construct with members of oppressed groups the new "central values."* While Pico College fell short of its lofty goals, it arguably set the stage for future work in diversity in higher education that would more successfully engage all the members of a diverse campus community.

A second larger finding in this study was that *efforts to alter the hierarchical effects of culture and power would need to provide new sources of "buy in" for wealthy alumni and other donors—and make those factors an inviting part of the overall change process.* For example, it was shown in this study that wealthy white alumni were complaining about the cover of the college catalogue that featured five people of color—and "no Whites." During the same period, the alumni office withdrew from the alumni magazine a feature story about a black professor who had captivated students with a course called "Reggae and Rastafarians." Citing a wish not to alarm their wealthy white alumni, the alumni director could not have been more prescient. In the ensuing months, alumni giving began to plummet. Wealthy white alumni were apparently finding their alma mater "unlike the campus we attended." In other words, there is a large price tag associated with binary approaches to diversity that fail to re-engage the white (and other dominant) members of an institution and its graduates.

From the Pico College study, it was clear that researchers would need more information about the impact of student racial demographic shifts on white students at colleges and universities nationwide. Are other U.S. campuses having the same experience as Pico College? Will future college students be forced to choose between multiculturalism and Western Eurocentrism, or will a third, non-dichotomous approach begin to take shape? On a more fundamental level, what is it that white students want in learning about diversity? Will they want to learn the skills needed to be successful citizens and leaders in increasingly diverse U.S. and global societies? And if they want to learn those skills, are there other underlying changes in their own identities they will need to investigate in order to take full advantage of those new skills?

To address these questions, I turned next to the greatest source of data about "difference" encountered in my eight years of research, a database containing survey responses from 25,000 white students attending 159 colleges and universities in the U.S. Since this study would require an examination of large amounts of information from many campuses and individuals across the country, the analytical approach would by nature be quantitative.

CHAPTER THREE

Why White Students
Still Want Diversity

This chapter presents evidence that white college students want to learn about diversity as part of their college-going experience and offers specific steps a college or university can take to attain the full benefits of diversity. The conclusions reached in this study are the result of an analysis of a comprehensive survey returned by 25,000 white students attending 159 U.S. colleges and universities from 1985 to 1989 (Cooperative Institutional Research Program, UCLA). In addition to showing specific benefits from having diversity programs, this chapter will examine evidence indicating white students will need new sources of identity, meaning, and belonging if they are to be successful citizens in diverse U.S. and global societies—and suggest that higher education now arguably has a duty to nurture that discovery process.

To examine diversity's effects on white students, this study employed multiple regression analysis to probe the factors that most heavily impacted their: (1) overall satisfaction with college, (2) sense of cultural competence, (3) desire to promote racial understanding, and (4) perceived sense of community. These measures became the *"dependent variables,"* constituting the primary focus of this study.

To explore how the above variables were impacted by the kinds of interactions students engaged in with others on their college or university campuses, I further examined student responses along three forms of possible involvement at each campus: (1) whether or not students from different racial backgrounds on that campus communicate well, (2) whether or not the student became personally involved in cross-cultural experiences, and (3) whether or not the student was a member of a social fraternity or sorority. Testing for "high" versus "low" scores in each of these three *"involvement variables"* (constituting six possible outcomes), I then examined the four dependent variables along those six dimensions. Altogether, this would equate to twenty-four regressions each examining the causal impact of different degrees of student involvement with diversity on a dependent variable.

To "operationalize" the particular impact of race and ethnic diversity on a given campus by translating the impact into measurable terms, I hypothesized five steps an institution might take to promote diversity on its campus. What this meant was that for each of the 24 regressions noted above, I evaluated what would happen if a campus implemented diversity by: (1) enrolling more students of color on campus, (2) placing emphasis on creating a racially/ethnically diverse campus environment, (3) adding more race/ethnic issues to the course content, and (4) hiring more faculty of color. These four measures constituted the independent or *"environmental variables"* for this study. The goal of the multiple regression analysis used in this study was to evaluate whether greater emphasis in any of these four environmental variables would lead to an increase or decrease in student "satisfaction with college," "cultural competence," "desire to promote racial understanding," or "sense of community."

When beginning this study, I also suspected that many campuses had been "reacting" to increased race diversity in the U.S. by implementing changes related to the five factors above in a piecemeal fashion rather than proactively planning a comprehensive institutional transformation that could enhance learning for all students. I was concerned that these reactions might also have the goal of trying to "keep the peace," through measures like hiring an African American counselor to assist African American students, allowing students of color to have their own separate dorms, supporting the creation of race-based student organizations, or holding "diversity workshops" for student affairs administrators. My concern, especially after the Pico College study, was that *ad hoc* approaches like these might have the unintended result of reinforcing divisions between white students and students of color, a development that would worsen rather than lessen the effects of campus racial fragmentation. My hope was that a nationwide analysis of the five environmental diversity variables noted above would shed light on how a college or university might build a more effective basis for campus unity while surfacing new forms of belonging for its white students.

To summarize, the research design included four dependent variables and six strata, making for a total of twenty-four regressions in which the impact of four campus policies promoting diversity would be examined. The analytical approach I employed was the "I-E-O," or "inputs-environments-outputs," model based on the "involvement theory" of college student development propounded by Alexander W. Astin (1975, 1984, 1991). One of the important benefits of this analytical framework is that it allows a researcher to "control for inputs," meaning that factors like gender, socio-economic status, and the political leanings of all the respondents surveyed can be taken out of the equation so that any causal effects surfaced by the regression can be held *not* attributable to those factors but instead to the ones the researcher is seeking to evaluate.

The unit of analysis for this study was white students on campuses having large proportions of students of color with the focus being on their subjective responses. I will present these findings below in two forms: (1) as major findings and (2) as specific recommendations for leaders at racially diverse colleges and universities. In the interest of letting each reader form her or his own opinion about harsh claims about diversity by conservative commentators in recent decades, I present the major findings in some detail.

Major Findings

Student Satisfaction With College

I will begin this chapter by examining one of the most important measures of success available to a college or university: "overall student satisfaction" with the institution. People who do research in higher education commonly hold this measure sacred in that it justifies the existence of the institution and at the same time serves as a useful way for an institution to "take its own pulse" about whether or not it is succeeding in the eyes of its students. Viewed within a context of diversity, it asks, "How have campus policies favoring race and ethnic diversity impacted white students' overall satisfaction with college?"

This is an important query for another reason. As indicated earlier, conserva-tive think tanks have been conducting well-funded attacks on diversity programs in education for a number of years. Included in their wave of criticism was an early campaign attributing a feeling of "disunity" in America to multiculturalism and its decentering of Western Eurocentrism (e.g. D'Souza, 1991; Bennett, 1988, 1992; Hughes, 1993). It should not go unnoticed that the message in these attacks was that efforts to bring cultural diversity into the college-going experience must be eliminated because, as these commentators argued, they are not considered important by white students.

Findings in this study will show, however, that *creating an ethnically/racially diverse campus environment has a net positive effect on overall student satisfaction with college for white students.* The most powerful finding in this study, this gives diversity proponents a powerful weapon in responding to attacks by conservative writers leveled at such initiatives as freshman diversity course requirements, ethnic studies programs, and ultimately, affirmative action in admissions. To probe more deeply into this powerful argument in favor of diversity, I examined whether it mattered that white students communicated well across difference on a particular campus, whether the white student actually participated in cross-cultural activities, and whether the white student joined a social fraternity or sorority.

Does It Matter Whether Students on Campus "Communicate Well" Across Race Difference? This regression explored whether the positive impact of diversity on white students will change depending on whether a context has been created in which students on campus communicate effectively across race difference. To examine whether this makes any difference on overall student satisfaction with college, I stratified white students' responses into two groupings corresponding to campuses where students believed there was effective communication across race difference and campuses where students did not.

The findings were not what I expected. In essence, the results showed that having "a diverse campus environment" will lead to higher overall satisfaction with college *at both* kinds of campuses, at campuses where students communi-cate well across difference *and* at campuses where students do not. In other words, the data regarding the impact of making a campus environment "more culturally diverse" on overall satisfaction with college is "robust": the positive impact of having a diverse cultural environment on student satisfaction with college applies regardless of whether or not students feel they can communicate well across race difference (B = .05 in each case):

Table 3A

"Student Satisfaction with College":

Does It Matter Whether People from Different Racial Backgrounds
Communicate Well on the Student's Campus?

	Final Betas for White Students Who Believe Students from Different Racial Backgrounds	
	Communicate Well N = 11,311	Don't Communicate Well N = 5,891
Independent Variable		
Creating a Diverse Campus Environment	.05**	.05*
Racial/Ethnic Issues In Course Content	.02	a .03
Faculty Diversity	b -.02	-.02
Student Diversity	.01	-.01

** p < .001
* p < .01
a p = .043
b p = .027

What this means, contrary to what some critics have claimed, is that creating a more diverse campus environment will generally lead to greater overall satisfaction with college for white students. As indicated above, it did not matter whether or not students from different racial backgrounds knew how to communicate well on a particular campus; satisfaction with college increased for white students when their campus placed greater emphasis on establishing race and ethnic diversity in the campus environment. In other words, even at institutions where the campus as a whole had not yet learned "how" to communicate well across difference, the white students attending that institution found value in the opportunity to be exposed to and learn about difference.

This was also one of the most significant findings in this study because it confirmed that, developmentally, an institution will be seen in a positive light by its own students for at least making the effort to introduce diversity into the learning and social environment. Simply put, the effort to add diversity to the college experience would be viewed as a "good" by its white students. Even leaders at campuses where students have not yet learned how to communicate well across race difference can draw courage from knowing that students will appreciate their exposure to diversity.

There are other important findings in the above table. It is also clear that increasing the number of faculty of color *negatively* impacted white students' overall satisfaction with college in all six regressions. This is a little unsettling for those committed to making their institutions both diverse and safe learning environments. It is something that needs to be examined in further detail if college and university campuses are going to make the diversity experience a positive one for both white students *and faculty of color*. This is a tension I will examine later and, indeed, it became one of the reasons for later designing and testing a new, "intercultural" model for campus diversity.

It should also be noted in the above table that adding more race/ethnic issues to course content had a generally *positive* impact on white students' overall satisfaction with college, although these effects were not significant ($p > .01$). (In three of the six regressions, the coefficients had levels of confidence at the .05 level and are therefore only suggestive.) What this means is that there can be a slight positive effect on satisfaction with college when institutions add more diversity content to the curriculum. In contrast, it can be seen from the same table that increasing the number of students of color attending an institution did not enter any of the regressions and so this was not a factor one way or the other affecting overall satisfaction with college for white students. In other words, contrary to what conservative commentators have claimed, satisfaction with college for white students is *not* negatively impacted when more students of color are admitted to a college or university student body.

Will Participation in Cross-Cultural Activities Impact White Students' Satisfaction with College? If creating a more diverse campus environment clearly has a positive effect on overall satisfaction with college, one might next ask, will it make a difference whether these white students actually participate personally in the diversity programs or activities?

This inquiry surfaced another highly important finding in this study. In the jargon of education researchers, an interesting "multiplier effect" occurs when white students participate personally in cross-cultural activities on campus.

That is, whenever a college campus places high priority on creating a more diverse campus environment *and in addition* the white students on that campus participate personally in those cross-cultural activities (B = .06), the coefficient for overall satisfaction with college becomes even more pronounced, that is, highly significant (p < .001). In contrast, when white students choose not to participate personally in cross-cultural activities on campuses placing high priority on promoting a diverse campus environment (B = .03), the coefficient is only suggestive (p < .05, > .01). Thus, while not significantly different from each other, these coefficients mean that when it comes to overall student satisfaction with college, direct participation in cross-cultural activities will yield greater positive results for white students.

While the findings are highly encouraging for leaders of campus diversity programs, it should be noted in the table below that increasing the percent of faculty of color on a campus had a negative effect on overall satisfaction with college for white students *even when* those students participated personally in diversity activities (the B was -.03 and p < .01). This raises a continuing concern about whether a college campus can be a safe place for faculty of color. Why would white students tend to be more dissatisfied with their college experience when there are more faculty of color? The answer is not clear, but this finding does raise large implications about the nature of the student/faculty relationship in a cross-cultural setting and whether student course evaluations of faculty of color can be considered fair and unbiased:

Table 3B

"Overall Satisfaction with College":

Whether or Not a Student Participates in Cross-Cultural Activities

Final Betas for Students Who	
Participated in One or More Cross-Cultural Activities N = 10,475	Did Not Participate in One or More Cross-Cultural Activities N = 6,602

Multicultural Variable

		a
Creating a Diverse Campus Environment	.06**	.03
		b
Racial/Ethnic Issues in Course Content	.02	.03
		c
Faculty Diversity	-.03*	-.03
Student Diversity	-.02	.01

** $p < .001$
* $p < .01$
a $p = .035$
b $p = .021$
c $p = .019$

Does It Matter Whether a White Student Joins a Fraternity or Sorority?
This part of the study focused on whether overall student satisfaction with college would be affected one way or the other by a white student's decision to participate in a social fraternity or sorority and in particular whether it makes a difference that the campus places a high priority on creating a diverse campus

environment. What I found were significant measurable differences depending on whether white students participated in a Greek organization:

Table 3C

"Overall Satisfaction with College":

Whether or Not the White Student Joined a Fraternity or Sorority

	Final Betas Where Student	
	Is a Member of a Sorority or Fraternity N = 4,866	Is Not a Member of a Sorority or Fraternity N = 12,635
Independent Variable		
Creating a Diverse Campus Environment	.03	.07**
Racial/Ethnic Issues in Course Content	a .04	.02
Faculty Diversity	-.03	b -.03
Student Diversity	.02	-.01

** p < .001

a p = .020

b p = .012

In essence, white students' exposure to a campus environment placing high priority on having an ethnically/racially diverse campus environment had a clear positive impact on overall satisfaction with college when those students *did not* join a social fraternity or sorority (B = .07). In contrast, when white students elected to become members of a fraternity or sorority, the coefficient was smaller (B = .03) and non-significant (p < .05, > .01).

This is a particularly important finding for campus policy makers. What this means is that Greek participation has "a dampening effect" on the positive impact of ethnic/race diversity for white students. In other words, *the otherwise positive effects on overall satisfaction with college at campuses emphasizing cultural diversity are greatly reduced when the white student participates in a social fraternity or sorority.*

But why would this be the case? One possibility is that joining generally more conservative and racially homogeneous organizations like social fraternities and sororities can serve to "insulate" these white students from the beneficial effects of being on a culturally diverse campus. Here it should be remembered that political orientation had already been taken out of the equation so that any differences in the findings linked to participation in a Greek organization derive from that activity and are not a result of the student having a more conservative or liberal political orientation. The larger implications of having Greek organizations on increasingly diverse campuses—and the potential for attitudes to solidify later in life in the form of a "foxhole mentality" with respect to race and ethnic diversity—will be discussed later in this chapter.

In summary, what the above regressions show in a rather dramatic fashion is that *white students show a strong positive overall impact on satisfaction with college when they are on campuses that place high emphasis on having an ethnically/racially diverse environment and this benefit is enhanced when these students participate personally in the diversity activities.* Under such circumstances, overall satisfaction with college goes up. In contrast, when white students at these campuses join social fraternities or sororities, the beneficial impact of having a diverse campus climate on "overall satisfaction with college" is greatly diminished. Given the unequivocal nature of these findings, I decided to explore whether student participation in different forms of diversity would impact other outcomes in a positive manner.

Cultural Competence

The positive impact of a diverse campus environment on overall satisfaction with college seems beyond dispute. What about cultural competence? When a college or university places a high priority on creating a more diverse campus environment, will such a policy lead to gains in cultural competence for its white students? If answered in the affirmative, this question would in and of itself seem to justify adopting a more pro-active approach to diversity on college and university campuses—and particularly so as the U.S. faces a diverse, shrinking world that seems at times to demand greater facility with cultures different from its own.

To examine this line of inquiry, I created a composite dependent variable for "cultural competence" by combining item scores from two separate questions in the nationwide CIRP survey, "cultural awareness" (self-reported gain by students in their cultural awareness after four years of college) and "acceptance of different races and cultures" (another self-reported measure of gain after four years of college). I reasoned the combination of awareness of other cultures different from one's own and the ability to accept other races and cultures would be a proxy for "cultural competence" in that these factors taken together would enable future citizens to be more effective in situations characterized by high levels of race and ethnic diversity.

What I found was that *placing a high priority on creating an ethnically/racially diverse campus environment has a clear, positive effect on "cultural competence" for white students.* This is another important finding for proponents of diversity and one that further warrants creating and expanding diversity programs in U.S. colleges and universities. Plainly stated, having a culturally diverse environment will enhance cultural competence for white students. At the same time, it turned out that the magnitude of this positive effect will clearly shift under different sub-conditions. As explained further below, the kinds of steps an institution chooses to take in offering diversity programs will have a direct impact on whether a white student gains cultural competence. In technical terms, the data suggested the presence of significant "interaction effects" between the key variables.

Does It Matter Whether Students on a Particular Campus Communicate Well Across Race Difference? While the impact of creating a diverse campus environment on cultural competence was uniformly positive regardless of whether students of different racial backgrounds communicated well on that campus (B = .07 and .05 respectively), the magnitude of that impact was much higher for students who participated in cross-cultural activities (B = .08) than for students who did not participate (a non-significant B of .01). This makes intuitive sense. When white students participate directly in cross-cultural activities, their cultural competence increases. When they don't participate, there is very little gain:

Table 3D

"Cultural Competence":

Whether or Not Students from Different Racial Backgrounds
Communicate Well on Their Campus

Final Betas for "Cultural Competence" Where Students Perceive
That Students from Different Racial or Ethnic Backgrounds

	Communicate Well N = 11,299	Don't Communicate Well N = 5,891
Independent Variable		
Creating a Diverse Campus Environment	.07**	.05*
Racial/Ethnic Issues in Course Content	.04*	.02
Faculty Diversity	-.02	-.02
Student Diversity	-.00	.00

** p < .001
* p < .01

Clearly, colleges and universities seeking to promote cultural competence among their students should carefully consider making some of their diversity experiences mandatory for all students. In fact, in the larger context of a racially and ethnically diverse global society, it can reasonably be argued that a nation's future leaders will need to possess high levels of awareness and acceptance of cultures different from their own. When U.S. colleges and universities fail to teach cultural competence, they run the risk of educating future leaders who will lack the skills and perspectives to interact successfully with leaders from ethnically diverse nations.

Here it should also be pointed out while adding more race and ethnicity based content to courses will have a positive impact on cultural competence at campuses where students from different racial backgrounds communicate well, this effect is somewhat reduced at campuses where communication across race difference is not as well developed. What this suggests is that efforts to include race diversity in course content should ideally be *paired* with efforts to teach students how to communicate well across difference. Stated differently, the addition of stories from previously silenced or marginalized cultures will not by itself lead to enhanced cultural competence; students will need to be taught specific cross-cultural communication skills along with this content knowledge. As I will suggest later, this lends further momentum to the idea of shifting the overall framework for diversity to an approach that is cross-cultural.

How Does Participation in Cross-Cultural Activities Affect Cultural Competence? This part of the analysis examines whether it makes a difference that white students participate or do not participate directly in cross-cultural activities when it comes to cultural competence. Here the findings show that participation in cross-cultural activities does not affect gains in cultural competence when it comes to the impact of various diversity policies, with one notable and intuitively obvious exception. When a campus places a high priority on creating a more culturally diverse environment, this has a highly significant positive (B = .08) effect on cultural competence, *as long as* the student participates personally in one or more cross-cultural activities. By the same token, the table below shows this positive effect is nonexistent (B = .01) if the student does not participate in such activities.

In other words, *when a campus places a high priority on developing a diverse campus environment—but the student does not bother to take part in any cross-cultural activities—there are no significant positive gains in cultural competence.* This confirms with empirical data the intuitive belief that cultural competence will be affected by how a student acts or behaves (that is, what s/he chooses to do during the college-going years) and that a positive effect on cultural competence will be magnified when a college reflects cultural diversity in its overall campus atmosphere:

Table 3E

"Cultural Competence":

Whether or Not the Student Participated in Cross-Cultural Activities

	Final Betas for Students Who	
	Participated in One or More Cross-Cultural Activities N = 10,468	Did Not Participate in Cross-Cultural Activities N = 6,599
Independent Variable		
Creating a Diverse Campus Environment	.08**	.01
Racial/Ethnic Issues in Course Content	.04*	.02
Faculty Diversity	-.03*	-.02
Student Diversity	-.02	.01

** p < .001
 * p < .01

One other implication from these findings is also clear: campuses seeking to prepare their graduates to be successful citizens and leaders in a diverse global society by making them more aware and accepting of different cultures and perspectives will want to combine the presence of diversity enrichment programs on campus with a requirement that students actually participate in some of those learning experiences.

Is Cultural Competence Affected by the Decision to Join a Fraternity or Sorority? In the same way, the positive impact of creating a diverse campus environment on gains in cultural competence is substantially greater when these students do not join a social fraternity or sorority (B = .08) compared to white students who do join (a non-significant B of only .01). These different effects, it should be repeated, already take into account any preexisting differences in gender, socio-economic status, and political orientation among students responding to the survey. What this suggests is that if college and university administrators want to see the maximum benefits from creating a more diverse campus environment, it is exceedingly important that they undertake other institutional changes consistent with that policy.

At the same time, it appears from this study that increasing the diversity of the student body results in no significant gains in cultural competence for white students in any of the six regressions. This data was quite straightforward and has large implications for those seeking to maximize learning about diversity for white students. The finding reaffirms that simply adding more students of color to a student body is not necessarily going to lead to greater cultural competence for the institution's white students. In addition to adding students from different racial/ethnic backgrounds, an institution seeking to enhance students' competence with cultures different from their own will want to provide formal programs on diversity and require students to actually participate in those programs.

As indicated below, placing a high priority on developing a diverse campus environment has a positive effect on cultural competence among students who are not members of social fraternities or sororities (B = .08), but has no effect among students who are members of these social organizations (B = .01). In other words, the positive impact of a campus creating a diverse environment on white students' cultural competence appears to be nil when a student is a member of a social fraternity or sorority or when the student does not participate in any cultural diversity activities. *In contrast to this, the inclusion of racial/ethnic material in course content appears to enhance cultural competence among white students, regardless of whether they are members of social fraternities or sororities* (the Betas of .05 and .03 are not significantly different):

Table 3F

"Cultural Competence":

Whether or Not the Student Is a Member of a Social Fraternity or Sorority

	Final Betas Where Student Is	
	A Member of a Fraternity or Sorority N = 4,864	Not a Member of a Fraternity or Sorority N = 12,621
Independent Variable		
Creating a Diverse Campus Environment	.01	.08**
Racial/Ethnic Issues in Course Content	.05*	.03*
Faculty Diversity	-.00	-.02
Student Diversity	-.01	-.01

** significant at .001 level
* significant at .01 level

This is an exceedingly important finding. What this means is that it is crucial for college and university campuses wishing to nurture cultural competence among their white students to add race and ethnic issues to the curriculum. This is a form of exposure that proves particularly beneficial for white students who join fraternities and sororities and who, as a result, might not otherwise have much contact with cultures different from their own. In other words, adding race and ethnic content to courses will have a "compensating effect" in that it can overcome the culturally narrowing effects of participating in homogeneous Greek organizations and help the white student achieve a higher level of competence with cultures different from her or his own.

At the same time, it must be underscored that cultural competence does not increase as a result of having greater race diversity in the faculty or student body. This finding is both surprising and troubling given that one of the prime arguments for diversifying the student body and faculty in colleges and universities is that it will increase white students' cultural competence. No such positive effects were revealed in this study, suggesting that *the mere presence of students of color and faculty of color will not necessarily enhance cultural competence among white students*. On the contrary, it is clear from this data that new ways are needed to recontextualize future increases in student and faculty diversity for enhanced cultural competence to inhere.

To summarize, these findings suggest that course content can be an effective vehicle for reaching white students who are ensconced in predominantly white social fraternities or sororities. When white students are in fraternities or sororities, their cultural competence will increase if they take courses that have racial/ethnic content in them. Given the promising nature of these findings, one could next ask whether policies promoting cultural diversity on campus have a positive effect on a white student's desire to promote racial understanding.

Desire to Promote Racial Understanding

Here it is important to keep in mind how the question probing racial understanding was worded in the survey instrument. Students were asked to indicate how important it was to them, as a personal goal, to promote racial understanding. This question is therefore a deeper inquiry into the student's values about race and privilege and not a measure of cultural knowledge. Promoting understanding among different races is held important in this study because it represents an important step toward creating an environment in which social unity and cultural difference will coexist. Without racial understanding, one might expect different racial groups to stay in racial and ethnic enclaves on campus and perhaps, as a result, later in life as well.

Does Having a Diverse Campus Environment Impact a Student's Desire to Promote Racial Understanding? Findings show that assigning high institutional priority to creating a diverse campus environment has weak and scattered positive effects on promoting racial understanding. Including racial or ethnic content in courses also has weak and scattered positive effects on desire to promote racial understanding ($p < .01$, $> .001$). No significant effects were observed either for student diversity or faculty diversity:

Table 3G

"Desire to Promote Racial Understanding":

Whether Students from Different Racial Backgrounds Communicate Well

	Final Betas for Students Who Believe That Students from Different Racial Backgrounds	
	Communicate Well $N = 10,776$	Don't Communicate Well $N = 5,657$
Independent Variable		
Creating a Diverse Campus Environment	.03*	.02
Racial/Ethnic Issues in Course Content	.03*	.02
Faculty Diversity	-.00	-.01
Student Diversity	-.02	-.02

* $p < .01$

Once again, it appears that white students' commitment to promoting racial understanding is not necessarily enhanced simply by having more students of color or faculty of color in the institution. What this table suggests, therefore, is that current approaches to diversity do not necessarily lead white students to want to take action in promoting social justice through racial understanding and this is of course troubling. While current approaches may expose white students to diversity, these efforts do not ultimately lead them to take an interest in making their campus (and, one might reason, their society) more egalitarian. If the goal of diversity leaders on college campuses is to encourage their students to envision and then construct a more egalitarian society, it is apparent from this data that they will need to initiate new approaches to diversity that succeed in reaching white students at a deeper level of commitment than is currently taking place. Wholly new approaches appear to be needed.

Does It Matter Whether Students Participate Personally in Cross-Cultural Activities? Similar results are indicated in the regressions examining differences that might arise between students who participate in cross-cultural activities and those who do not (with "cross-cultural activities" consisting of participation in a racial awareness workshop, enrollment in an ethnic studies course, and socializing with persons from other racial or ethnic groups on campus). There is only one borderline effect ($p < .01$, $> .001$): a negative coefficient ($B = -.03$) arises when there is an increase in percent of students of color. Otherwise, *none of the primary environmental characteristics linked to creating a more diverse campus environment has a significant effect on a white student's desire to promote racial understanding.*

While the relationship between student diversity and promoting racial understanding in the table below is only borderline, the fact that it is negative (Beta = -.03) is troubling, as it suggests that increasing the number of students of color on campus may actually serve to weaken white students' commitment to promoting racial understanding, even when they participate in cross-cultural activities during their first four years of college. This finding suggests the need to examine more closely the dynamics of interactions between white students and students of color where student bodies are diverse, and discover fresh ways to re-direct diversity efforts that specifically improve those relations.

This data is also reason to pause and consider that a more comprehensive shift in institutional strategies may be necessary if the goal is to instill in white students a more progressive desire to promote racial understanding as part of a larger process of training them for citizenship in a diverse global society. This table reveals that current practices to create a more diverse campus environment, introduce race and ethnic content into courses, and increase the number of faculty of color do not make a difference one way or the other in attaining this important goal when it comes to participation in cross-cultural activities by white students.

Table 3H

"Desire to Promote Racial Understanding":

Whether or Not the Student Participated in Cross-Cultural Activities

	Final Betas for White Students Who	
	Participated in Cross-Cultural Activities N = 10,029	Did Not Participate in Cross-Cultural Activities N = 6,240
Independent Variable		
Creating a Diverse Campus Environment	.03 [a]	-.01
Racial/Ethnic Issues in Course Content	.02	.01
Faculty Diversity	.01	-.02
Student Diversity	-.03*	-.02

*   p < .01

a   p = .018

Will a White Student's Desire to Promote Racial Understanding Be Impacted by That Student's Participation in a Fraternity or Sorority? Separate analysis for members and non-members of social fraternities and sororities produces only one possible interaction effect. Creating a diverse campus environment has a borderline (p < .01, > .001) positive impact on white students' desire to promote racial understanding when students are not members of a fraternity or sorority (B = .03). Inclusion of race/ethnic content in courses produced two non-significant positive coefficients (p<.05, >.01).

In other words, the only possible significant interaction in the table below follows previous patterns with fraternity or sorority membership: namely, creating a more diverse campus environment has a positive impact on white students' desire to promote racial understanding, but only when they are not in social fraternities or sororities:

Table 3I

"Desire To Promote Racial Understanding":

Whether or Not the Student Was a Member of a Fraternity or Sorority

	Final Betas Where Student	
	Is a Member of a Fraternity or Sorority N = 4,568	Is Not a Member of a Fraternity or Sorority N = 12,091
Independent Variable		
Creating a Diverse Campus Environment	-.00	.03*
Racial/Ethnic Issues in Course Content	a .04	b .02
Faculty Diversity	.00	.00
Student Diversity	-.03	-.01

  * p < .01
  a p = .041
  b p = .026

Later in the chapter, I will discuss the policy implications of these findings. At the same time, he inability of current diversity approaches to generate a greater desire to promote racial understanding across groups does raise a more basic threshold question: Are there diversity approaches that will generate a greater sense of community for a diverse campus?

Sense of Community

The question examined here is whether different campus policies in relation to race and ethnic diversity will impact in one way or the other the "sense of community" experienced by white students on a campus. In this regard, I will point out that Astin's 1993a study and my own 1992 study had already demonstrated that institutional diversity emphasis (in student admissions, multicultural events on campus, and hiring faculty of color) and faculty diversity emphasis (race and gender issues included in course content as well as faculty research) will have a positive impact on sense of community for white students. My own study had revealed, however, that high institutional emphasis on diversity will be *negatively* associated with sense of community when faculty members fail to match that emphasis by increasing the race and gender diversity of their course content and research (Tanaka, 1992). In other words, these earlier studies also stand for the proposition that college and university campuses would do well to coordinate their incorporation of diversity policies.

Given the great volume of commentaries asserting that multiculturalism causes divisiveness in U.S. society, often based not so much on empirical evidence as anecdotal evidence (e.g., Bennett, 1988; D'Souza, 1991) and personal experience (e.g., Bloom, 1987; Kristol, 1991; Schlesinger, 1991; and Hughes, 1993), this study seeks to dis-aggregate the variables used in both the Astin study and my own study so that the separate impacts of diversity policies on sense of community can be evaluated with hard empirical evidence.

As shown below, *the findings from this analysis reveal that creating a more diverse campus environment has a uniformly positive effect on sense of community as perceived by white students.* This positive effect is especially strong where students elect to participate in one or more cross-cultural activities. The findings indicate that where a campus places a high priority on creating a diverse environment and white students participate in those activities, there is a heightened perception that building community is valued on that campus. These findings are uplifting and directly contradict the argument advanced by Schlesinger and others that diversity content in education will automatically have the result of "disuniting" America. Given the importance of these results, the expectation is that education research can add much by examining alternative approaches to community building for diverse campus environments and by uncovering approaches that are more successful than others at involving white students in these activities.

Second, *the findings show that including race issues in course content has a uniformly positive effect on sense of community as perceived by white students.* This also contradicts the arguments advanced by conservative writers like Schlesinger, Lynne Cheney, and D'Souza that American education needs to return to a Western Eurocentric curricular emphasis. Further, this positive effect does not appear to depend on the quality of interracial communication or on whether students join fraternities or personally participate in cross-cultural activities. The positive result remains strong under varying campus conditions.

Third, *increasing the percent of faculty of color ("faculty diversity") has a uniformly negative impact on sense of community among students and faculty as perceived by white students.* This finding is rather disturbing and fits the pattern surfaced earlier with respect to overall student satisfaction with college. Of large importance to diversity leaders on college campuses, this negative impact on sense of community applies even when white students participate in cross-cultural activities, do not join a fraternity or sorority, or attend campuses where students of different racial backgrounds communicate well. As more and more colleges and universities in the U.S. make concerted efforts to hire faculty of color, it will clearly be important to study why the presence of faculty of color seems to have a negative impact on white students' sense of community and devise new approaches that turn the presence of faculty of color into a positive.

Fourth and equally alarming, *increasing the percent of students of color on a campus has a strong negative effect on sense of community as perceived by white students (B = .-12) and these are the strongest negative effects of this study.* This effect does not appear to depend on the quality of interracial communication or on whether the student joins a fraternity or sorority or participates in cross-cultural activities. In other words, one of the risks run in increasing the percent of students of color (or the percent of faculty of color) is a potential decline in perceived sense of community in the eyes of white students. These are among the most important findings of this study and they demand, if nothing else, a reexamination of the approaches to diversity currently used on college campuses and the basis for a white student's sense of self and community that might make those approaches appear less successful than desired.

What is particularly puzzling about these findings is that having a high percentage of faculty and students who are of color is positively associated with creating a diverse campus environment. The latter variable, as is demonstrated in this data, has a positive effect on perceived sense of community. In other words, a high percent of people of color in the campus community, which has a direct negative effect on perceived community, tends to be associated with institutional priorities that have a positive effect. (In technical terms, this anomaly is reflected in what is called a "suppressor effect" that occurs when the variable for placing a high priority on diversity in the environment enters the regression. At this point of entry, the negative coefficients for faculty diversity and student diversity get even *stronger*.) This finding may have important implications for educational policy, as will be discussed later in the chapter.

To further study the conflicted nature of this data relating to sense of community in the eyes of white students, I examined whether these outcomes might shift depending on the nature of their involvement with diversity, that is, whether students communicated well across race difference on their campus, whether they chose to be personally involved in cross-cultural experiences, and whether they chose to join a social fraternity or sorority.

Is the Impact of Diversity on Sense of Community Different When Students from Different Racial Backgrounds Communicate Well? This analysis shows that putting a high priority on creating a culturally diverse campus environment has a positive impact on sense of community for white students, whether or not it is a campus where students from different racial backgrounds are perceived to communicate well (B= .07 and .09, respectively). In other words, it makes no difference: the impact of having a more diverse campus environment on perceived sense of community for white students is positive whether or not the campus they are attending is one in which communication across race difference is believed effective:

Table 3J

"Sense of Community Perceived by White Students":

Whether Students from Different Racial Backgrounds Communicate Well

	Final Betas Among Students Who Believe That	
	Students of Different Racial Backgrounds Communicate Well N = 11,272	Students of Different Racial Backgrounds Do Not Communicate Well N = 5,868
Independent Variable		
Creating a Diverse Campus Environment	.07**	.09**
Racial/Ethnic Issues in Course Content	.06**	.05*
Faculty Diversity	-.05**	a -.02
Student Diversity	-.06**	-.12**

** significant at the .001 level.
* significant at the .01 level.
a p=.14

Similarly, including more race issues in the course content has a positive impact on sense of community for both types of students: those who believe, and those who do not believe, that students from different racial backgrounds communicate well on their campus (B = .06 and .05, respectively). These findings suggest that efforts to include race or diversity issues in course content will have positive effects on perceived sense of community, even on campuses where students believe that cross-racial communication is poor.

One especially interesting finding in the above table is the stronger negative effect (B = -.12) of increasing the percent of students of color on white students on campuses where interracial communication is poor, in comparison to campuses where interracial communication is good (B = -.06). *What this suggests is that the negative effects of increasing the number of students of color on sense of community are exacerbated when campuses have poor inter-racial communication.* (Stated differently, the negative effects of large numbers of students of color on sense of community are mitigated to some extent when campuses begin to promote effective cross-cultural communication.) What this means is that campuses that have diverse student bodies will want to make concerted efforts to improve communication across race difference for their students, and that as the number of students of color in the institution grows, the need for such pro-active training will be even greater.

Clearly, a comprehensive strategy for diversity on campuses that have large numbers of students of color will need to include a component for learning and communication across difference. This is one of the findings that prompted the drive to create an intercultural campus as discussed in the next chapter.

Is Sense of Community Impacted by a White Student's Participation in Cross-Cultural Activities? The strongest positive effect of creating a diverse campus environment on sense of community, however, occurs where white students have chosen to become engaged in one or more cross-cultural activities (i.e., participated in a racial awareness workshop, enrolled in an ethnic studies course, and/or interacted socially with persons of different racial groups).

In the table below, the beta associated with creating a diverse campus environment is a highly significant .11 where white students engage in one or more cross-cultural activities, but non-significant (B = .02) when white students do not engage in cross-cultural activities. This is another finding of large importance to leaders at diverse institutions.

In other words, *creating a diverse campus environment as an institutional priority enhances white students' sense of community, but only if the student has direct personal experience with some kind of diversity activity.* By contrast, when students have little or no direct ethnic/racial diversity experience, sense of community is not significantly affected by placing a strong emphasis on diversity in the campus environment.

Table 3K

"Sense of Community":

<u>Whether the Student Participated Personally in Cross-Cultural Activities</u>

	Final Betas for Students Who	
	Engage in One or More Cross-Cultural Activities N = 10,394	Do Not Engage in One or More Cross-Cultural Activities N = 6,536
Independent Variable		
Creating a Diverse Campus Environment	.11**	.02 [a]
Racal/Ethnic Issues in Course Content	.04*	.08**
Faculty Diversity	-.06**	-.04 [b]
Student Diversity	-.10**	-.07**

** significant at .001 level
* significant at .01 level
a p=.26
b p=.013

The policy implications of this are undeniable: if an institution wishes to get maximum "mileage" out of its efforts to make cultural diversity a high priority, it must make sure all its white students have the opportunity for direct personal experience with that diversity. In other words, the benefits of having white students learn and be exposed personally to experiences that are cross-cultural can now be viewed as compelling. Given the powerful nature of these findings, it is evident that a campus strategy for diversity will need to include policies that encourage (or even require) white student participation in such activities.

Is the Impact of Diversity on Sense of Community Altered When a White Student Joins a Fraternity or Sorority? What this regression shows is that the pattern of positive environmental impacts on sense of community is similar to what was found earlier when examining how well students from different racial backgrounds communicate on a particular campus. That is, the positive effects of creating a diverse environment and of including race/ethnic issues in the curriculum are the same regardless of whether the student is a member of a social fraternity or sorority.

In other words, when colleges try to build a sense of community by placing a high priority on creating a culturally diverse environment and by including race/ethnic issues in their courses, they can be equally successful with students who join and those who do not join Greek organizations. This is an important finding for those who promote ethnic studies and other diversity programs on college campuses. *What it shows is that it is exceedingly important, when seeking to build a sense of community, to pair efforts to create a more diverse campus environment with an initiative to include race and ethnic issues in course content—and that this strategy will be particularly effective in reaching white students who have joined social fraternities and sororities.*

Consistent perhaps with the reader's expectations, the negative effects of increasing faculty diversity and student diversity on sense of community are greater among fraternity and sorority students (B = -.08 and -.10, respectively) than among students who do not join fraternities or sororities (B = -.04 and -.07). While one might expect that the kind of student who joins a fraternity or sorority might be more conservative on race issues, it is important to remember that we are observing the greater negative impacts of racial composition on sense of community after controlling for political orientation and such social stratifiers as class, gender, and parents' education, and so this makes the differential all the more powerful. The clear indication is that the negative effects of both faculty and student diversity on a white student's sense of community are *exacerbated* by membership in social fraternities and sororities.

Table 3L

"Sense of Community":

Whether or Not the Student Joins a Fraternity or Sorority

	Final Betas Where Student Is	
	A Member of Fraternity of a Sorority N = 4,767	Not a Member of a Fraternity or Sorority N = 12,373
Independent Variable		
Creating a Diverse Campus Environment	.07**	.06**
Racial/Ethnic Issues in Course Content	.07**	.07**
Faculty Diversity	-.08**	-.04**
Student Diversity	-.10**	-.07**

** significant at .001 level

In summary, the factors examined in the above regression form a clear pattern in which: (1) the positive effects of a college's emphasis on creating a culturally diverse campus environment are greatest when the white student is not a member of a social fraternity or sorority, and (2) the negative effects of faculty and student racial diversity are greatest when the white student is (a) a member of a fraternity or sorority, or (b) does not participate in cross-cultural activities. In other words, you cannot just set out to diversify the faculty and the student body and expect white students to benefit. To attain maximum benefit, a college or university has to change its overall campus approach to diversity by adding more racial/ethnic material into the curriculum, providing more culturally diverse activities on campus, and establishing programs that require white students to participate personally in racially mixed groups to study and discuss racial/ethnic issues. These findings should provide a renewed sense of mission and inject fresh confidence into college and university diversity programs.

Ten Recommendations for Leaders
at Diverse Colleges and Universities

This portion of the chapter will reduce the above findings to specific recommendations for leaders at colleges and universities where the student racial demographics are shifting toward greater diversity. Projecting the findings from this study, it can also be suggested that the following policies will have the added benefit of enhancing student preparedness for citizenship in a diverse global society.

1. To Maximize Learning, Campuses Should Combine the Decision to Admit a Diverse Class with Other Diversity Initiatives

One of the generalizations from this nationwide study is that admitting a racially diverse class of students must go hand in hand with other steps in institutional transformation if white students are to experience the full benefits of diversity. Simply put, admitting students of color will not alone lead to gains in cultural competence, desire to promote racial understanding, sense of community, or satisfaction with college for white students. Stated differently, merely exposing white college students to classmates who are of color—without also offering the formal programs, courses and student activities to explain this diversity to them—will not prepare these students to be effective citizens and leaders in an increasingly diverse global context for the U.S.

For example, it was expected that an increase in students of color would have a positive effect on cultural competence for white students on the belief that there would be more personal interaction and, therefore, greater appreciation of cultures different from one's own. There were no such effects. What this means is that just adding more students of color to a campus will not automatically lead white students to learn more about the cultures of their classmates of color. Either white students will choose not to bring the topic up or instead choose to remain in homogeneous white groups. Whichever may be the case, it appears that campuses with growing numbers of students of color will need to do more than just throw the students together and "hope for the best."

As a further example, it was hoped in this study that greater diversity in the student body would have a positive effect on white students' desire to promote racial understanding. Instead, there was a weak negative effect. This finding may constitute special cause for concern because it means that increasing the number of students of color will not, in and of itself, motivate more white students to want to involve themselves in achieving greater racial understanding and, by implication, equality, in U.S. society. This is consistent with the classic work of Gordon Allport (1954) who found in his exhaustive study that merely placing together people from different racial backgrounds may not ease racial tension and can in fact lead to greater racial tension. Under Allport's "contact hypothesis," in order for increased racial contact to lead to better race harmony, there would have to be equal status between the racial groups. Applying Allport's analysis to diverse U.S. college settings today, the admission of a racially diverse entering class of students—without also having organized attempts to carve out a greater sense of equality among students—can be expected to lead naturally to greater racial tension on a campus.

One possible interpretation of the findings in this study is therefore that white students, if left to their own devices, might tend to maintain preexisting notions or beliefs about other cultures and people of color they might have brought with them from their high school communities which were often homogeneous and white. In other words, whatever misunderstandings or notions of their own superiority they might have harbored toward people of color *before* entering the diverse college or university setting will be reinforced or magnified absent an organized attempt by the institution to guide new learning about diversity. This makes sense. In Allport's terms, any preexisting beliefs these entering students might have brought with them about race or racial superiority might be expected to lead to racial conflict in interactions with classmates of color. Arguably, the campus that does little to promote equality and positive learning about diversity in the context of changing student racial demographics would in effect be *creating* the conditions that cause racial tension and conflict.

At the same time, it seems obvious that having a diverse entering class is a necessary prerequisite to meaningful learning about diversity. If no students of color are present with whom white students can interact, their learning about diversity will remain abstract and lack practical, personal meaning. This can also be stated in another way. In the context of today's complex global society, U.S. colleges and universities assume a special role by providing a common point of learning where future leaders can acquire the skills and perspectives to work effectively across difference instead of being fearful or anxious of people from other nations. It makes intuitive sense that having diverse classmates will help this learning process take root in practical, day-to-day terms and that personal exposure to diversity in college—in combination with formal instruction about this in the curriculum and co-curriculum—will bear fruit many years later when these young people are called upon to interact with world leaders who are of color and from different cultural backgrounds.

In fact, in the absence of constructive learning about diversity, one can infer from this study that the college experience can *worsen* any fears and anxieties white students may bring with them from homogeneous high school communities. Under such conditions, the opportunity to develop and redirect perspectives and skills for future leadership roles in a diverse world will have been lost. Indeed, findings from this nationwide study show that the negative effects that large numbers of students of color have on white students' sense of community can be *softened* to some extent by placing high priority on creating a culturally diverse campus environment, introducing more racial/ethnic content into the curriculum, and encouraging cross-racial student interaction.

If one buys the notion that Allport's contact hypothesis is in effect on today's college and university campuses, then one aspect of a new approach to diversity would be to include planned, proactive programs that create equal status between racial groups. This conclusion gives impetus to the creation of a new framework for diversity that promotes interaction across race and ethnic difference—with the added requirement that it provide for interactions that reflect equality. The problem, as might be expected, is that any attempt to model and test an approach that creates equal status among all racial and ethnic groups can too easily come into conflict with the identities of white students if those identities continue to be based on race or race superiority.

What this suggests is that future approaches to diversity will need to provide white students with new opportunities to connect with others—and new ways of belonging to the campus community—that do not leave them tracked in modes of race or race superiority but still grant them full membership. As the lessons from the Pico College experiment showed earlier, a "multicultural approach" can too easily leave white students, faculty and staff feeling alienated or personally blamed in an increasingly diverse community. Perhaps the most significant finding of the present study is that a new framework for diversity must be hatched and tested that allows white students to have a sense of belonging at a diverse campus while promoting a level playing field for all identities. It is this larger conclusion that ultimately drove the final research project, discussed in chapter 4, to model and test "an intercultural campus."

2. Even in Tight Budget Times, Colleges and Universities Should Continue to Provide Funding for Diversity Programs

Findings from this study also confirm that creating a culturally diverse campus environment (through student social activities promoting interaction across race or ethnic difference, ethnic studies courses, and race awareness workshops) will lead to clear-cut gains across a number of important dimensions. Significantly, an overall campus emphasis on diversity will lead to greater satisfaction with college among white students. This data thus provides powerful evidence in favor of increasing institutional support for diversity programs.

At the same time, there are other factors that campus leaders will want to take into account when designing, funding, and maintaining the shape and orientation of such programs. For example, it was noted earlier that there is a clear pattern indicating that the positive effects of creating a diverse campus environment will only lead to greater satisfaction with college, cultural competence, desire to promote racial understanding, and sense of community for white students when those students participate personally in cross-cultural activities and programs. It does not do any good to have race awareness workshops or ethnic studies courses if white students do not experience the activity personally. As one example of how to nurture interaction through institutional support, some campuses are experimenting with ways of linking funding for student organizations to projects that require joint sponsorship and co-planning by diverse organizations like the Black Student Union, Greek fraternities or sororities, MEChA, Sistah Friends, LGBT Alliance, and service clubs.

What this study shows is that campuses that may have entertained any doubts about the value of allocating resources to diversity programs—like ethnic studies courses, race awareness workshops, and activities that promote social interaction across difference—now have clear evidence that there is a high pay-off in making such allocations in terms of immediate student satisfaction with college. I will even venture a guess that the real gains will come years later when these students go on to become government, business, education, and arts leaders and interact with people of color from other countries around the world. It is logical to presume that leaders who have cross-cultural skills will be more effective than those who don't.

3. Students Should Be Required to Participate Personally in Cross-Cultural Activities

Indeed, it should by now be clear that direct personal participation in cross-cultural learning and social activities on college and university campuses must be actively encouraged for white students. Participation in cross-cultural activities was shown in this study to magnify learning about diversity for white students by enhancing the positive impact of creating a more diverse environment on "sense of community," "cultural competence," "desire to promote racial understanding," and "overall student satisfaction with college." Consistent with this, the beneficial effects on all four of these variables associated with promoting a culturally diverse learning environment are enhanced when the student participates personally in some kind of cross-cultural activity: socializing with persons from different racial or ethnic groups, taking ethnic studies courses, or taking a race awareness workshop. One of the broadest patterns in the findings, it helped me turn a corner in my own thinking and provided the impetus to design a new kind of campus that would emphasize positive social and academic interaction between racial and ethnic groups, that is, an "intercultural" campus.

In other words, a campus can maximize the gains that come from creating a more diverse overall campus environment by combining this with programs that directly involve white students (and by implication, all students) in cross-cultural experiences. While it is true that creating a culturally diverse environment will have a positive impact on both perceived sense of community and cultural competence, there is also suggestive evidence that such an approach will have a similar, although weaker, effect on student satisfaction with college and commitment to promoting racial understanding. In addition, when white students as a whole participate in cross-cultural activities, this will *soften* the negative effects of diversity they might experience.

What this study therefore suggests is that the biggest key to establishing positive approaches for diversity on college and university campuses will be to find ways to increase white student engagement with it. This conclusion is wholly consistent with the classical assertion in higher education research that student development will be enhanced when college students increase their "involvement" with their college campus (Astin, 1975; see also Tanaka, 2002a). What this means in today's terms is that if colleges and universities with racially diverse student bodies can identify new ways to involve their white students personally in cross-cultural experiences, it will enhance even further the benefits of other policies that expose white students to diversity. In other words, educators who wish to get the maximum "mileage" out of their attempts to build a culturally diverse campus environment will be well advised to do everything possible to provide each white student with at least some kind of direct experience with American cultures different from her/his own. This set of data has enormous implications for the future of U.S. higher education. It means that in some ways, colleges and universities have barely scratched the surface when it comes to promoting learning based on diversity.

At a time when U.S. government and business leaders seem to fall too easily into a "foxhole" mentality of fear and arrogance toward other countries, particularly ones populated by people of color, it seems imperative that colleges and universities take steps today to better prepare future leaders to be more successful in cross-cultural interactions and possess greater facility and understanding about difference than our current leaders. Stated differently, higher education may bear part of the blame for failing to train today's generation of national leaders to better understand and negotiate a constructive role for the U.S. in a shrinking, multiethnic global society. To promote peace, harmony, and cross-cultural understanding decades down the road, higher education will want to expose future leaders to diverse personal experiences while they are in college.

4. All U.S. Colleges and Universities Should By Now Include Race and Ethnic Issues in the Core Curriculum

This study also confirms what many have suspected for some time—that there are clear benefits to including race and ethnic issues in the curriculum. Campuses that do this will tend to promote higher levels of cultural competence among white students as long as they take these courses. The benefits of course content diversity are even greater at campuses where students from different racial backgrounds communicate well. For example, having greater race and ethnic course content will have a positive impact on white students' desire to promote racial understanding—on campuses where students from different racial backgrounds communicate well and where white students are not members of social fraternities or sororities.

At the same time, it is not enough for campuses to convey the substantive content of many cultures; campuses must also teach students how to apply that understanding in their daily lives. Needless to say, students will find it difficult to apply their learning in their daily lives if their classmates are not racially and ethnically diverse. These findings add further impetus to the creation of a new framework for diversity that emphasizes cross-cultural interaction while incorporating the stories and identities of all students.

There is yet another positive conclusion from these findings. It is clear that including race and ethnic issues in the curriculum will have an "ameliorative" impact on some white students where other diversity policies have failed to reach them. This is powerful information for campus leaders. Where white students might otherwise shy away from diversity experiences in social activities, student programs, and race awareness workshops, they can nonetheless be reached through formal course content that addresses race and ethnicity. *On campuses where students tend to remain in homogeneous Greek organizations or choose not to become involved in cross-cultural student activities, having these students take courses that have diverse content will tend to promote cultural competence and sense of community among white students and also have a weak positive effect on overall satisfaction with college.*

This suggests that colleges and universities will want to revisit their policies on race and ethnic culture in the curriculum. Where they do not currently require entering students to take a course on American cultures or race diversity, this study shows they should now consider doing so. What this finding also establishes is that even if a campus is unable to combine diverse course content with other diversity policies, like promoting cross-cultural student social interactions or requiring race awareness workshops, there is still great value to at least starting with diversity in the formal curriculum.

This also brings to mind the earlier questions raised by conservatives about the value of diversity and whether it has a divisive effect on sense of unity on a campus (and, by implication, in a nation). Where campuses create a more diverse cultural environment and include race issues in course content, white students will register a more positive sense of campus community—whether or not they participate in cross-cultural activities, join a fraternity or sorority, or are on a campus where students communicate well across race difference. These findings are quite robust and directly undercut the earlier assertions of Allan Bloom, Dinesh D'Souza, William Bennett, Arthur Schlesinger, and others who have long claimed that cultural diversity has a divisive effect on America.

5. Campuses Should Hire More U.S. Minority Faculty as Part of Their Overall Approach to Diversity

I had anticipated when beginning this study that a policy of hiring more faculty of color might have a small negative impact on satisfaction with college because it would be unsettling for white students to have instructors (people in positions of authority) who are not white. That hunch was partially confirmed. The more shocking finding, however, was that having a diverse faculty will *also* have a weak negative effect on cultural competence, sense of community, and desire to promote racial understanding for white students.

Even more unsettling, while having more faculty of color has a negative effect on sense of community for white students, this is the case *whether or not* these students participate in cross-cultural activities, join fraternities or sororities, or attend campuses where students of different racial backgrounds communicate well. As might be expected, the negative effect of faculty racial diversity is even stronger among white students who are members of social fraternities or sororities. As a side note, the regressions show that the negative effects summarized here will likely be magnified in the case of large institutions, public institutions, and universities, since these institutions tend to have larger percentages of faculty of color and students of color and since they are less likely to incorporate race issues into the curriculum or place a high priority on building a culturally diverse campus environment.

One would normally expect that greater exposure to professors of color would enhance both cultural competence and an interest in promoting racial understanding, but this was decidedly not the case. The reasons for this will need to be examined in another study. Are professors of color still so small in number that white student contact with these professors is minimal? Another possible explanation is that professors of color are being hired primarily to teach courses about race and not to teach the core academic subjects. This pigeonholing may tend to isolate them in sensitive courses that require white students to learn about race privilege for the first time. This could have the result of reinforcing negative stereotypes white students may have been holding about race. A third possibility is that professors of color may themselves feel so marginalized on predominantly white campuses that they redouble their efforts to mark and defend their own cultural identities, and further alienate their white students.

The interpretation I find most immediate, however, is that having faculty of color who are in positions of authority as persons who give grades can undermine the sense of power that white students experience from having identities based on whiteness, whether or not students are aware of it. In this regard, the reader may wish to review ground-breaking work in "whiteness" studies by McIntosh (1988), Roediger (1991), Morrison (1992), hooks (1992), Frankenberg (1993), West (1993), Scheurich (1993), Brodkin (1994), Young (1995), Chesler (1996), Ignatiev and Garvey (1996), Fine et. al. (1997), Delgado and Stefancic (1997), Lipsitz (1998), and Daniel (1999), among others. These scholars agree that whiteness has associated with it internalized and unexamined privileges that grant people who are white positions of social superiority over people who are of color.

What is clear from this study, however, is that the scholarship on whiteness now needs to be directed at the place where U.S. scholars themselves reside, their own colleges and universities. For example, when white students find themselves taking a course from a professor of color, the position of power the professor of color enjoys by virtue of that teaching position is, under whiteness analysis, in direct conflict with the race-based view that people of color are "inferior." This begs the next question: What will identity, sense of belonging, and central community values be like under campus conditions *after* whiteness, and what will be the role of higher education in promoting the new identity construction?

For example, if new identities are to be constructed by white students that are not based on race, all professors and staff will likely need to become involved in this effort so they are not left out of step with new developments. It should be obvious that this new duty should not devolve solely to faculty of color. And if all members of a campus are to participate in such an enterprise, one likely outcome is that the identities of faculty of color will no longer need to be constructed as the binary opposite of "whiteness." In other words, the act of creating new sources of identity for white students may go a long way toward creating safe places for U.S. minority faculty to teach and seek tenure. Along the same lines, it will be equally important for colleges and universities to teach students of color how to form new identities that aren't based on race, and do not leave them in opposition to the identities of their white classmates by celebrating their victim status, what Nietzsche (1967) termed *"ressentiment"* (see also Cocks, 1991; Tanaka, 1999). In a post-racialized campus setting, there would conceivably be new, non-dichotomous sources of meaning for all members, not just white students and white faculty. At the time this study was completed, no such reformulation of identities was forthcoming.

Whichever direction new identity formation takes in the future, this study strongly suggests that college officials will need to study the relationships between white students and their faculty of color, how faculty of color are integrated into a campus, and the roles that faculty of color are expected to play in a strategy to enhance diversity on campus. The findings here demonstrate that any campus seeking to create a new framework for diversity will want to ensure that in any department culture, professors of color can join white faculty and students as full members of the community.

6.   Diverse Campuses Must Now Offer Formal Training in Interethnic Communication

As student bodies become more racially and ethnically diverse, it makes intuitive sense that colleges and universities will want to do more to promote positive interethnic communication and have specific programs for this that all students are required to take. It should not be taken for granted that students enter college having those skills. In fact, where students enter diverse institutions and come from homogeneous high school communities, colleges and universities are missing a significant opportunity when they do not provide them skills in interethnic communication. This study confirms that colleges can mitigate the initially fragmenting effects on community from rapidly increasing numbers of students of color by improving communication between students from different racial backgrounds. These interaction effects were among the strongest in the study, meaning this finding is quite powerful and should be accorded great weight in determining campus policies.

While this conclusion is based on a study of white students and their perceptions, it might also be interesting to extrapolate from it to other members at an increasingly diverse campus. Given the powerful nature of the findings, it might be inferred that white faculty and staff might also have increased feelings of belonging and sense of community on diverse campuses when they are themselves given opportunities to learn cross-cultural communication skills.

Stated differently, it would be logical to expect that when staff and faculty can come to model preferred behavior through their own enhanced interethnic communication skills, they will further improve the interethnic learning of their students. Taken together, the discussions above argue strongly in favor of designing and testing a cross-cultural framework for diversity on college and university campuses that reaches all members of a campus community.

7. Desire to Promote Racial Understanding Is a Particularly Sensitive Issue and Must Be Addressed Strategically in the Campus Framework

Scholars have shown that a student's desire to promote racial understanding yields the largest racial differences in the nationwide database used in this study, anchored at one end by the African Americans and the other by white students, with Latinos and Asians in between and the Latinos above Asians (e.g., Astin, Wingard & Trevino, 1991). This paradox seems to constitute the crux of some of the racial and ethnic differences we see on U.S. college and university campuses today: namely, that most African Americans and many Latinos want action and are willing to commit themselves to practical action to achieve equality, whereas most white students are more content with theoretical sorts of engagement, like discussion and learning as opposed to action to create a level playing field. It is worth pausing for a moment here to consider the possible reasons for this.

One possible interpretation is that there is a distinction between being satisfied with the experience of learning about diversity and being motivated to take action based on that experience. In other words, white students might be hesitant to commit themselves to a much more active engagement in "promoting racial understanding"—which is the way the question was worded in the survey instrument—as opposed to simply appreciating being exposed to diversity and multiculturalism. But this thinking seems simplistic and does not view white students within the historical context of race relations in the U.S.

A second possible interpretation is that racial understanding is so loaded a concept by now that invoking it forces white students artificially into one of two camps, one consisting of students who are willing to change themselves and their notions of community and personal worth to accommodate people of color, and a second group consisting of those students who are resistant to any such change. The former group seems predisposed to learning about diversity and would be expected to engage in such learning activities voluntarily. The latter group would be found in one or more of the following categories and require direct interventions by their colleges to encourage their participation in an increasingly multiethnic world: (1) students at campuses where students from different racial backgrounds do not communicate well, (2) students who are not participating in cross-cultural activities, and/or (3) students who are members of social fraternities or sororities.

Still another possible interpretation is that there is a practical distinction between ethnicity and race, such that the same white students who are willing to learn about differences in ethnic cultures (in classes that address different ethnic traditions, beliefs, and behaviors) may find it more difficult to confront difference based on race (recognizing issues of power and privilege that may make their own "whiteness"-based identities obsolete). The latter interpretation would be more in line with the recent work in whiteness noted earlier. Since this interpretation is not directly supported by the findings of this study, further research will be needed to examine the relative merits of all three possibilities.

Any way you view this issue, it is clear that future work in diversity in U.S. higher education will need to include an ongoing assessment of what makes for identity and belonging for white students on diverse campuses. If left to their own devices, this group cannot be expected to know how to maintain identity and belonging of their own accord. This research acquires even greater significance with the following thought: that the same inability to know one's connection to community on a diverse campus can reappear later in life in the form of an inability to "connect" with others as leaders in a diverse global society.

8. Colleges and Universities Should Reexamine the Nature and Purpose of Social Fraternities and Sororities

The findings in this study document with surprising directness the ways in which Greek organizations in U.S. colleges and universities tend to (1) remove white students from the benefits of diversity and (2) magnify the preconditions for negative effects from diversity. In fact, being a member of a social fraternity or sorority produces virtually a mirror image opposite of what was found with white students who participate in cross-cultural activities. Beneficial effects on satisfaction, cultural competence, and commitment to promoting racial understanding that come from being on a campus that puts a high priority on cultural diversity are *lost* if the student joins a social fraternity or sorority—and the negative effects of greater faculty diversity and student diversity on sense of community are *magnified* for white students who join fraternities and sororities, even after controlling for political orientation and socio-economic status. While these findings should not be taken to mean that all fraternities and sororities have a negative effect on diversity efforts on college and university campuses, it is clear that as a general practice, membership in social fraternities and sororities will lessen the positive effects of diversity for white students and enhance the negative effects.

A clear conclusion from this study is therefore that joining a fraternity or sorority tends to deprive white students of the positive effects of diversity. For example, creating a culturally diverse environment has a positive effect on cultural competence, but only when students are *not* members of a fraternity or sorority. Similarly, the positive impact of emphasizing a culturally diverse environment on desire to promote racial understanding occurs *only* among students who are not members of a fraternity or a sorority. The only benefit from having a culturally diverse campus that does not disappear when students join a social fraternity or sorority is with respect to the perceived sense of community. One possible explanation for this exception is that being in a small "community" like a social fraternity or sorority strengthens the students' perceived sense of community on the campus, because on a diverse campus, a heightened sense of belonging can derive from having white students "draw themselves together."

The implications of these findings are compelling. If white students wish to acquire the knowledge, perspectives, and skills to interact successfully with people in increasingly multiethnic U.S. and global societies, they will want to think twice about entering a racially homogeneous social fraternity or sorority while they are in college. By the same token, college and university leaders wishing to promote the goals of student satisfaction with college, cultural competence, and desire to promote racial understanding will want to reexamine the usefulness of having Greek organizations on their campus.

To prepare students to be leaders in a fast evolving global society, colleges and universities may want to either change the focus of their Greek organizations or create alternative (non-race-based) forms of social support that will be equally engaging for their white students. Organizations reconstituted in this way could find it easier, for example, to co-sponsor joint activities with minority student organizations on a campus and this could lead to positive social development for all students. From the practical standpoint of teaching future leaders, diverse colleges and universities may now be reaching a juncture where they must decide whether to continue to support Greek organizations given that the continued existence of these organizations appears to be in direct conflict with institutional goals of promoting cultural competence and racial understanding and teaching skills necessary for future citizens to negotiate increasingly heterogeneous U.S. and global societies.

This data also adds fuel to the argument that artificially separating white students from other students on campus may well create a separatist mind-set that manifests itself later among U.S. leaders in government and business in the form of arrogance, uncertainty, and fear of other cultures and peoples. As a group, these students clearly do not possess the same levels of "cultural competence" and "desire to promote racial understanding" while they are in college as white students who were not in fraternities or sororities. Equally significant, white students who join fraternities and sororities will tend to leave college with a "sense of community" based on a narrow formula for cohesion and belonging that only includes white people. This is a mind-set that can later mature into an even greater pull toward isolationism later in life. It would not be too great a stretch to conclude that a tendency of homogeneous Greek organizations to reinforce homogeneous definitions of community could lead to a generation of national leaders who are unable to understand, empathize with, or collaborate with people of color years after leaving college.

Stated in a more positive light, it would be reasonable to conclude that business decision makers and government policy makers will be much more effective in their positions of leadership if they experience, during their college-going years, direct exposure to and daily negotiation of ethnic and race difference that will lead them to discover mutually beneficial relationships and outcomes rather than operate out of an "us-against-them" frame of reference. Arguably, the U.S. pattern of foreign relations leading up to and following the 9/11 bombing represents just such a frame of mind, characterized by fear, mistrust, condescension, and belligerence. While this would clearly demand a separate study, it seems logical to conclude that direct interaction with classmates of color while in college might translate to a greater capacity among U.S. leaders to be compassionate with, rather than "demonize," leaders of other countries.

As evidence of merit in this line of thinking, a recent note in the *Chronicle of Higher Education* reveals that Greek organizations produce an "old boy network" that is racially homogeneous in college and years later, when these individuals become national leaders. In its February 14, 2003, issue, it states that, "In addition to the 120 CEO's on the *Forbes* list, fraternities have accounted for 48 percent of American presidents, 42 percent of senators, 30 percent of representatives, and 40 percent of Supreme Court justices."

One troubling conclusion from the current study is therefore that U.S. higher education may have failed its democracy and the interests of the nation by missing an earlier opportunity in the 1960s, 1970s and 1980s to train future American leaders through direct exposure to people and cultures that represent perspectives different from their own. This study strongly suggests that admitting a racially diverse class, having race and ethnic content in the required curriculum, promoting student engagement in cross-cultural activities and workshops, and teaching how to communicate cross-culturally together constitute a "pedagogical set" that would be very useful to leaders in business and government who interact with people of color from other countries where the stakes are so high.

Unless the purposes and practices of social fraternities and sororities are recast, colleges and universities that continue to allow these organizations to operate as binary, "racializing" mechanisms on their campuses are conceivably undercutting their own efforts to foster cultural competence, racial understanding, and student satisfaction among their white students while *magnifying* the kind of conflict Allport predicted would occur in non-egalitarian, racially mixed settings.

Just as campus officials must find ways to reposition diversity programs to better accommodate white students and their needs, it perhaps behooves those same leaders to end the divisive impact of racially homogeneous Greek organizations now and in the future.

9. Leaders Must Reexamine the Central Values on Their Campuses That Define What Makes for "Community"

College and university campuses appear to be at another crossroads. Either they will continue with current approaches to diversity that perpetuate existing divisions between racial and ethnic groups while leaving dominant group members without the skills to change their own modes of interaction with people different from themselves, or they will initiate a new framework for diversity that better prepares all students, including white students, for successful participation in a diverse global society. The most self-conflicting findings in this study deal with precisely this concern in the context of "sense of community." While having a culturally diverse campus environment and placing an emphasis on race/ethnic diversity in the curriculum will clearly lead to gains in satisfaction with college, cultural competence, and desire to promote racial understanding, increases in the number of students of color and the number of faculty of color will lead predictably to *declines* in sense of community for white students.

Here it will be asked one more time, why should white students perceive a greater sense of community when there are significant institutional efforts to create a culturally diverse environment and to have more racial/ethnic material in the course content, and a *lower* sense of community when there are greater numbers of persons of color in the faculty and student body?

As indicated earlier, there are at least two possible interpretations. One is that having a student body that matches one's own racial background makes it easier to find a basis for commonality; that is, community is easier to imagine if members of the student body and faculty are racially homogeneous. Under this interpretation, it is easier to find a common bond among students who are all white because there is no need to concern oneself with race when seeking community. If, on the other hand, there is a significant mix of races in any setting, the notion of community or commonality is harder to find, simply because it is more difficult to find a common ground for creating community. Community may be easier to see, in other words, if there is racial homogeneity among its members. Of course, this kind of reasoning might be better suited to a world society in which racial groups stay in their own geographic enclaves and there is little need for interaction with others, but this is arguably an earlier period of simplicity to which the world can never return.

A second and more complex interpretation is sociocultural. This suggests that having more classmates of color will force white students to examine for the first time how they will form connections with people from different racial or ethnic backgrounds, and this in turn forces them to confront who they are (what makes for *their* own social and cultural identities). This interpretation looks beyond a common racial basis for community and focuses instead on the way identity and community interact. "If I can't identify myself with the others, then there must not be 'community,'" anthropologist Dorinne Kondo (1990a) notes wryly. In U.S. colleges and universities, this means asking candidly whether identity and community for some white students continue to be based on a sense of advantage or power over people who are *not white*.

Expanding on this, Ruth Frankenberg (1993) found through interviews of thirty white women that their identities were based on a form of whiteness that equated to white superiority. Prior to Frankenberg's study, Peggy McIntosh (1988) had demonstrated through her classic list of questions dealing with race distinction that white identity is based on unexamined daily privileges that give white people an advantage over people of color in U.S. society. In getting loans, being able to rent a house or finding people who look like you on television, people of color do not possess the same "invisible knapsack" of privileges that help white people navigate their social world with relatively greater ease.

In college, a white student's encounter with students of color may therefore differ in both magnitude and nature from the difference one finds between engineers and English majors, or the encounter between one's own culture and another culture when reading a book. Under the face-to-face, daily encounters one experiences from a racially diverse student body, the contact is more immediate and calls directly into question one's own sense of worth. In 1996,

Chesler confirmed this was the case where colleges and universities were adjusting for the first time to increasing race diversity and multiculturalism.

If the work of Frankenberg, McIntosh, and Chesler holds true in the diverse college setting, the white student's challenge of having to include students "who don't look like me" in a new definition of community will conflict with internalized differences in power that had marked these same people as "inferior." Seeing large numbers of those individuals would make that dissonance even greater. In other words, the desired institutional goal of maintaining sense of community at an increasingly diverse campus (that is, a diverse community) is in direct contravention of the mechanism by which the "white" student had previously affirmed her/his own sense of worth. Such an interpretation would be consistent with the conclusion reached by Morrison (1992) who, after conducting a review of early American literature, argued persuasively that white identity and its defining sense of superiority was historically created by and dependent upon the construction of blackness as inferior (see also hooks, 1992, and West, 1993).

Under Morrison's analysis, race will always be a marker that locates one group as inferior and another as superior. This is intrinsic to the operation of race. In the newly multiethnic campus climate, however, the white student who wants to feel part of a new community made of members coming from "lower" positions of power is now being asked to treat these people as equals, even when doing so would erode her or his own basis for self-worth. In other words, the problem with leaving white students in the position of having identities based only on race is that their only source of rootedness must be "surrendered" in order for them to participate as equals in an egalitarian campus community. Simply put, this leaves the white student with no identity.

If further research proves this to be the case, then colleges and universities experiencing rapid increases in the number of students of color will want to think more seriously about how to help European American students find new sources of worth and meaning in diverse social spaces. *Applying Morrison's analytics, the key to new identity and belonging in a diverse community would be to help white students discover connections to past and place that do not employ race as the underlying basis of worth.* This may well be the greatest challenge for U.S. educators doing work in human development in the twenty-first century.

Could it be that both interpretations are operating together? That is, upon entering racially heterogeneous college campuses, white students are finding it difficult to see a basic commonality with others who don't look like them *and also* finding themselves forced to reconcile that diversity with a set of old values about how to assign worth? If so, then in all likelihood that dual dissonance is magnified for white students who come to diverse college and university campuses from racially homogeneous high school communities and then affiliate themselves with homogeneous social organizations like fraternities and sororities.

Whichever interpretation one embraces, it seems clear that white students can benefit from academic experiences that enable them to value people from other racial and ethnic backgrounds, while valuing themselves. With this study demonstrating that adding racial/ethnic issues to the curriculum will lead to gains in cultural competence, it behooves college leaders to devise approaches that enable white students to see the possibilities in creating real "community" from a diverse faculty and student body. In other words, being able to interact with faculty of color and students of color should be viewed as part of the positive experience of going to college rather than as a threat to views of community linked to "whiteness." Needed next is a framework for diversity and individual worth that reinscribes the central values of a community *after whiteness*.

10. Every U.S. College and University Should Have a Comprehensive, Multi-Faceted Plan for Diversity

It should also be clear by now that institutions undergoing shifts in student racial demographics will need to establish strategies for diversity that contain within them aspects of all the above policy recommendations. It should be evident that different campus policies for diversity will impact white students in different ways depending on the activities the students choose to participate in during their college years. Creating a more ethnically diverse campus environment will impact "cultural competence" differently for students who join social fraternities or sororities than for those who don't. The combination of greater numbers of students of color with direct student involvement in cross-cultural activities may yield yet another result.

In fact, the larger patterns in the data confirm that colleges and universities will ideally want to combine (1) opportunities to participate personally in cross-cultural activities, (2) opportunities to learn how to communicate across race difference, and (3) campus efforts to formally introduce race issues into the course content. In other words, it is not enough to change the campus by admitting a diverse class or making course content more diverse (arguably just the first steps a campus might take); campus leaders will want to combine those changes with specific programs that increase skills in cross-cultural communication and promote cross-cultural interaction among students.

Given that the individual policies toward diversity examined in this study have also had differential impacts on different segments of a student population depending on how those students spend their time, it makes sense that *a college that has a goal of teaching its students how to develop more positive relationships with people from different racial and ethnic backgrounds will want to take a well-planned, multifaceted approach to race and ethnic diversity.* In other words, institutional policies to incorporate diversity on college campuses must now be viewed as steps that are coordinated rather than piecemeal if campus leaders are to maximize the positive effects of diversity for their white students.

In addition, absent a teaching component that specifically addresses the need for white students to incorporate and articulate positive sources of meaning not based on race, the progressive efforts of many colleges may prove to be deficient in exactly that regard most needed by white students. What I will suggest here is that identity-making as an academic thrust may next need to move to a higher level of sophistication by including within its scope sources of identity not based on race *or* ethnicity. This may ultimately mean having higher education participate in the production of new sources for meaning for white Americans that are not vestiges of a race-based Western colonial project or derive from specific countries of origin in Europe. One promising way of achieving this result will be presented in the next chapter.

In sum, this nationwide quantitative study confirms in rather detailed fashion the earlier findings of the Pico College experiment: (1) that current campus approaches to race and ethnic diversity need to be modified to better accommodate the needs of white students and (2) that a new template is needed to teach all students how to learn and interact *across* difference rather than leave groups in racial or ethnic enclaves. Most importantly, however, this study reveals that (3) learning about diversity is an important ideal held by white students: simply put, white students want to learn about diversity as part of their college-going experience and are not as satisfied with college when denied that opportunity. The analysis of surveys returned by 25,000 white students at 159 institutions thus reveals that earlier assertions by writers funded by conservative think tanks that diversity should not be viewed as a "good" and that white students do not want to learn about diversity are wrong headed. Not only is diversity perceived as "a good" by white students, it is a *desired* part of their undergraduate education.

When presented as part of a larger institutional strategy that weaves together various elements—in course content, race awareness workshops, social interactions, policies toward fraternities and sororities, training in cross-cultural communication, and by implication, wholly new approaches to community building and minority faculty integration—diversity will lead to enhanced cultural competence, greater desire to promote racial understanding, and most impor-tantly, higher overall satisfaction with the college experience for white students. Further, the positive impacts of diversity are maximized when white students are urged to participate personally in these cross-cultural activities. In other words, the first misconception raised at the beginning of this book is resolved in unequivocal terms by this study: *white students want to learn about diversity while in college and, if they do not, their satisfaction with college declines.*

At the same time, it is clear from this study that efforts to promote learning about diversity must be introduced in ways that do not increase racial fragmenta-tion on campus. Sneaking into this study are persistent issues of identity, power, and sense of belonging for white students who attend campuses that are increasingly diverse. Any new approach to diversity will have to take on and overcome these issues of culture and power that do seem to leave groups in enclaves and uncover creative precursors for community building on diverse campuses. One holds out hope that any success created on diverse college and university campuses might serve as a template for the U.S. as a society seeking to redefine its identity and place in a shrinking and diverse world.

But is it even possible to initiate a comprehensive long-term plan for diversity at a college or university campus that builds on the strengths of multiculturalism while overcoming its shortcomings? If so, then what might be the components of such a strategic plan and how might that plan represent an improvement over the approaches already taken at Pico College?

While many colleges and universities have been successful at adding the multiple cultural voices that make up America's social landscape (multiculturalism), it is becoming increasingly clear they must now explore specific strategies that focus on learning and sharing *across* cultures, that is, they must focus on the *inter*cultural. With this nationwide study demonstrating that white college students benefit in major ways from "intercultural" experiences and skills as part of their college-going experience, the pressing question then becomes, how will colleges and universities formally teach this? To address these questions, I initiated a study that was theory building in nature and "action research based," meaning that the ethnographer collaborates with others in planning and carrying out change in an organization that affects them.

CHAPTER FOUR

How to Build an Intercultural Campus

This chapter presents findings from a four-year action research study of one university as it attempted to become the first "*inter*cultural campus" in the U.S. by teaching how to learn across difference in a context where no culture dominates. While many of the hopes and dreams of this collaborative project would prove to be somewhat utopian, the lessons learned about how to incorporate diversity into an organizational change effort and overcome current limitations in uses of culture and power will likely lend fresh enthusiasm and momentum to progressive education in an increasingly diverse U.S.

A New Framework for Diversity

A small, private institution with an undergraduate student body of 4,300, Del Rey University (fictitious name) rests on the edge of an urban sprawl in California. Founded in the early 1900s, the university's student body was until the 1970s mostly white. From 1988 to 1998, the percentage of students who were of color increased from 27 percent to 42 percent, with many of these students immigrants or sons and daughters of immigrants from Asia, Latin America, and Africa. While nearly 50 percent of the entering class is now of color or mixed race background, 84 percent of the faculty remains white. There are no U.S. racial minorities in the top administration.

Several years ago a number of racial incidents marred the campus climate. The frequency and severity of these events—occurring over a relatively short period of time—triggered a heightened sense of alarm among campus leaders and led the institution to seek a new model for diversity that could reestablish racial harmony. While Western Eurocentric approaches had long had the effect of marginalizing minority students and employees on this campus, leaders were also finding that attempts to introduce a multicultural perspective into the curriculum and student affairs only seemed to inflame existing conflicts between racial groups. Needed next was a framework that could nurture all identities while building a new sense of campus unity.

The year before this study was launched, an African American basketball player was expelled following an altercation over a parking space. African-American students questioned why it was the black student who was expelled from school and not the white student who had brandished a baseball bat. Not long after this, groups of African American and Latina students were sprayed with a water gun by fraternity members from a dorm window above a walkway, with one prankster yelling to the Latinas, "Hey, I buy oranges from your father at the freeway exit!" With so many ethnic groups streaming into the adjoining city, these events became coded expressions of race fear, racism and lack of understanding about diversity in the eyes of some in this campus community.

In the ensuing weeks, the letters "KKK" were scratched on an African American student's dorm room door, forcing him to move off campus; bright red swastikas were painted on the interior hallway walls of an upperclass dorm; three white male students yelled "Homo!" at an Asian American student as they peeled out of a parking lot in their car; and a plate of food was thrown at the door of a black housing staff member who served as a judicial officer and lived with his wife on campus. During this time, Latino students were reporting that a professor in class was describing Mexicans coming into the U.S. as "wetbacks" and African American students reported that a different professor had stated in an American history class that, "Blacks were partly to blame for being slaves."

With news of these incidents spreading like wildfire through minority sub-communities on this campus, the cumulative effect was an overwhelming sense of alienation among minority students and the minority faculty who consoled them. Black students tended to associate more closely with each other and the same held true for other minority groups. While some students dreamed of a better place (e.g., Harris, 1997), the campus had already formed protective enclaves.

The great paradox was that while minority members felt they were under significant racial stress, many white members believed the campus was a place defined by racial harmony. A campuswide survey of students, staff and faculty (with over 1,000 surveys returned) showed that as a group, white students and faculty believed that race was not a problem on campus. As a Catholic institution, Del Rey prided itself for an atmosphere nurturing social justice, development of the whole person, and open intellectual exchange. The same survey showed, however, that being on campus was a different experience for minority students (p < .05) with particularly high racial stress reported by African American students. Beneath a "veneer of civility," as one senior white professor put it, the experience was apparently not so positive for many on campus who were not white.

These events, of course, did not take place in a vacuum. A senior white professor of education perhaps captured developments best when he exclaimed at a department meeting, "With multiculturalism, now there's no way for us to belong!" Indeed, American higher education seemed at an impasse with two warring approaches to knowledge. Multiculturalism had sought to add silenced voices to the education mix and this remained a valuable thrust. Not unlike Pico College, however, multiculturalism was apparently leaving out the interests of European Americans. In "binary opposition to" a U.S. legacy of whiteness, it was apparent that multiculturalism could never be the binding force that brings the members of racial minority and white groups together. The second approach, one of "Western retrenchment," sought to promote order by returning the focus of education to a European or European American tradition, at the expense of the histories of minority groups in America. No resolution seemed imminent and Del Rey was not immune to this unresolved tension.

To address the alarming rate of racial fragmentation on this campus, Del Rey University sought and obtained $800,000 in grants to begin an "action research" project that would, if all went well, turn the university into "the first intercultural university campus" in the U.S. The first part of this chapter will be devoted to reporting *practical* steps and pitfalls in this project as they are highly instructive to those who wish to devise new strategies for diversity on their campuses.

At the same time, it might be possible to view the events in this project in more abstract terms and pose the urban U.S. university as a site for renegotiation of meaning and space in an increasingly heterogeneous democratic society. Intrinsic to this view is the opportunity not only to reexamine whether social change can be modeled in the American scholar's backyard, the university, but also whether current analytical tools are adequate to track radical change in uses of culture and power in "transnational" education settings impacted by the influx of so many cultural meanings into one space. To evaluate this transformation in *theoretical* terms, the second half of this chapter will apply frameworks from sociocultural and linguistic anthropology that may ultimately lead progressive educators to explore and apply new concepts and tools.

In *Culture & Truth,* Renato Rosaldo (1989: 102–104) indeed found after studying border crossing situations in the Philippines and with U.S. Chicanos that culture would now have to be defined not so much as a fixed set of shared meanings but rather "a process of change over time in which people alter the conditions of their existence." In *Crafting Selves,* Dorinne Kondo (1990a: 300–307), a Japanese American who studied gender and class relations in Japan, extended this thinking by suggesting that culture was not a reified thing or system at all but a "meaningful way of being in the world inseparable from the deepest aspects of one's self." Kondo further reasoned that one's conception of "inseparability" could be equated to establishing a connection to community. Under Kondo's analysis, "power" is created when a person finds meaning through connection to community. In the study presented here, I will note that Kondo's view of how to be in the world (connection to community) can apply equally well to connections based on gender, sexual orientation, class, religion and other socially constructed categories.

So if culture has to do with altering conditions of existence, as Rosaldo would hold, and connecting oneself to her or his world, as Kondo suggests, then an intercultural campus might conceivably allow groups to create conditions enabling each to create *and connect to* a common community across race and ethnic, gendered, sexually constructed, and class-based differences. At the same time, a further caveat seems in order when examining the increasingly heterogeneous space of the urban U.S. campus. I found people seeking to build campus harmony would need to heed Gayatry Spivak's (1988) admonition that cultural contact between an oppressive culture and a subordinate one will lead to a form of "incommensurability" in which the members of one culture would never truly know the meanings of the members of another culture. Amended to reflect this, an "intercultural" educational framework would feature learning and sharing across difference *in which no culture dominates*.

Would it be possible for an entire university to make itself intercultural? The impetus to do model building on the scale contemplated in this study came from work on resistance theory by Emily Martin (1987: 183), who after studying the gendered treatment of women by the medical profession observed, "At the heart of people's ability to question the social order is their ability to conceive of an alternative kind of regime" (referencing Goran Therborn, 1980). Accordingly, this case study raised three initial questions:

1) *Can you affirmatively set out to create an alternative regime?*
2) *How can you organize thinking about cultural contact in a transnational urban space?*
3) *What is required for human interconnectiveness in a polycultural public sphere?*

Del Rey's Intercultural Plan

In an excerpt from a book on moral collapse, Vincent Crapanzano (2001) issues a call for forthrightness about one's scholarly agenda by reminding researchers that, "However well masked, interpretive practice is always implicated in plays of power." Since critique is an interpretive action and itself susceptible to plays of power, this study was an attempt to examine whether the 1990s love affair with "critique" might give way to "model building." Given the racial fragmentation at Del Rey University and dissatisfaction nationwide with existing approaches to diversity, a shift to "model building" seemed both necessary and timely. While the presumption was that model building would surface new ways for power to operate on a particular campus, it was also suspected that research methods and scholarly reward mechanisms for researchers might need to be revised to accommodate the longer term work to evoke organizational and social change of this magnitude.

In performing model building, a turning point thus presented itself: whether to turn education research back to a restorative form of Deweyan pragmatism or constructivism that might overlook historical asymmetry (Popkewitz, 1998: 560) or instead take up more directly the study of opportunity and surprise associated with the breakdown of a social order. As Popkewitz articulated with unsettling clarity, constructivism, with its tendency to view problem solving as a universal disposition in each student to the exclusion of historical oppressions, too easily "remakes the problem of inclusion/exclusion." Michele Foster (1997) further crystalized this issue when she noted at an ethnographic methods conference that researchers in critical pedagogy and postmodern ethnography often exhibit a tendency toward "structural overdeterminism" and should begin to change how power operates in their *own* workplaces.

Bauman and Briggs (2000: 140) evinced similar cynicism about current methods when they concluded that a recent overemphasis on "not leaving something out" of one's critique had formed a kind of "Derridean gap" in progressive U.S. scholarship wherein a scholar becomes preoccupied with the act of critique, and by implication, never conducts actual change. With a growing need for new models leading to different patterns of culture and power, the larger question becomes, "How?"

To facilitate new uses of culture and power on one campus, I helped Del Rey University launch a four-year "action research" project that would be guided by six campus committees composed of members of all strata and racial groupings. Under an action research philosophy, the researcher joins with leaders of an institution to collaboratively plan, implement, and assess a particular organizational change that will ultimately affect them (e.g., Elden & Chisholm, 1993; Tax, 1975). To track the desired change, this project employed a "pre/post" assessment strategy in which baseline measures of social and cultural interaction would be taken at the beginning of the project and again at the end to see whether there would be any measurable effects from the interventions. *The research question was whether a university could make itself into "an intercultural campus" by introducing intercultural practices into all its major functions.*

Three Patterns of Cultural Interaction

Pre-test data deriving from focus groups, surveys, and observations indicated a preexisting co-presence of three competing patterns of cultural interaction, and this was a finding that would dictate the implementation strategy to follow. This pre-assessment included a campus racial climate survey administered to students, staff, and faculty, eleven focus groups conducted by affinity groupings with students, staff, and faculty, and two years of observations.

One preexisting pattern of culture and power on this campus centered around an expectation that minority groups would eventually assimilate into the dominant culture on campus. In three focus groups consisting of senior white professors, participants expressed an ideological position that racial minority students needed to "fit into American culture." Similarly, in focus groups of white students, some argued the campus didn't have any race tension because it had successfully become "a melting pot" where minority students were integrated nicely into the campus milieu. As further evidence of this ideology, when offered the opportunity to hire a "minority" professor, two academic departments nominated scholars of color who came to them from Asia and Africa—a practice that might suggest the word "minority" was equated with "foreign." It was because of early experiences like these that the intercultural project at Del Rey University was compelled to switch its terminology from "person of color" to "U.S. minority" despite abhorrence of the term "minority."

With so many pieces of data implying that U.S. minorities should fit into a dominant Eurocentric culture, this belief system recalled Homi Bhabha's (1994: 38) description of that in-between space of *"hybridity,"* where cultures come into contact with each other. It is interesting that the hybridity to which Bhabha referred in a colonial or postcolonial context often traced the assimilation of a subordinate culture into a dominant one, a result that many on campus not in the "dominant" group would reject out of hand. At the same time, this interpretation characterized the world view expressed so forcefully by several senior professors in their focus groups discussions, one of assimilation.

A second pattern of beliefs about the influx of people of color into Del Rey University reflected a view that different cultures would not merge at all but be "at war" with each other. Invariably, this was the view of people from racial groups subordinate to the white culture. In minority student focus groups, students described the university as "a white campus" where, for example, the core requirement of having to take courses in European history was just one more device "to keep the dominant group in power." Noting how racial incidents had left minority students feeling hurt and confused, several minority professors contended that before this campus could ever become a safe environment for learning, "white professors have to change." White staff members, who worked in racially diverse job settings every day, expressed a particularly high need for formal training in race sensitivity.

For many minority members of this campus, it seemed the vicissitudes of their work made for daily border crossings, a term developed earlier by Anzaldua (1987) to describe the experience of Latinos coming north into the U.S. Under border theory, it is presumed that when two cultures come into contact—one dominant and the other subordinate—they will each impact the other. To the extent that minority groups and white groups were at war on this campus, that behavior might well be described by the metaphor *"border crossings."*

The third pattern of cultural contact that appeared at the outset of this study was one where members of all cultures interacted with equal status and generated positive emotion that bridged across racial and ethnic difference. This occurred where students studied together in racially heterogeneous groupings, in extra-curricular activities where students from different backgrounds worked together on a common project, in racially diverse social interactions by staff or faculty, or where minority faculty had more than a token presence in an academic department. In such instances, people interacted across race and ethnic difference as equals and power was shared.

In addition to the above, a quantitative analysis of pre-assessment survey results showed that encouraging students of the same racial group to associate with each other would not result in Balkanization of the campus into separate racial enclaves *as long as* those students also had positive interactions *across* groups ($p < .05$). This was an important finding because it confirmed that members of ethnic groups could be encouraged to associate among themselves while also interacting with members of other groups. In other words, multicultur-alism would not need to be sacrificed to make way for an intercultural framework and, arguably, could be viewed as a critical prerequisite for it. That is, there could be no sharing of cultures if those stories and histories were not developed and nurtured to begin with.

Still the exception rather than the rule, the last kind of intercultural contact arguably approximated the egalitarian interaction across cultures that Mikhail Bakhtin (1984/1929: 88) termed *"intersubjectivity."* In an intersubjective exchange, all participants retain the subject position from which to author and validate their own ethnic and family histories (e.g., Tanaka & Cruz, 1998: 144; Tanaka, 2002b). But just as importantly, under an intersubjective frame of cultural interaction, no participant or participant's culture would be turned into an essentialized "object" of another person's speech (e.g., Burbeles & Rice, 1991; Lenkersdorf, 1996; Flores, Tanaka & McLaren, 2001; Tanaka, 2002a).

In contrast to hybridity where cultural contact is presumed to lead to assimilation of a subordinate culture into a dominant one, intersubjectivity nurtures participation on a level playing field without sacrificing individual social identity. The term "intersubjective" can thus describe moments where every student has voice and agency, one's identity is not established at the expense of any other student or group, and there is an overarching sense of connection to others even in a highly heterogeneous community.

Depending on whom you asked then, there were at least three broad forms of intercultural behavior at this campus—behaviors that theorists might describe as hybridity, border crossing, and intersubjectivity. The implementation strategy in this action research project was to build an intercultural campus by maximizing moments of intersubjectivity for students, staff, and faculty.

Del Rey's Action Research Project

Organizational change of the magnitude contemplated here was not without its early advantages. First, Del Rey University was a small institution and this meant that changes affecting individual functions of the university might one day coalesce and result in a transformation of the organization as a whole. Second, the university was a Catholic institution and obligated by its mission statement to promote the aims of social justice. The idea of creating a level playing field for members of all ethnic and racial backgrounds was consistent with the cherished doctrine of founding priests. Third and perhaps most importantly, university leaders were committed to placing the institution on the map and saw in the chance to become "the first intercultural campus" an opportunity to do just that. Eight hundred thousand dollars in grants provided added incentive.

To maximize the development of intersubjective moments within the university, leaders at Del Rey University initiated a multi-pronged approach. The action research plan would ultimately consist of five parts, each directed by a separate campus committee composed of people who would be affected by the change, and aimed collectively at impacting the major functions of a university.

Staff intercultural training would be offered on a volunteer basis with the intention of building a positive word of mouth reputation for the workshops rather than making them mandatory or risk building resentment toward diversity. There would be a Level I workshop teaching cultural awareness, commonly used terms, and issues of power and privilege. At a Level II workshop, participants would be asked to exchange stories of their family's history coming into and moving across the United States—their "geo-ethnic family histories" (Vigil & Roseman, 1998)—and then discuss strategies to make their own workplace egalitarian and intercultural. As noted below, geo-ethnic family histories would prove to be one of the most effective techniques in building an intercultural campus and have large implications for future work in diversity. The workshops would also make liberal use of small-group discussion combining workers from different units of the university and across different strata. The first staff workshops were devoted to academic deans and vice presidents with the aim of enlisting their early support.

Importantly, these approaches were designed and implemented by the Staff Intercultural Committee, composed of employees from different strata and responsibility within the university. Initially, this committee consisted of, among others, office assistants, middle managers, a service worker, the director of training, the vice president of operations, and the director of human resources.

A Student Certificate Program in Intercultural Competency would consist of two semester-long courses and a three-day mountain retreat that would culminate in a high school summit planned and facilitated by certificate students. Focus would be on listening and conflict resolution skills, learning about power and privilege in the students' own lives, intercultural team building and leadership skills, and learning how to facilitate small group discussions about race and power. It was hoped that all students entering the university would be given training in intercultural skills. In addition to the certificate program, all entering students were to participate in a two-hour workshop during orientation weekend and all leaders of student organizations would go through a similar training session on cultural awareness and power. The Student Intercultural Planning Committee would include the dean of students, a professor of psychology, the director of student intercultural affairs, and four students.

Minority faculty hiring would be initiated through a grant that paid for the first-year salaries of four full-time teaching equivalents (FTE's). To initiate searches for these individuals, departments could nominate candidates in open competition with other departments, with the prize being a full-time teaching equivalent for the winning department. Under this novel approach, departments would be urged to search high and low for strong candidates. In seeking U.S. minority candidates who were "extraordinary" and then nominating them to the academic vice president, this process was identical to the preexisting practice where any department could nominate an extraordinary person from outside the university at any time. But not only would this candidate have to show very high promise of scholarly success, s/he would have to show a track record as a mentor and role model for U.S. minority students and be able to contribute in a positive way to the intercultural learning environment.

To plan and coordinate minority faculty hiring and changes to the curriculum (see below), a Faculty Intercultural Committee was formed, consisting of associate deans from multiple colleges within the university, faculty from the ethnic studies departments, and two senior white male faculty members who were former presidents of the faculty senate. One former faculty senate president would turn out to be the co-chair of this highly important committee and prove to be a major reason for its success.

Curriculum development workshops and **workshops in how to teach a diverse classroom** would also be instituted through several different approaches. Curriculum development would take place through summer course development grants to induce professors to convert existing core courses into ones that could be cross-listed with the American Cultures requirement examining three of five major racial or ethnic groups in the U.S.

Second, there would be an incentive program inviting departments to bring in outside consultants paid for by the intercultural project who were from their own discipline and could tell them how their departments made the curriculum multicultural or intercultural at their own universities. Workshops in how to teach a diverse classroom would be provided to selected professors from four colleges of the university using a combination of outside consultants and internal professors as facilitators. These sessions would expose professors to the possibility of different learning and teaching styles. The Faculty Intercultural Committee would also oversee the design and testing of these initiatives.

An ongoing assessment, using surveys and focus groups, would be conducted on a regular basis to track change in campus racial climate and sensitivity toward diversity. The committee formed to oversee this process would include the director of the Office of Institutional Research, a researcher from the School of Education, a researcher from the psychology department, the director of research in the campus intercultural project, and an undergraduate student research assistant. This committee would supervise construction of the campus climate survey instruments, coordinate the surveys and focus groups, and hire and supervise several outside consultants who were to provide technical assistance and analysis for the campuswide assessment.

In addition to the five committees described above, *an Oversight Committee* was formed to make budget decisions, oversee and coordinate the work of all the intercultural committees, and help open important doors in the university administrative structure. This committee would come to play a large role in the early success of the project and include such individuals as the academic vice president, the dean of the College of Business, the vice president for administration and finance, the associate dean in the College of Liberal Arts, and the director of human resources. As the action researcher and grant director, I served on all six committees and chaired the Oversight Committee.

Why an Intercultural Approach Worked

Now four years into the project, initial testing has been completed for model intercultural interventions in all the major functions of the university. The indication from the findings in the post-assessment is that another five or six years of implementation will be needed to fully complete the process of building an intercultural campus. Results from the post-test qualitative and quantitative assessments are presented below.

Interculturalism a Successful Framework

Data from the post-test campuswide survey show that intercultural interventions have already led to positive measurable outcomes for students, faculty, and staff. To prepare this data, a blocked, stepwise regression analysis was performed on surveys returned by students (15 percent return rate) and faculty and staff (55 percent return rate). Results indicate that:

1) When students, staff, and faculty participate in intercultural activities, they feel more comfortable discussing ethnic issues with others in the campus community, are more likely to have positive interactions with people from different ethnic backgrounds, believe race relations are good on campus, and experience enhanced feelings of control over campus policies relating to race (p < .05). In contrast, when members of the campus community do not participate in intercultural activities, they do not experience improvement in intercultural skills.

2) Where there is high university commitment to interculturalism, the faculty and staff indicate higher satisfaction with the environment for teaching and learning and their intercultural understanding and skills are improved over the previous year (p < .05).

3) While African American students reported higher racial discrimination than other students in year one of the project (1998), by year three there was no significant difference in reported rates of harassment between African American students and white students. One highly encouraging conclusion from this data is that interculturalism is having a positive effect on the campus racial climate even though not everyone is participating.

A second conclusion born, confirmed by observations and focus groups, is that racial stress has increased slightly for white students who are finding that whiteness and privilege no longer go unexamined. This suggests that declines in racial stress for racial minorities may go hand in hand with an initial increase in racial stress for white students when creating an egalitarian field for learning. At the same time, this finding is clouded somewhat by the fact that many students did not participate in intercultural training and could be inferred to be in a mind set of "early multiculturalism." While not inconsistent with the findings in chapter 2, the initial stress for white students in an intercultural social environment is more than compensated for in this study by larger gains in sense of belonging and interconnectiveness, as I will discuss below.

Collectively, the data from the post-assessment surveys and focus groups suggest that intercultural interventions have already had measurable, positive impacts on students, staff, and faculty after just two years of programming. This is an encouraging development for diversity efforts in U.S. higher education and for foundations that provide support to institutions for organizational change through grants. Simply put, multi-year grants can clearly be an impetus for organizational change that, if applied more extensively throughout a campus, may well lead to the creation of new kinds of universities in the United States. In this case, the two large grants that funded this project came from The James Irvine Foundation and The Hewlett Foundation.

At the same time, it should be remembered that only a fraction of the campus community at Del Rey participated in planned intercultural activities, about 50 percent of all staff, 20 percent of the faculty, and 45 percent of the student body. While well on its way, this university's effort to make itself into an intercultural campus was not yet finished.

What Worked Best

A deeper qualitative analysis of the data will show that particular programs had much to do with the early success of this project and should each be considered in their own right for use at other U.S. universities and colleges. At the same time, the success levels of each intervention differed significantly.

Staff Intercultural Training. The staff intercultural training sessions were arguably the most successful part of the project and led to innovations other campuses may wish to emulate. Two years into the project, 50 percent of all staff members had voluntarily participated in Level I sessions and almost 25 percent in Level II sessions. This high level of participation alone was enough to make the overall project a success. Word spread that these training sessions were positive experiences in which "the white male" was not made into a target but difficult race issues like privilege and victim status were nonetheless addressed.

In the staff training sessions that worked best, participants were divided into diverse groups of four or five and asked to tell stories from their own lives or the lives of their ancestors. Invariably, the set of questions ran as follows: (1) Tell your group a brief history of your family's entry into and movement across the United States. (2) Can you describe a situation where you or a family member experienced a sense of privilege in relation to others, and why? (3) Can you describe a situation where you or a family member experienced oppression, and why? (4) Dream of the same place where oppression occurred but describe what it would be like if the oppression were removed. In some sessions where there was time, the small groups were asked to address a fifth question: (5) Given what you have learned today, what would you do tomorrow to make your workplace more egalitarian and fair?

During these sessions the small-group storytellings—with people from different ethnic backgrounds and levels of responsibility sprinkled throughout each group—proved exceedingly engaging and rewarding for participants. At one small-group dialogue, a senior administrator described his family's negative experiences with religion and class difference in the Midwest before moving to California; an African American female service employee told how a grandparent had been lynched in the South before her family moved to California; and a department secretary told her group that she used to cry on her porch at home after returning from elementary school in central Oahu in Hawaii where she had been taunted and teased for having curly light brown hair by Asian classmates who had long straight black hair. At another session, I watched as the academic vice president discussed "how to share power" with a grounds crew member, two administrative assistants, and a middle manager. (For a fuller account of these and other stories, see Tanaka, 2002b.)

The advantage in having mixed groups of participants was that everyone engaged in a storytelling could arrive at an understanding that there was both privilege and oppression in their family histories, no matter their family background, and that others in the group did not personally cause those power differentials to occur. Perhaps even more importantly, the last two questions elicited dreams of a future place where the ugliness of past or present oppression is removed—and this took participants out of the enhanced understanding of pain and oppression to a new place of release from that mentally and spiritually taxing state. As will be explained in the next chapter, this may have been the single most important discovery in the three studies presented in this book. The stories of pain, and then dreams of a better place, took participants out of a "binary" mind-set that had always nominated a victim and an oppressor and left individuals in a permanent state of binary oppositionality.

In general, the staff intercultural training sessions proved extremely successful in that all participants no matter their rank or gender or race could listen at the same table with others different from themselves and tell their own stories. The intercultural storytelling component of these workshops, along with other awareness pieces, were among the most transportable interventions of this project and can be readily adapted to other colleges and universities.

Student Intercultural Training. One of the first interventions in the intercultural project, the Student Certificate Program in Intercultural Competency, proved so successful in its first year that it should be modeled and tested at other universities and colleges. Students who completed this program say it changed their lives. They became more complete, felt fulfilled, and were better able to know themselves in relation to others. A major reason for the success of this program was the director, who instilled a positive attitude about difference in all its forms while moving students of color out of their oppressions and white students out of guilt or fear about diversity. A second reason for the success of this intervention was again the storytelling techniques that proved extremely effective at breaking down student fears, anxieties, and false assumptions about culture, race, gender, class, sexual orientation, religion, and power.

Thus, while Del Rey's 1980s "multicultural model" had earlier left many white students feeling alienated and too far removed from countries of origin in Europe to know their cultural histories—that is, they were without "ethnic culture"—an intercultural storytelling approach let all individuals discover they had family histories here in the United States that were worthy of telling others. As suggested in chapter 3, it did indeed seem that the declines in sense of community under a multicultural model could be attributed to the fact that the appearance of so many students and faculty of color and their histories made "raw" a recognition that many white students had no specific ethnic identity they could call their own; they had no particular connection to past or place in Europe. With an intercultural storytelling, however, this all changed. The exploration of one's rootedness to past and place became reestablished by exploring and telling the history of one's family in the United States—an activity that did not automatically stake one out as "the oppressor."

At a campus troubled by race tension, the feeling of release for all students that derived from this new program of study and training led to a kind of overall experience that seemed almost spiritual. One lesson from this is that it was exceedingly important to find skilled individuals to lead the student and staff intercultural training sessions. In the case of Del Rey University, the director of student intercultural affairs was a rare soul who could reach students from all ethnic and racial identities and move them to a new place of sharing and interdependence.

As suggested earlier, another key lesson was that storytelling will likely be a critical component in any approach to intercultural learning that seeks to achieve a heightened sense of community. As will be discussed later, the benefits of intercultural storytelling go far beyond the learning of other people's histories and cultures and hint at the onset of deeper values like compassion and learned interdependence with others different from oneself. In a shrinking global society, it might be persuasively argued that these skills and perspectives are more valuable in building world harmony than norms of competition, superiority, selfish individualism, or victim status.

Third, and perhaps most importantly, it became readily apparent from this four-year project that having a highly diverse student body constitutes a critical prerequisite if an institution is to promote the kind of intercultural learning that took place here. Absent diversity in the student body, staff, and the faculty, there could be no richness of stories, and the full benefit of an intercultural storytelling would not inhere. As I will explore further in the next chapter, this finding confirms how affirmative action in admissions is a necessary precursor to a racially and ethnically diverse student body that makes possible the particularity and richness deriving from a sharing of diverse stories.

At the same time, while intercultural awareness was being introduced to all entering students during student orientation at Del Rey University, only forty-five students completed the formal certificate program during the first two years. With the increase in positive interactions across difference and feeling of control over one's life—and with declines in racial harassment for minority students after these limited interventions—it would be reasonable to predict that extending the certificate program to the entire student body would lead to even larger positive results. The hope is that one day this institution will expand this successful program to reach all students when they become juniors and seniors.

Minority Faculty Hiring. The minority faculty hiring initiative also achieved a major breakthrough that can serve as a model for other institutions to follow. I personally found this approach so novel and so successful that I believe it should be tested in other institutional contexts like corporations and government agencies. In contrast to the early 1990s when minority scholars were "given to" academic departments—there to be either stigmatized as "the minority hire" or rejected outright by the existing faculty—the academic departments under the approach used in the intercultural project typically fell in love with their candidates as a result of the open nomination and competition process.

In the first full year of this initiative, four of six finalists were hired, two with funds provided by the grant and two who departments insisted be hired through other means. In addition, there was a kind of "penumbra effect" in which many departments campuswide determined that it would be a good idea to start to "stockpile" U.S. minority visiting scholars and lecturers in anticipation of getting one of the much sought after grant-funded FTE's in a future year. In effect, the goals of minority faculty hiring were "institutionalized" into the culture of academic departments, where, as a practical matter, future hires would often come from the ranks of part-time lecturers and visiting artists and scholars.

What this also meant was that the litany often heard in previous years of "no qualified minority candidates available" was of no weight, after aggressive departmental searches for potential candidates at conferences and through phone calls to contacts teaching in doctoral programs led in almost every case to a strong departmental pool of U.S. minority applicants. In one year alone, so many academic departments became excited about minority faculty hiring that another ten U.S. minority scholars and artists were brought into the cultures of those departments outside the auspices of the grant-funded positions. In other words, the excitement from the open candidate search and nomination process had a "ripple effect" that attracted in one year a total of fourteen U.S. minority scholars as either visiting faculty or tenure track professors. With a total university faculty of only 275, these gains were extraordinary.

The Curriculum. Curriculum transformation became yet another success and was initiated, as indicated earlier, through the use of *"outside consultants."* In early dialogues with faculty, it had become quite clear that professors—who were not inclined to listen to a "diversity consultant" coming to their department to help them make the curriculum more diverse—would be open to listening to the views of another professor from their own discipline. These departments believed an outside visitor from their own discipline could address the specific research methods and concepts that would resonate with them. It should be underscored here that the invited outside professors from other institutions were selected for a visit by the departments themselves.

In this case, it was in the Departments of Theological Studies and History that faculty members came to feel an immediate sense of connection with the person coming to visit them, since each visitor could state how it felt to go through a similar change of curriculum at his own institution, describe the fears and concerns among faculty at those other institutions, and tell how those doubts could be overcome in ways that made sense in that discipline. While these seminars were highly successful, they next needed to be followed up with discussions to explore how many of the professors changed their course content as a result of meeting with these consultants from their own field.

In addition to curriculum consultants, *course development grants* were employed to evoke change in the freshman American Cultures program, and this led to further changes in core courses offered in English and Theological Studies. Co-listed with courses in American Cultures in a novel pairing, these courses had the effect of "institutionalizing" intercultural learning by integrating the new diversity content with previously offered core curriculum courses.

Pedagogy. In contrast to the intercultural successes in the curriculum, a separate attempt to conduct *workshops in how to teach a diverse classroom* met with only partial success. One possible reason was that neither outside nor internal faculty consultants used the kind of "small-group" format that was proving so successful in the staff intercultural training workshops. Lecturing about what they considered "best practices," some facilitators addressed the faculty only on an intellectual register and, as a result, did not lead participants to investigate their own feelings, perspectives, or assumptions about diversity. With attendees "intellectualizing" their involvement rather than learning from each other through storytelling, there was less self-introspection concerning their own positions of power and their own rootedness in family history than was taking place with staff and students.

There was another factor that should be reported here and it has large implications for the future of multiculturalism. In many faculty pedagogy workshops, there were only small numbers of U.S. minority faculty. In contrast to staff and student intercultural training workshops where almost 50 percent of the participants were U.S. minorities, faculty workshops lacked a "critical mass" of minority faculty necessary to make the experience itself diverse. In these sessions, minority faculty seemed marginalized and white faculty members did not seem compelled to examine their own identities or basis for knowing. Even if there had been more storytelling, the stories would not have been intercultural in the absence of stories from more U.S. minority faculty.

What this suggests is that there must be a healthy degree of multiculturalism (in the form of many participants of color and their family and ethnic histories) before intercultural learning for faculty can truly occur. Just as a diverse entering class will create the opportunity for intercultural learning and sharing that could prove useful later in life, a U.S. college or university will want to seriously consider diversifying its faculty ranks with U.S. minorities if the goal is to educate future citizens and leaders who will help the United States interact respectfully with people from other countries. The implication from this conclusion is that the multicultural and the intercultural modes work best when in combination with each other. Without the "polyphony" of a diverse student body and faculty, there would be limited intercultural learning; by the same token, without an intercultural emphasis on learning and sharing across difference, a multicultural emphasis would tend to leave groups in enclaves.

In the case of Del Rey University, 45 professors out of a campus total of 275 went through intercultural pedagogy training in the early years of the project. The intention was to have these participating faculty members engage in follow-up sessions as a means of getting them to share what worked and didn't work as they went about altering their teaching approaches for diverse audiences. The long-term aim then would be for every faculty member on this campus to undergo this kind of training and to in effect teach each other the "best practices" so the entire faculty body would benefit and learn from each department's innovations.

Assessment. One of the unexpected gains in this long-term action research project was the high success of the *"pre/post" assessment* strategy, in which the attitudes, skills, and knowledge base of the campus community was evaluated at the beginning and at the end of the project. Introduced by a professor in psychology, the idea of "pre/post" measurement became one of the most important contributions to the project and should constitute a critical component in organizational change efforts at other institutions exploring models for diversity. In this case, the dual use of quantitative methods based on surveys and qualitative findings from focus groups and observations enabled leaders to form conclusions about what worked and didn't work, plan future adjustments, and begin to theorize about what it meant in abstract terms for a university campus to become "intercultural."

Other Success Factors. In reviewing the successes and partial successes of the intercultural project, the significance of three other factors cannot be emphasized enough in a model building process. First, *support from the top administration* was very high, as two deans and four vice presidents took personal responsibility to help introduce intercultural initiatives into their colleges and divisions. The academic vice president was particularly visible in stating the value of this effort to the institution and in opening the door to corridors of institutional power at key moments. Where this kind of support can be expanded in future years would be in having intercultural dialogues and workshops for critical units like the board of trustees and the priests who live on campus.

Second, *the use of town halls* was an unexpected surprise and was quite helpful in eliciting broader support for the project. As a result of this, leaders of the change initiative concluded that there needed to be greater use of town halls in the future. It was during these town halls that leaders of the intercultural project could see with their own eyes the benefits of an intercultural perspec-tive—and the crying need to expand these programs to reach more students. In particular, the unmet needs of white students became even more evident as they used this forum to express in unrestrained terms their own plight as participants who found multicultural approaches unhelpful and who wanted more from their undergraduate education in the form of skills and perspectives that could help them interact more successfully with people of color.

Third, there were three *key leaders in the institution* who each took personal responsibility for the success of a particular program and used their committees to develop these programs into models that could be worthy of replication at other campuses. One senior faculty member, who was white and male and skilled at campus politics, became a major force in encouraging other faculty members and departments, through their chairs, to take up this idea of interculturalism and see what it could mean for them. Based on his contributions, it would be highly advisable for other institutions to identify a leader from the "dominant cultural group" on campus who could go on to enlist yet other leaders from that group.

In addition, as mentioned previously, there was a staff administrator in student affairs who was a large factor in the success of the overall project. After watching his work, it would be highly recommended that other institutions interested in undergoing a similar transformation hire at least one or two individuals who have experience directing diversity training efforts that do not place blame on the white person but who nonetheless can get every participant in a workshop to examine their own positions of power and ultimately discover spiritual reasons for wanting to learn how to share across difference. The third individual who played a prominent role in the success of the project was the director of training in human resources. Her special contributions were an even-handedness and sense of fairness that made every initiative she facilitated a complete success. With people trusting her intuitively because of her openness and forthrightness, people essentially flocked to the workshops and the success of her workshops basically set the tone for the entire project.

For all three individuals, it was clear that an extraordinary sense of decency and humility combined with a strong commitment to social justice helped make these people into role models that others on campus would want to follow. As a result, I now think every institution wishing to undergo an organizational transformation of this nature will want to identify this kind of leadership in the early going. Together, the above "key success factors" underscored how the original research question could essentially be answered in the affirmative: it is indeed possible for researchers to set out to create a new social space that approximates a level playing field—and model a new kind of campus.

Barriers to Building an Intercultural Campus

A number of developments suggest, however, that the full transition to "an intercultural campus" has not yet been completed. First, the interventions that became effective models now need to be refined and applied to all departments and divisions in the university. To be fully participatory, the action research nature of this project *needs to spread to all units,* where every member of the community can feel invited to participate. The next group of project leaders is seeking to do this by asking each major unit to design a plan indicating how they will make themselves intercultural and offer a timeline.

Second, it turned out that the Division of Student Affairs insisted on *housing the new Student Intercultural Affairs Program within the Department of Minority Student Affairs,* over the protest of minority administrators and intercultural project coordinators. White students now had to walk through the minority student wing—past the Office of Black Student Services, Chicano/Latino Student Services, and Asian American Student Services—before they could enter the Student Intercultural Affairs office. While this ultimately made sense from a budget perspective, there were important ramifications about this decision that made it counter productive. Minority students felt that locating the intercultural office in Minority Student Services violated their "safe space" to let their hair down about race stress. On their part, some white students campuswide came to see the Student Intercultural Affairs unit as "a minority program," since it was housed in Minority Student Services. Thus, with this decision was lost the opportunity to present interculturalism as a fresh mechanism that could fully engage and bind together all the factions on campus, including all white students.

Arguably, the decision to locate Student Intercultural Affairs in the minority students section of Student Affairs could also be construed by some members of the campus as a place where minorities can be kept safely away from white students in a kind of "super ghetto" that minimizes the "contamination" of an otherwise white campus. This could also have the effect of perpetuating the very binary, "us-against-them" mind set that led to racial incidents in the mid-1990s and forced the campus to seek grants to ease the race tension. If a wish by one administrator comes true, the Minority Student Services Department will change its name to the Department of Ethnic and Intercultural Student Affairs, thus potentially allowing the minority program to "appropriate" the novelty, momentum, and growing budget of the intercultural project.

In other words, the potential for full appropriation of interculturalism by Minority Student Services hints at the university's larger problem of viewing cultural diversity through an obsolete, binary lens of a *dominant/minority construct*. This frame empowers the institution to keep white students "over here" (in Greek organizations and service organizations, for instance) and minorities "over there" (in minority programs). Arguably, it was this kind of dualistic thinking that enabled the university leadership to believe it was "helping" minorities earlier when minorities were suffering.

Further, the decision to artificially hold minority students in spaces removed from white students too easily "reproduces" the notion that minorities are "in deficit" and exacerbates racial tensions rather than showing students how to work with and understand each other. Learning the language of social critique well enough to escape criticism, these white *and minority* leaders might in fact be perpetuating the dualisms that keep them in power while disguising each as "a negotiation" (see Aaen, Parker-Hayes et al, 2000; Darder, 1991: 55–60). Missing from this binary approach to diversity is a better, more inclusive theoretical framework that elides such dichotomies and rescues members of the community from the superficiality of carefully regulated oppositionalities.

The biggest bar to creating an intercultural campus, however, may be *the missed opportunity of this campus to expose more white students to the new sources of identity and meaning that derived from geo-ethnic family histories.* Those students who did perform this storytelling gained a greater sense of self and connection to past and place. The students who did not do this storytelling seemed to be lost or suspended in the complex space of a diverse campus. Simply put, they lacked the personal base from which to comparatively investigate the personal histories of others. For example, at two town hall meetings each attended by over sixty students, faculty, and staff, it was the white student who had not experienced intercultural training who expressed pain and anger at having to learn about diversity in ways that treated their identities as the source of the problem. One student asked in frustration, "Does this mean I should start a White Students Club?" Other white students criticized a required American Cultures core course that was in their eyes a form of "white male bashing." With these outcomes, the campus would clearly benefit from having all its students engage in the kind of storytelling that Certificate Program students enjoyed.

Another development, and one I had not personally anticipated, was that U.S. racial minorities sometimes had difficulty letting go of a personal need to have power over and "beat the white person." One minority officer, for example, seemed to use his newfound power as an administrator to suppress the development of white women under his charge. Two other minorities who chaired committees in the intercultural project could not accept the idea of working with outside consultants who were white and ultimately had to step down. This behavior also translated to leaders of color criticizing other leaders who were also of color. One Latino leader continually cast aspersions about other Latino leaders involved in the project and a minority dean complained about the intercultural project because it "had resources" he did not have.

What this behavior may well reflect is a preexisting sense of *victim status mentality* that all university transformation projects will need to anticipate and address. Under this internalized "celebration of victim status," some of these individuals seemed unwilling to give up a vested interest in being resource dependent even when it would mean "putting down" other racial minorities in their own group or other groups. Clearly needed were new rituals that would help oppressed members find a clear path out of an investment in victim status, or *ressentiment* (e.g., Tanaka, 1999) as mentioned earlier. In moving away from simple, binary understandings of culture and power that reproduced themselves through this victimology, the intercultural was clearly creating new challenges that could also be viewed as fresh opportunities to conduct yet other forms of action research and storytelling in the future.

What these entrenched behaviors also indicate is that the transition to an intercultural campus will require people of color to undergo a kind of soul searching that will be every bit as challenging as the ones initiated by "dominant" members of the campus. Like many of their white counterparts, some who were of color tended to see the world in binary "us-against-them" terms, and this was a bar to their own intercultural learning. Needed at base was a new framework for human development that would enable campus leaders and researchers to theorize, rationalize, and assess new patterns of being in the world for individuals of all racial or ethnic backgrounds in an increasingly diverse community.

Another theme that appeared was the ubiquitous presence of *economic class distinctions* within the university. Staff and students indicated over and over again that Del Rey was an upper-class institution that treated people with money differently from those who didn't have money. Staff members pointed out that race, class, and gender discrimination conspired to make the grounds crew black, custodial crew Latina, and operations middle managers white and male. One vice president who championed the cause of interculturalism when it came to ethnic culture insisted that the same level playing field did not need to apply to class-based differences on campus. Other administrators insisted that staff training and faculty development should be kept separate—a policy that was likely to forestall the effort to make the university "intercultural" in the sense defined here because there would always be a group of second class citizens.

In addition, there was throughout this four-year project clear evidence of *a special "class" distinction that separated staff from faculty* and this of course is not unlike the same division that exists at many other U.S. universities. What was interesting here was that early probes by intercultural leaders to break down this barrier were quietly turned back in academic affairs for fear that the overall project would never get off the ground if the project were to tackle that distinction at the same time it was addressing race. But in forming separate intercultural committees for staff and faculty, the project itself arguably became complicit in perpetuating this very distinction. What I will suggest from the perspective of hindsight is that the larger intercultural project was already considered so valuable to the institution that the accommodation of this form of "difference" could have been made part of the implementation plan without losing momentum in the overall project. Even now, it remains feasible to import some of this thinking into the future work of the intercultural committees.

Another factor that looms large in the march toward becoming an intercultural campus was the growing significance of *sexual orientation*. In this Catholic institution, top administrators at Del Rey had time and again issued clear instructions that this was one form of diversity that would be better left alone. The campus was loathe to "run afoul of" the church even in the interest of promoting its mission of social justice. While at one point the vice president for student affairs was forced to block a student initiative seeking student government funds for a student gay/lesbian club, the students and staff issued calls over and over again at town halls and staff intercultural training sessions for fresh thinking about this. If it becomes the last step, official recognition of this oppression will in my view be the one that finally makes this campus "intercultural"—that is, where no culture dominates.

While there are committees on campus addressing gender discrimination, it also appeared that a *male-centered philosophy* continued to dominate the upper levels of management in this university. Criteria had been developed to provide recourse for sexual harassment and the human resources division conducted workshops on this. At the same time, however, women faculty and staff still felt they had unequal status in relation to men on this campus. Most of the top positions in the institution are filled by males. In fact, the stress from so many forms of difference on this campus seems to have driven some to "competition between subjectivities." On losing three U.S. minority middle managers, for example, one white female administrator elected to fill the vacancies with two white women and a white male despite the availability of highly qualified minorities. With a clear preference for "white women" in a division charged with overseeing interactions between highly diverse individuals on campus, one hierarchy was potentially replaced by another.

Even with all the above barriers to building an intercultural campus, there is still one more source of resistance to change that seems more entrenched than all the others put together. The most unsettling data in this study came from untenured faculty members who indicated their continuing fear of senior white male professors who continued to wield firm control over faculty hiring and promotion. On multiple occasions, junior faculty members reported that senior white professors did not want them to bring up race or gender issues—if they themselves wanted to have tenure one day. A shocking revelation, this struck at the heart of a faculty member's life and way of being in a university.

In other instances, U.S. racial minority professors expressed deep disappointment at the hypocrisy of teaching students about social justice as part of the mission of the university but not teaching them "how to actually do it on campus." Too often, these professors indicated, there would be one white student who was determined to write a scathing course evaluation of the professor's performance no matter what the professor did to strengthen her or his teaching. As they noted quite persuasively, this was not a barrier that junior white faculty had to overcome in their march toward tenure. With this qualitative data, it would seem that the biases against faculty of color reported in chapter 3 were confirmed in this action research project. This provides further evidence of the need to study the unique difficulties encountered by U.S. minority faculty in relation to their white counterparts. If nothing else, it might be useful to regard the occasional outburst by a white student toward a faculty member of color as an "outlier" that should be removed from the evaluation process. And clearly, before Del Rey University could become a fully intercultural campus, it would need to change how power operates at the senior faculty and tenure review levels.

In summary, the attempt to create an intercultural campus climate surfaces larger issues beyond race and race inequity. This study also demonstrated that you cannot expect to address race issues to the exclusion of other subjectivities or ignore longstanding traditions that leave one group or another in power—and expect to build an intercultural campus. Addressing one historical asymmetry will always trigger discussion about the others. The greatest surprise to me in this study, however, was not the ideological resistance by senior faculty, but that some minorities would continue to undermine the work of a project that would create a level playing field for all identities. Needed next was a new way of posing the evolution of the individual in a transnational urban space.

Culture and Power

When I began this four-year study, I had three questions in mind and will re-examine them here in light of these research findings. At the same time, new theoretical questions were raised by this research that made me realize that organizational change of this magnitude could not be completed without also examining the impact of intercultural training on the individual student or professor or staff person. I was forced, in other words, to re-see the individual, or "self," as a subject and agent. The sections below will examine some of the theoretical implications of these findings.

Revisiting the Three Questions Posed

Can you affirmatively set out to create an alternative regime? Data from this study would indicate the answer will one day be "yes." While it had been unrealistic to expect an entire campus to make broad changes after just two years of full programming—there being no templates for this—the real breakthrough in the study came in creating model intercultural programs for each major function of a university. Taken together, it seems realistic to expect these interventions will one day amount to a complete transformation of the institution. At the same time, as indicated above, a number of thorny problems must be resolved if Del Rey University is to become a fully intercultural campus.

How can we organize our thinking about cultural contact in a transnational urban space? Two things stand out here. First, it is apparent that an intercultural approach can be an effective third alternative to the diametrically opposed thrusts of Western retrenchment and multiculturalism. While I first learned about intercultural frameworks from performed art (Marranca & Dasgupta, 1991; Hwang, 1994; Tanaka, 1994) and applied them to my work in education (Tanaka, 1993, 1995, 1996, 1996–1997, 1997; Tanaka, Bonous-Hammarth & Astin, 1998; Tanaka & Cruz, 1998), others were quick to see its potential significance to education research (e.g., Cornwell & Stoddard, 1994; Arratia, 1997). Cornwell and Stoddard (1994: 44) were most hopeful in suggesting that interculturalism would be "a less polemicized and politicized term because it has not been bandied about the media as a buzzword for the breakdown of Western civilization." Their work injected a degree of intellectual confidence into this project and crystallized the question of whether an entire institution could become "intercultural." A successful initial testing of an intercultural model at this university suggests an intercultural perspective can now be introduced into the wider theory base for higher education.

Second, among the three intercultural frameworks examined in this study, it is "intersubjectivity" that offers the greatest promise of rationalizing a reconstitution of urban education settings having an influx of multiple subjectivities. Intersubjectivity is thus posed as a means of promoting constructive engagement across difference without forcing diverse voices to conform to one set of norms regarding knowledge. Nurturing whole subject positions for all students—where no one else is turned into an object of one's own discourse—the goal of an intersubjective pedagogy is to create a learning environment where individual voices and positionalities can interact with each other on a level playing field.

This means, ideally, the creation of communicative spaces for storytelling where each person becomes a subject with full voice and agency for her/his own story and achieves this result by helping others to become subjects (tell their stories). In other words, in the kind of intercultural storytelling that took place in staff and student workshops, each individual told stories from her or his own family history and helped others to do the same. The sharing of stories thus enacted a "subject-to-subject" exchange. In the sense that personal storytelling moves away from binary, essentializing treatments of racial and ethnic categories in favor of the "complex multiplicity of every individual" (Cornwell & Stoddard, 1994: 46), the establishment of intersubjectivity via storytelling constitutes a clear alternative to monocultural and multicultural pedagogies.

Here it is important to acknowledge that if each person is still labeled "white" or "female" or "bisexual" rather than seen as having complex, shifting subject positions, intersubjectivity will itself devolve to the formation of tinier but still reductionistic categories (Kaplan, 1997; Shohat, 1997). It will also be useful to draw a distinction between two types of subjects, one being what Michael Jackson (1998: 7) refers to as an "empirical person endowed with consciousness and will" ("the subject") and the other being the social identifiers that Jackson refers to as "abstract generalities such as...class (and) gender" (what I call "subjectivities"). In remaking each individual as a subject (Tanaka, 2002a: 289, 2002b), I will mean helping a person enhance her/his own ability to exercise and occupy a subject position that accommodates all her/his subjectivities based on race, gender, sexual orientation, class, religion, etc.

To avoid the trap of essentializing either subject positions or subjectivities, progressive educators will want to promote the kind of "interdependence" among individuals that appeared in intercultural storytelling sessions for staff and students at Del Rey University, where each individual subject's agency helped fulfill the agency of another. To evaluate how to promote interconnectiveness in a polycultural environment, I will next suggest that an intercultural, storytelling-based pedagogy changes how we see identity, culture, and power.

Connection to Past and Place

In intersubjective spaces created at staff intercultural training sessions, student discussions in the Certificate Program, and minority faculty hiring deliberations, the relationship between culture and power indeed seemed to shift. Where "culture" had before been a tool to keep other groups at bay (the unstated universality of whiteness reproducing relations of asymmetry, as one example), the culture for white members in an intersubjective space seemed more like a feeling of belonging to a new community they were able to co-define with others who were not white. Here, it was critical that white participants could uncover and tell their own stories about their family's history of movement into and across the United States—a process that instantly placed them on the same level playing field with other "tellers" who were of color.

Here it can be suggested that intercultural storytelling lends credence to the argument that category-based approaches to identity and culture can too easily reduce to essentialized treatments of subjectivity that paint individuals as "token characters lacking complexity and completeness" (J. E. Davis, 2002: 31, citing with approval Ferguson, 2000; Talburt, 2000). In critiquing the current tendency toward entrenchment in "identity categories," Davis issues a strong call for "critical examinations that go beyond commonplace identity representations" (id at 32).

This critique of ready categories in education research trails a long line of work in cultural studies that traces overreliance on categories to binary thinking. In *M. Butterfly: Orientalism, Gender and a Critique of Essentialist Identity,* for example, Dorinne Kondo (1990b) provides an early critique of conventional representations of gender and race, noting how David Henry Hwang's intercultural play "subverts notions of unitary, fixed identities" (Kondo, 1990b: 26). Unlike identity representations that are universal and ahistorical, Kondo contends a performed approach reveals identities that are "multiple, ambiguous, shifting locations in matrices of power." In "De-Essentializing Interracial Representations," Diana R. Paulin (1997: 166) extends this argument further when she notes that, "Binaries that reduce identity to one exclusive position obscure historical complexities and contemporary realities." As will be discussed in the next chapter, the impetus to discover and test new ways of posing identity and belonging that are *not binary* gain further momentum from the capacity of intercultural storytelling to position *each individual* as "a subject" who goes through space helping others also to become subjects.

For white participants then, the intercultural storytelling experience at Del Rey University was not a rediscovery of some essentialized ethnic culture from a Europe long removed. Nor was it a rearticulation or rebirth of whiteness and its unstated universalities. In contrast to a generalized, totalizing notion of history and connection to place, the sharing of highly particularized "geo-ethnic family histories" rooted each individual "white" participant and other tellers in the common geographical space of a California campus and, arguably, constituted the onset of a new, collective history. In other words, the telling of geo-ethnic family histories made possible, for all members, a connection to past and place. In asking for the histories of people coming into and moving across the United States, the intercultural project thus encountered a way of bringing together people in a common storytelling experience who might not otherwise find commonality, and instantiated a co-emergence of unity and diversity.

Rosaldo had argued in border crossing situations (with Latinos coming north into the United States) that culture is a process of change in which people "alter the conditions of their existence," and it would be useful to revisit that conclusion here. What's different in the intercultural campus is that *both* members of oppressed groups and privileged groups are altering the conditions of their existence *together*. Thus, while the term "culture" still has currency, it is becoming too simplistic to deploy the term superficially to distinguish one "homogeneous" group from another. In an intercultural storytelling, there are as many different family histories within a group of Latinos as there are Latino storytellers. No longer linked to a common set of "shared meanings" to which every person must adhere—an increasingly strained use of the term "culture" in a transnational social space—the intercultural campus creates a condition where there are as many meanings as there are individuals in attendance. Here the word "shared" refers instead to what happens when diverse stories are told.

Power

What this line of thinking suggests is that notions of power must also be re-examined in the spaces of an intercultural campus. In place of one group using its culture as a mechanism for control—distinguishing one group from another in asymmetrical terms—intercultural participants on this campus discovered a different kind of power that was spiritual, shared, and reconstitutive of community, not unlike what Kondo had found among women shopworkers in Japan in their struggles with shop owners for survival and identity. Unlike the experience reported by Kondo, however, both "oppressed" and "privileged" members at Del Rey University participated in this storytelling process *together*.

What this equates to, then, is a radical shift in how power gets deployed and interpreted in progressive work, away from opposition and resistance in Kondo's reporting, to an "interdependence" among storytellers. In exchanging binary oppositionality for interdependence, the latter contextualization makes it more likely that individuals will achieve a heightened sense of release from preexisting patterns of generalized fear (of the "Other"), blame (for inequities in society), or celebration of victim status (from feeling oppressed).

Interdependence

Traveling well beyond binary notions of power and resistance, the onset of intercultural storytelling thus forces a reconceptualization of power into a more complex typology that encompasses different forms of spirituality reflecting the individual's soul in relation to the souls of others. Here power is no longer seen as derived from a dominant discourse (after Foucault) but instead from a storytelling process in which multiple agents get to tell their stories to each other—and become dependent on those other storytellers being good listeners. In place of competition and individualism there is a kind of "interdependence," in which one's own coming into personal power becomes dependent upon helping others also to come into personal power. In this way, the idea of a dominant discourse (already in retreat on this "transnational" campus) is superceded by the onset of multiple stories told by multiple, inchoate storytellers. If the Del Rey University experiment is to be perfected and replicated at other venues, the challenge will be for future intercultural efforts to engage and teach people who are not naturally inclined to be empathetic and good listeners.

While interdependence is not new (e.g., Chickering & Reisser, 1993) and autonomy has in human development circles been conceptualized as a precursor to socialization and interdependence (id, citing with approval Erikson, 1959: 115), it is something else to pose individual development as an event that occurs *as a result of* helping others also to come into being. The latter formulation would extend the reach of Chickering and Reisser (1993: 143), who wrote in more subdued terms:

> Growth occurs when relationships of reciprocal respect and helpfulness are developed with parents and peers and when mutually satisfying interrelationships are sustained through vagaries of distance and disagreements.

In a diverse, transnational education space, this newer conceptualization of interdependence seems quite critical and needs to be developed further. In the space of multiple storytellers, autonomy and interdependence seem to be co-present and may even merge. I will examine this further in the next chapter.

So what is required for human interconnectiveness in a polycultural public sphere? At the most successful intercultural storytelling sessions at Del Rey University, participants and facilitators alike spoke of their own family histories—of family difficulties encountered with respect to race or gender or class or religion. In these exchanges, students of color learned that many white students were not aware of their privilege and did not mean to hurt others because of that privilege. White students learned that the pain and rage felt by some students of color were real and based on specific incidents in their lives or their family histories. But what is even more important is that all students, no matter their race or ethnicity, learned there are moments when they are privileged (because of their education status as college students as one example) and other moments when they may feel oppressed. The value of this recognition alone more than justified the time and expense of this project and, indeed, delivered the students to a new, shared place that was non-binary.

Toward a New Epistemology

In these storytelling sessions, the primacy of "theory" also seemed to decline. Meaning about how the world works was constructed not so much from abstractions as from the storytelling itself. In lieu of one author offering a theoretical construct to explain how the world works *on behalf of all others,* the realization from each storytelling was that there will be different meanings constructed by different people from the same experience (polysemy) and an overarching quality of new group meaning through this shared process. In this urban campus, there was something of a feeling that ways of knowing might proceed more accurately from story and storytelling than from the totalizing function of a "theory" advanced by one person or group on behalf of all others.

Similar success was encountered when dialogues or workshops for staff began with personal storytelling—in contrast to faculty workshops where there was very little storytelling and a lower level of success was experienced. In effect, storytelling seemed to level the playing field by exposing all participants equally to vulnerability, risk, and reliance on each other not to ridicule, judge or belittle. The emphasis on dreaming of a different kind of campus in the years to come placed a further gloss on the success of the storytelling: beyond promoting a sense of race harmony, there was for all participants an increased personal connection to past, a more direct rootedness to place, and an incipient interconnectiveness with each other in dreaming of a new social space.

Story vs. Theory

The power of storytelling as a tool to improve social relations at Del Rey University of course comes at a time of great soul-searching by scholars about the distancing of theory from original experience. It was Edward Said (2000: xvii, xxxi) who perhaps summarized developments best when he observed:

Looking back from the present, one can discern a trend in much of the great criticism of the early twentieth century that draws readers away from experience and pushes them instead toward form and formalism...I have been using the term "historical experience" throughout because the words are neither technical nor esoteric but suggest an opening away from the formal and technical toward the living, the contested, and the immediate.

Here Said is unable to suppress his personal disappointment in the fact that inequities of the world have continued unabated despite two decades of vigorous social criticism, much of which he helped shape. Cultural critique, postcolonial and subaltern studies, poststructuralism, critical theory, feminist theory, queer theory, postmodern self-reflection, neo-Marxist analysis, multicultural studies, New History, and critical race theory are some of the theoretical frameworks that have directed themselves to hierarchy and urged its dismantling. Even with all this critical work in theory, the U.S. race-based, capitalist, gender-directed hierarchy appears more entrenched than ever—and its global reach is being reinvented and strengthened daily.

Coming at the end of his career, and this by a brilliant theorist, Said's urgent call to original experience and his reservations about the sole eminence of theory would almost seem to imply a recanting of his own original contributions (Tanaka, 2002b). In his ruminations, Said of course recapitulates the earlier work of writers like Barbara Christian (1987: 52), who has argued that some individuals do not theorize *only* in the form of abstract logic:

I am inclined to say that our theorizing (and I intentionally use the verb rather than the noun) is often in narrative forms, in the stories we create, in riddles and proverbs, in the play with language, since dynamic rather than fixed ideas seem more to our liking.

What is different about the Del Rey University experiment is that storytelling came to be a medium of exchange for *all* participants—those from marginalized groups and those who had been "privileged." Taken in concert with the observations of Christian and Said, the advent of successful *inter*cultural storytelling in the Del Rey experiment may therefore signal a turning point in U.S. higher education and a transition to a storytelling pedagogy that would counter the tendency of one person to theorize on behalf of all others. In fact, in that it could not reflect the multiple stories of multiple storytellers, a way of knowing based on one person's theorizing about the presumed meanings of others now seems to leave out much, to be "incomplete," and at each utterance, to reinscribe the binary. In contrast to this narrow monovocality, the power of a "storytelling pedagogy" to remove incomplete knowledge from the learning process and replace it with an inchoate sense of polysemy was arguably the most positive, unexpected conceptual discovery in this action research experiment.

What I now suspect, based on the positive effects of storytelling at Del Rey University, is that researchers and educators will be forced to consider that "story" (or original experience) may be displacing "theory" as the primary vehicle for learning in heterogeneous social contexts. What I am suggesting here is that story—and its multiplicity of perspectives—may be *more* important than having one theorist summarize in abstract terms the perspectives of others, for others. But in the very least, I would think, students will want to leave college with the skills to perform in both registers, through story and with theory.

From Critique to Model Building

While completing this project, I also discovered the reward system for scholarship in education research places large emphasis on journal articles that perform critique and are written in a relatively short period of time. In doing work in the field to actually change an organization, I did not have time to turn out large numbers of such articles. With the success of this organizational change project, I now suspect that reward systems for progressive scholarship will need to be modified to give credit for the long, hard work to test new organizational models, or on a larger scale, to create new democracies or economies that promote the aims of social justice. Put differently, such change efforts would be far more effective with contributions from scholars than without them.

Thus, while much of the work by progressive scholars in recent decades has been directed to critiquing power relations and with good success, they have not always led to actual change in hierarchies of power within the university structures where those scholars reside. Divisions along race, gender, and class lines remain hierarchical. One result of this emphasis on theory and critique has been that the progressive movement launched in the 1960s now seems to have dissipated somewhat; arguably, in following the current system that rewards piecemeal or abstract work, the progressives lost the initiative to deeply funded conservative think tanks whose work is strategic, long-term in focus, and oriented toward practical change. To extend the fine work of interpretation and critique in such movements as critical theory and cultural critique, the success of the Del Rey University intercultural project offers evidence that future diversity efforts will benefit from greater emphasis on achieving actual change through new model building and from scholarship that doesn't stop at the act of critique. One possible way of promoting such a shift is presented below.

Anticipatory Action Research

At Del Rey University, this particular action research project meant changing an organization into a larger "model" that has the potential to give rise to still larger "social change" in the wider society. Based on the lessons learned from the Del Rey University project, future approaches to model building might also benefit from the key components of what I will term "anticipatory action research" below (see also Tanaka, 2002b). As will be explained, the use of the word "anticipatory" derives from the emphasis placed on having a diverse group of people sharing visions and dreams about a better place.

The notion of "anticipatory action research" I will present derives directly from the *intercultural storytelling* that cultivated feelings of interdependence at Del Rey University. Consistent with the work of Foucault and drawing from work in anthropology, an anticipatory action research approach will look behind the stories of pain and oppression of all participants and *examine how power operates* in historical context for different groups (structural critique). At Del Rey University, this analysis revealed, for example, that men still held dominant positions on campus and that the interests of LGBT students were "swept under the rug" by an administration that remained beholden to a Catholic Church that continued to regard sexual orientation as taboo.

We also know from the successes of staff and student workshops that a storytelling must then move to a stage of *dreaming of a new social arrangement* that establishes a level playing field for all members. In that this social space is dreamed of and not yet real, this step is "anticipatory" of actual change to come even as it addresses past harms, fears, or inequities. Importantly, this stage was the one that seemed to transform each storytelling workshop from one that might otherwise celebrate victim status, self-pity, or fear to a new place of healing, rootedness, renewal, and interconnectiveness for all participants.

In addition, this research revealed another innovation. In anticipatory action research, participants go beyond the dreaming stage to *construct and test models* to actually change a site by making it more egalitarian. If truly collaborative, a model building project of this nature might result in spaces where individuals re-establish "soul" through enhanced *connection to place, memory, and ritual*—while also helping others do the same. The hope then is that these connections will form a foundation for each individual to evoke larger change "in anticipation of," for example, a more diverse democracy.

In combining the advantages of intercultural storytelling, social critique, dreaming, model building, and soul creation, an anticipatory action research approach can, in broader terms, lead educators and students to envision new campuses where notions of the self, reinvented within a larger goal of interdependence, will work hand-in-hand with the construction of new forms of civic governance that are diverse and intercultural. In summary, an anticipatory action research project would seem to have at least five components:

1) Small group storytelling about past and place
2) Examining how power operates
3) Envisioning or dreaming about a new social arrangement
4) Actual model building in anticipation of wider change in society
5) Greater personal connection to place, memory, and ritual

At Del Rey University, an anticipatory approach was carried out where students co-planned and implemented what they would be learning in their intercultural activities or where staff at intercultural workshops co-dreamed of new practices for their workplaces and mapped out those changes. In all such cases, no one was turned into an object of another person's discourse and the development of each individual seemed tied to helping other participants also to grow. While "anticipatory" methods have gained some sway in such disciplines as anthropology, a long-term project to change an entire university by applying those methods remains rare in higher education research. One way to teach others how to promote actual change in an increasingly diverse U.S. society would be to offer schoolteachers and college professors a continuing education practicum that teaches them the methods of anticipatory action research.

In summary, this study demonstrates one means through which U.S. higher education can depart from a 1990s preoccupation with theory and criticism by placing less emphasis on rigid categories of culture and power in favor of new forms of meaning-making that are anticipatory and mutually beneficial for diverse groups of individuals. While an abstract deconstruction of historical asymmetry will continue to constitute a useful starting point for positive change, it is no longer enough to stop there. What progressive movements must now do is instigate and fund research-based projects that perform actual change in social relations at specific sites—through the kind of storytelling, model building, and ethics of interdependence and collaboration that worked so well on the playing field of this intercultural campus.

At the same time, this was only one campus. This university's intercultural project was directed at only one kind of "macro" social force, a transnational racial demographic shift. The final chapter investigates several larger ramifications of the findings in this book and outlines the contours of a pedagogy that shifts the focus for diversity from analysis of "mediating" systems of culture and power to a closer examination of the individual (the micro level) and the larger (macro) social forces that are acquiring so much significance in today's world.

CHAPTER FIVE

The U.S. after 9/11: Diversity in the Twenty-First Century

It would be simplistic to conclude the events of 9/11 and larger global context of anti-U.S. sentiment are a result of higher education's failure to train today's generation of leaders to be compassionate and understanding toward people different from themselves. At the same time, it is impossible to ignore that the global racial fragmentation linked to recent U.S. economic policy mirrors the racial fragmentation that plagued Del Rey University in the mid-1990s and led that institution to launch its "intercultural project." With this in mind, a fresh question presents itself: *If one U.S. university can teach its students, staff, and faculty the intercultural skills to build community among people who differ from each other in ethnic or racial background, might an intercultural model provide the next generation the skills to be more effective leaders in a diverse global society?*

Stated differently, would it be possible to extrapolate from "model building" at one organization, a university, to larger prospects for peace and social justice in both U.S. and global societies? If so, how would the shift be made from one organizational change—through action research—to transformation at the macro level of society, that is, "social change?" This chapter will investigate the initial components of a social change pedagogy posing education as the primary vehicle to build a more just and "diverse democracy" (Musil & Wathington, 2002).

While the following probes can constitute the elements of a new framework for diversity, my hope is that they will reveal the need for a larger philosophical shift in the work of progressives. The areas that beckon are: (1) a change in focus for diversity work away from essentialized categories like race and culture to the individual as an agent or *subject;* (2) the notion that each individual's development can be linked to helping others also to grow, that is, *complementarity;* (3) redirection of the rationale for social change work *away from "resistance" and binary oppositionality* to norms of interconnectiveness based in interdependence and soul creation; (4) *alternative storytelling* as a means of engaging individuals in positive social change; and (5) the high promise of *parallel systems* as sites for social change where energy need not be wasted protesting or fighting against entrenched hierarchies. While the following discussion will be somewhat abstract, it is offered in the spirit of initiating further dialogue about how to renew and redirect diversity work in the decades to come.

Departing Essentialized Categories

One of the larger findings in these eight years of research was that the usefulness of *categories* defined by "race," "culture," and "identity" fell off quickly when applied to emergent behavior in the complex, shifting social spaces of the urban campus. In assigning to all members of a class one uniform identity that is essential to everyone in that class, these category-based tropes became too inflexible, unwieldy, and undiscriminating when the task turned to tracking new uses of social space and personal meaning *as those shifts were occurring.*

Worse, a category-based analysis typically left white members out of the process of redefining community and in "binary opposition" to diversity rather than as full participants in it. The Pico College study demonstrated in particular how multiculturalism could lead white members to feel alienated or personally to blame for society's inequities. At times, a multicultural approach could even exacerbate existing tendencies toward racial fragmentation by driving people into enclaves and failing to reposition members of dominant groups for successful participation in the newly multiethnic community.

This difficulty is perhaps no more acutely seen than in the U.S. Supreme Court cases upholding race-based affirmative action in college admissions (*Grutter v. Bollinger*, 2003) while striking down racial quotas (*Gratz v. Bollinger*, 2003). In these opinions, the Court is unable to escape a deeper tension in its own history caused by a strong wish to avoid category-based thinking (like quotas) and an equally strong interest in protecting against inequities *linked explicitly to categories* like race and sexual orientation. This book presents one way of promoting learning across difference where diversity need not be conceptualized in the form of fixed categories, where the individual learner (as agent) becomes the focus of assessment, and where the research methods and outcomes are themselves re-unifying and participatory. In this regard, the non-binary constructions that proved so successful at Del Rey University—the individual as a subject, interdependence, the notion that each individual can have multiple, shifting subjectivities, and intersubjective storytelling, to name a few—suggest a shift is possible in diversity that will resolve some of the tensions encountered by the Court.

Thus, while the court cases clearly place a burden on educators to decamp category-based applications of diversity like quotas, it is important to note that education researchers had already identified the need for non-binary, non-essentializing practices (e.g. Nozaki, 2000: 374-375; J.E. Davis, 2002: 29; Gutierrez, 2002: 1079) and begun to explore alternatives. Missing from the U.S. Supreme Court's call for new frameworks is a recognition of its own complicity in hinging equal protection historically to the compartmentalized notion of a "suspect class" found in a footnote in *Carolene Products* (1938) and further developed in *Brown v. Board* (1954) and *Bakke* (1978). One objective of this chapter is therefore to deconstruct the analytics of difference based in homogenizing legal constructions and articulate a field based alternative that departs both essentialized categories and dichotomous uses of culture and power.

Relocating poststructural theory and social change analysis to the transnational urban U.S. campus, this chapter explores the disadvantages in research paradigms that place great emphasis on mediating notions of culture and power and outlines an alternative framework for diversity based in a form of agency called "subjectivity." As I will explain, the methods of building subjectivity tested successfully at Del Rey University demonstrate it is possible to engage in new uses of diversity that do not rest on binary, essentialized constructions.

Thus, while category-based analysis of race and other forms of difference formed a foundation for a flowering of U.S. diversity programs after the 1960s, it should by now be clear that this approach is too dichotomous and rigid for the transnational education space that is demanding explanations at the level of inchoate meanings for individual agents or subjects. In addition, it is a perspective that leaves many white Americans without sources of identity and belonging in an increasingly diverse America. Stated differently, the alienation of white members at institutions like Pico College reflects a wider inability of U.S. education to address constructively the *anomie* linked to demographic shifts in the U.S. and underscores how a missed opportunity could ultimately be mined by conservatives who had a larger purpose in mind.

In this regard, I argue a small group of free market conservatives have used the natural fears and uncertainty from these demographic shifts as a foil while appropriating the democratic institutions of government, education, and the media. With racial demographic shifts and global capitalism exerting great impacts on individual human development, I argue progressive scholarship now has no choice but to depart its 1990s reliance on a mid-range analysis of culture and power and focus more aggressively on: (1) the individual as agent (the micro) and (2) the larger social forces that impact that individual (the macro).

In focusing on each individual, a *"micro"* emphasis would begin by putting into play some of the lessons learned from the Del Rey University intercultural project. As I will explain below, this can include a learned capacity to link one's own personal growth to the act of helping others also to grow. A learned "micro" pattern of helping others grow as a part of one's own personal growth (that is, complementarity) can also constitute a key building block for larger change in creating a diverse and more participatory U.S. democracy. In place of posing the learner as a person in binary opposition to a dominant discourse, or privileged by it, an intercultural society would teach each individual to acquire agency by linking her or his own development to the growth and well-being of others in that society. With new norms supporting mutually beneficial interaction, a reconstituted U.S. would not only position its diverse citizens to participate in their own domestic self-governance, it would acquire the skills and perspectives to interact "in complementarity with" other nations in a diverse global society.

In relation to *"macro"* systemic change, it is clear that problems with the structure of the current U.S. representative democracy are mounting, and this leads many to wish for a democracy that better accommodates diversity and re-engages the average citizen (Association of American Colleges & Universities,

2002). A rare opportunity thus presents itself to locate future diversity strategies within a larger project to transform the U.S. democracy. It should go without saying that this project must also meet the needs of dominant group members who are finding their interests ignored by the current democracy. In other words, the process of making a new democracy must itself be intercultural.

Subjectivity and Place

Foucault (1971: 23) was one of the first to crystallize the notion that an individual person, or "subject," moving through social space is unavoidably dissolved into a "unity of discourse" (Jackson, 1998: 5; Deleuze, 1986). Under the abstract forces of discourse, meanings are assigned for individuals who in that process become "objectified" and are governed by the surveillance of state mechanisms (Foucault, 1975: 200, 220; M. Davis, 1990: 243–244; Bratich, Packer & McCarthy, 2003). For over a decade, Foucault (1972, 1976, 1984) expanded on his groundbreaking idea that knowledge and power are interconnected through discourse-based processes that make the individual small.

Here I want to draw attention to one of Foucault's last writings because it creates an opening through which to investigate the theoretical implications of an intercultural campus. In an afterward to a book by Dreyfus and Rabinow (1983), Foucault indicates a possible shift in his view of the individual as a "subject." Having spent a lifetime foregrounding how discourse-based systems of power operate to objectivize and make small the individual as a subject, Foucault goes on to say rather curiously, "Thus it is not power, but the subject, which is the general theme of my research" (id at 208). While Foucault passed on before he could explain this in detail, he does leave with us with a fresh thought. If you follow his words "not power, but the subject," he seems to want the emphasis in his prior work to be flipped, this time with the individual subject being the point of departure instead of abstract notions of power, resistance, or discourse that presume a subjugated individual.

In abstract terms, the complex, multisubjective context of a transnational campus like Del Rey University (where multivocality undermines the dominant discourses of Eurocentrism, Catholicism, heterosexism, and maleness) forces a recontextualization of Foucault's original notion of the dissolved subject and a reconceptualization of the individual student as agent. In an intersubjective, multiethnic storytelling space, where every teller acquires the status of a "subject/author" and no one is made into an object of another person's story, the binary relation of subject-and-object is superceded by a "subject-to-subject" exchange of story. At an intercultural campus, the individual subject (the student, the staff person, the academic vice president, the untenured faculty member) is not dissolved but "remade" in ways that do not turn others into objects of her/his storytelling (Tanaka, 2002a, 2002b). With individual agency created outside the operation of a subject/object split, subjectivity and place intersect in ways that aren't possible through structural *or* poststructural analytics—through story.

In *The Use of Pleasure,* Foucault (1984) extends his end-of-career shift by suggesting that individuals who possess sexual desires "can seek to transform themselves, to change themselves" (id at 10). From the self-directed nature of sexuality, Foucault reasoned a degree of personal agency can inhere that will "enable individuals to question their own conduct, to watch over and give shape to it, and to shape themselves *as ethical subjects*" (id at 13, emphasis added). While Foucault's passing prevented him from explaining how individual agency (an ethical self) might change the operation of discourse, knowledge, power, and surveillance, the intercultural storytelling at Del Rey University arguably created spaces where exactly this might occur—where individuals question and give shape to their own conduct outside the press of a dominant Catholic, male, Eurocentric, heterosexual, upper middle class discourse. Relocating Foucault's thinking to an intercultural campus, the logical extension of ethical conduct would be for educators to help each student become a "subject" and agent who *in an ethical act* helps others also to become subjects and agents.

It is no surprise that in recent years there has been an upsurge in scholarly interest in subjectivity, and this is a strand worth following. Davis (J. E. 2002: 29) joins others in noting the growing problems in essentialized treatments of identity and urges renewed emphasis on the individual as a subject (see also de Certeau, 1986; Kondo, 1990b: 26; Roth, 1992: 694; Butler, 1993: 15; Ortner, 1996: 294; Arextega, 1997; Paulin, 1997: 166; Popkewitz, 1997: 22; Tanaka & Cruz, 1998: 151; Mendoza-Denton, 1999: 287; Capps, 1999: 102; Coates, 1999: 123; Nozaki, 2000: 374–375; Sandoval, 2000; Talburt, 2000; Said, 2000; Chun,

2000: 572; Howe, 2001: 41; Rabinow, 2002: 135; Tanaka, 2002a: 283; Gutierrez, 2002: 1079; Demerath, 2003: 137; King, 2003). It was de Certeau (1986: 217) who noted the direct relationship between essentializing practices and objectification and reasoned that in a better world, we would all pass "from the subject-object relationship...to a plurality of authors...(where) hierarchy of knowledge is replaced by a mutual differentiation of subjects."

In a context of heightened interest in subjectivity, the storytelling at Del Rey University takes on added significance as a tool that *builds subjectivity* in a diverse world. Where patterns of subject-to-object education would only reproduce, by virtue of a dichotomous ethics, a prescribed binary relation of objectification and internalized victim status, intersubjective storytelling is by its very nature directed to nurturing multiple individuals, as multiple subjects.

Complementarity

One development from establishing an intercultural campus is that it therefore appears to alter the nature of "the self." Instead of posing the individual as a person moving through space under the directives of a dominant discourse (e.g., Eurocentrism) or of having groups advance their silenced histories at a risk of alienating others (early multiculturalism), the learner in an intercultural space acquires a meaning of the self that is developmentally deeper than an interdependence with others. In an intercultural storytelling, the very act of "being in the world"—of finding connection to past, place, and others—is defined by the act of helping others do the same. In an intercultural storytelling, each storyteller needs others present to be good listeners, to be supportive, and ultimately to help that individual complete her/his story. In other words, the coming to be of an intercultural storyteller places each person "in complementarity with" others who are also coming to be. In place of a person whose identity system tends to exclude others or turn them into objects, this definition of the self is indeed subject-to-subject, as it requires others also to become subjects. In a transition to complementarity, the operating palimpsest becomes, *"I am me, through you."*

With a subject-to-subject storytelling, a different relational status is thus established in which each storyteller's individual agency becomes dependent upon helping others *also* to acquire agency. In other words, the more particularized, non-binary mode of an intercultural storytelling can make possible for educators a different kind of assessment based not just in individual growth but in each individual's capacity to achieve personhood because others also are acquiring a sense of self. It is this emphasis on the individual as a "storytelling subject," who achieves both agency *and* complementarity, that can form a new foundation for teaching and learning diversity. Equally important, this larger focus on subjectivity could well be what progressives need to finally let go of structuralist tools that have become too rigid, dichotomous, and category-based to assess growth in a shifting, complex transnational setting. It is perhaps in this light that Sean Hand (1988: xliv) stated in such clear terms:

> This liberation of pure difference leads to the abandonment of dialectics and a move to an affirmative thought of disjunction and multiplicity...the abandonment of categories and the move to an acategorical thought.

Restated for the transnational educational context, Kondo's original definition of culture as a "meaningful way of being in the world inseparable from the deepest aspects of one's self" might now be amended to encompass a way of being in the world no longer confined to a particular category of the self but instead linked to helping others also to find a positive way of being in the world.

Located in an intercultural context, diversity thus becomes more than just an occasion to reevaluate regimes of knowledge, culture, and power (and it is certainly this); it forms a basis for fundamentally altering the nature of the self for a diverse world. And in this new personal growth process may lie an irrepressible form of power. For example, in the current global atmosphere of escalating racial conflict, the onset of complementarity may prove to be the most significant outcome of an intercultural approach to education because it suggests that before the U.S. can move away from a posture of global conflict and competition with others, its future leaders will need to learn how to be in mutually beneficial one-on-one relations with others in their daily lives.

In this regard, the words of Lizabeth Cohen (2003: B9) published for diverse U.S. college and university settings would be equally instructive in the context of future U.S. participation in a diverse world society:

> Deliberating for the general good means not denying inevitable difference but rather assuming collective responsibility for the well-being of each other... it is more important than ever that social groups not become competing, self-interested segments, or self-contained, oblivious islands.

Put differently, with complementarity, the notion of individual subjectivity is transformed and recast in a redintegrative frame. In small groups, classes, and social experiences in their college years, future leaders will learn how to be *in complementarity with* others who are different from them.

In contrast, it is possible to look at human development from the opposite perspective of the individual who never learns how to achieve complementarity in a diverse social space. At Del Rey University, it was the white student who did not participate in the Certificate Program who missed the chance to tell others about her or his own family history, and as a result, lost the opportunity to learn how to navigate a multiethnic social space. Of no small import in the U.S. context of 9/11, this inability to know connection to past and place could lead U.S. citizens to be fearful of other nations and cultures. It might even be inferred that when a nation of people loses connection to past and place, that nation can become an easy target of fear campaigns that drive wedges between racial or ethnic groups; if left unresolved for too long, this could even lead to a collapse of the social order. Under this analysis, the inability of many U.S. citizens to know their family histories could bear a connection with the last two decades of global capitalism, 9/11 terror, and related wars. In an era of rising global violence, this is an issue that clearly demands formal study.

After Resistance

With Foucault's earlier work on the "dissolved" subject having formed a basis for much progressive thinking, I argue that education and diversity efforts have been unable to address the "loss of meaning" facing dominant group members *because* they have too often been in a binary mode of "resistance." In other words, a progressive love affair with the notion "Where there is power, there is resistance" (Foucault, 1976: 95) has limited the reach of its own work.

Under resistance theory as applied, it has been argued that those who suffer from oppressive regimes are led to resist that oppression as an initial step toward attaining liberation (see e.g., Martin, 1987; Scott, 1990). The intercultural storytelling sessions at Del Rey University, however, revealed a different, non-resistance-based, non-binary pattern that can't be stressed enough. Whenever intercultural learning environments were established, participants demonstrated over and over again that they held within them a deep, unmet need to visit, rediscover, and validate their original sources of meaning and personal worth—and use their storytelling across difference as a means to do that. This was insistent. It was *sui generis*. It was as if an entire lifetime in the U.S. had not allowed these individuals sufficient opportunity to celebrate family history, to be rooted in time and place, or be at peace with their own personal path in life. These benefits of storytelling appeared for all students and all staff members who participated, no matter their social identifiers or status within the university.

This power of story was an unexpected development and perhaps a call to re-examine how "resistance theory" had come to rationalize ethnic minority and other diversity programs. The power of story led me to ask, "Could it be that all this time, the use of 'resistance' as a basis for social change has overlooked one of the most powerful forces available—the need for each individual human being to feel validated, find connection to past and place, be whole, and link that self-growth process to the project of redefining community?" Worse, "Could the strategic posture of resistance have been self-limiting for progressives in that it restricted their own behavior to responses to oppression?" If answers to these questions prove to be yes, then intercultural storytelling may well be a core component of a new strategy for diversity and social change, *after* resistance.

For example, we know from the Del Rey project that the particularity deriving from multiple, personal accounts in an intercultural storytelling can decenter the tendency toward dichotomy and essentialism. This is a step in a positive direction. But a storytelling's capacity to insert individual story into a learning environment also hints at a larger opening. Where binary constructions had been demeaning, destructive, even soul depriving for members of "oppressed" and "privileged" groups alike (e.g., Hemmings, 2000: 170), a non-binary approach makes possible new connections to past and place and, with this, the ability to connect with others. In a subject-to-subject way of knowing, the learning act does not position individuals in binary opposition to each other.

Once a resistance-based model for diversity is questioned, fresh thinking also becomes possible with respect to whiteness. The reader will recall the difficulty encountered with whiteness in chapter 3. Data from the nationwide survey showed many benefits from diversity in the eyes of white students but a conflicting discovery that their sense of community would decline significantly with increases in student and faculty diversity. In a "post-resistance," non-oppositional frame, however, new possibilities appear. As will be discussed further below, the non-binary social interaction contained within intersubjective approaches breaks the pattern of resistance and resistance back. It moves storytellers to a collaborative mode where members of oppressed and privileged groups can work together to identify new sources of meaning. A post-resistance model also releases the oppressed person from having to "celebrate being a victim." Stated differently, a non-oppositional approach to social interaction sustains storytelling spaces that exist *outside* the operation of the hierarchies of a campus. In this way, a "post-resistance" approach of storytelling makes possible a subtle but powerful shift to a more positive view of life.

In other words, the Del Rey University intercultural project may have surfaced a defining characteristic for an "ideally diverse campus" in the twenty-first century (Clayton-Pedersen, 2001): a feeling of "complementarity" that comes from relying on others for a rich, safe learning experience across difference. In contrast to the earlier tendency of students to stay in ethnic enclaves based on ethnic or racialized identities that compete with each other, students who participate in non-binary intercultural retreats and class discussions enjoy a sense of reliance on each other because they are telling their stories to willing ears—and listening to the stories of others. In the mutuality inscribed by a storytelling across difference, one encounters an alternative to resistance. What I will do next is deconstruct the way in which story operated and suggest there were at least two storytellings in every successful intercultural workshop or class.

The Importance of "Alternative Stories"

While not known to planners at the beginning of the project, it quickly became clear that each successful intercultural storytelling at Del Rey University entailed moving students or staff through at least two stages. In dealing with the wide array of diversity issues, it was important to begin with students' and staff members' stories of pain and privilege, as this enabled them to become personally vested in the cross-cultural learning process. At the same time, a transition to complementarity between participants seemed to occur only when they shifted to a second set of stories that were positive and forward looking. This second stage of storytelling occurred when facilitators asked participants to picture in their minds ("dream of") a better place in which the factors that had caused the pain, oppression, fear, or uncertainty are already eliminated.

In moving from stories of pain to dreams of a better place, this dual quality of intercultural storytelling parallels in compelling ways the two-staged process of healing that proponents of "narrative therapy" report in New Zealand and Australia, and it would be interesting to explore this similarity here. Narrative therapists hypothesize that in a counseling context, guiding a patient from stories of pain that reveal how power operates to "the generation of alternative stories that incorporate vital and previously neglected aspects of lived experience" will enable the patient to heal her or himself. With a dual storytelling, they reason, the client automatically begins a "performance of these counter knowledges" (White & Epston, 1990: 31; see also Land, 2003; Costantino & Greene, 2003: 44). Citing Foucault's belief that a dominant discourse will eradicate the histories of a disempowered people, narrative therapists conclude a second, alternative storytelling can lead storytellers to "refuse the objectification or 'thingification' of themselves and their bodies through knowledge" (White & Epston, 1990: 30).

Importantly, narrative therapists also link their work to Bruner (1986), who found earlier that people's own interpretation of their life circumstances would shift radically with the generation of new stories that present an alternative rendering of their histories (cited with approval, White & Epston, 1990: 10). Thus, while an initial storytelling might reveal the operation of a dominant discourse that oppresses individuals (like the initial impact of race-, gender- or sexuality-based discrimination at Del Rey University), this pattern is reversed through a second storytelling by these individuals that enables them to "perform new meanings, bringing them to desired possibilities, new meanings that persons will experience as more helpful, satisfying and open-ended" (id at 15).

It should be emphasized here that alternative storytelling also closely mirrors some of the most successful field-based work of feminist theorists (e.g., Noddings, 1984; Foster, 1990; Anzaldua, 1987; Kondo, 1990a; Trinh, 1991; Witherell & Noddings, 1991; hooks & West, 1991; Behar & Gordon, 1995; Bucholtz, Liang & Sutton, 1999; Wood, 2000; Cruz & McLaren, 2003) and critical race theorists (e.g., Williams, 1991; Bell, 1992; Delgado, 1995) who have often used storytelling to envision liberated, even fictive, settings where the individual escapes an oppressed state.

The notion of alternative storytelling about a future place employed by narrative therapists, feminist theorists, and critical race theorists thus offers an explanation for the epiphany experienced by staff at Del Rey University when they dreamed in groups of how to create new kinds of work spaces where the oppressions that plague them are removed. Arguably, this is what also occurred when groups of students participated in story-based learning at intercultural retreats and established safe places for dialogue across difference at a summit for high school students they planned and facilitated. While these moments of epiphany and deliverance from painful, repressed histories were often short-lived—with staff and students returning the next day to hierarchical work and school settings—it is also the case that these participants had tasted of this experience once in their lives. They had, collectively, been removed from a place of angst, blame, fear, or victim status to a more positive place.

With the unexpected success of intercultural storytelling, a number of other exciting developments becomes possible for educators who work in diversity, and I will explore some of these below.

Reversing the Effects of Objectification and Soul Loss

With the importance of dual storytelling, it becomes highly useful to examine the relationship between "objectification" and "soul loss," a connection that brings further clarity to the findings in this book relating to a subject/object split. What I will argue below is that the practice of objectification can lead to soul loss for all involved. To do this, I will first revisit recent interpretations of soul loss and soul recreation conducted in sociocultural anthropology.

In a comparative review of ethnographies on possession and trance healing, Andrew Strathern (1996: 129) states that every sickness results in a quantum loss of soul, or life force. In drawing this conclusion, he advances the notion that healers ultimately employ "objectification" as a tool to lead the individual out of sickness and bring soul "back into the body" (id at 128–129). "(T)hrough the mediation of others," Strathern (id at 164, 130) concludes a ritual healing will enhance "the connection between the communities of the dead and the living...as well as between the spirit and the body."

Applying Strathern's analysis to a racially and ethnically diverse college campus, I encountered a similar result but a very different process. While Strathern argued that a healer uses objectification to reconnect a person with her or his soul or past, I found in the transnational context of Del Rey University that the objectification of others was a factor *causing* the soul loss. When African Americans were turned into objects by white fraternity students, where lesbian and gay students were denied permission to establish a gay/lesbian student club, when untenured female faculty members were admonished by senior white male faculty to stay away from race and gender issues, the result was in each case the same—a deep sense of soul loss for all who were being turned into non-persons or essentialized objects, that is, all who were "objectified."

In addition, the onset of the intercultural campus revealed a second type of soul loss. This was soul loss for the dominant group member. The sheer critical mass of diversity on this campus revealed that the white person, the heterosexual, the senior male faculty member who insists on treating others as objects had also been laboring under a sense of self that was essentialized in relation to a presumed lesser person. Depriving himself of particularity, the so-called "dominant" person was substituting for a rich geo-ethnic family history (and the positive spirit deriving from that) a totalizing identity that was generalized, abstract, and without connection to a particular past or place. In fact, *both* the act of the white campus member to treat people different from her or him as lesser "objects" *and* the act of the multiculturalist to categorize all European Americans as dominant and white arguably constituted processes of mutual objectification. Both operated to interrupt in oneself and in the other a specific connection between memory and the body.

There is another important development here. While ascribing to "the other" the status of an "unfulfilled soul," each act of objectification also arguably prevented the speaker herself or himself from moving to a more healthy place of soul creation. Ironically, both oppressor and oppressed seemed linked in a dance of negativity that further distanced both self and other from particularizing family histories. In the words of Strathern, each individual's body became separated from her or his spirit or past community.

When a senior male faculty member told junior female faculty members not to bring up race or gender issues in faculty meetings if they themselves wanted to attain tenure, that senior faculty member was denying himself a sense of soul. When a "disadvantaged" senior Latino faculty member undermined the intercultural contributions of a younger Latino faculty member, he was arguably extending his own soul loss another day, by internalizing the objectification process and casting it upon another minority member. If there is one critical lesson to be learned from the experience of building an intercultural campus, it is that both objectifier and objectified experience soul loss together, producing and reproducing its effects both in her/his own body and the body of the other.

Restated, *it is the "objectification" of others* through both dominant and subordinate discourse that interrupts the connection between memory, ritual, and the body. This may well be the crux of all future work in diversity and social change. With the studies in this book showing that both privileged and oppressed social locations are reproduced by language use patterns that pose "the other" as a member of a homogeneous group inimical to one's own interests, it now seems clear there is heightened value to constructing scholarly research and diversity projects that develop communicative practices that are *not* objectifying.

In the same way, it might be argued, a decision to leave storytellers in a state of heightened awareness of pain from their stories—without steering them into a second, alternative storytelling—would be a disservice to them because it would lock the storytellers in a magnified state of pain without a path out of that condition. They would remain in a state of "soul loss." To escape the objectification trap that paradoxically locks both oppressed and privileged individuals in a common state of soul loss, educators will want to initiate new teaching practices that replace soul loss with soul creation.

What might happen if too many members of a society occupy a state of soul loss—lacking personal connection to past and place and the positive spirit that comes from that? One possibility is that this may give rise to a larger loss of meaning equating to a collapse of the moral order (see e.g., Crapanzano, 2000). At least one researcher has suggested that as more and more young Americans find their souls "administered" in schools by the homogenizing effects of neoliberalism and its free market capitalism (Popkewitz, 1998b: 12, 14), it becomes increasingly necessary to ask, how does one "remake the soul?"

It is in this vein that Strathern (1996: 164) queries, how "can the personality of the spirit be built up?" If the societies he studied employed faith healers and objectifying rituals to cure sickness, how would one cure the problems of social breakdown in transnational U.S. education where the very problem is objectification itself? Here I suggest we need not cast off Strathern's analysis entirely. Just as the faith healer will fill the role of mediator in a ritual healing (Strathern, 1996: 130, 164) and create soul via new connections between memory and body, I argue an intercultural storytelling will yield some of the same positive outcomes, even though arrived at differently.

What I contend is that an intercultural storytelling (engaging geo-ethnic family history, trauma in that history, and then dreams of a better place) operates as a "ritual" that establishes new connections between a storyteller's body and memory. In this ritual, soul creation results from each person's connection to her/his own family history and in a second way, from connecting with others who are listening. While differing from Strathern's analysis, there is something to the idea that a storytelling across difference inserts particularity and rootedness into a transnational fishbowl campus experience that would otherwise leave each member in a state of disorientation from the encroachment of diversity into a Eurocentric curriculum. Unlike in Strathern's analysis, the mediating force on the intercultural campus is not a faith healer but rather the storytelling itself.

Connerton (1989) and Fabian (1983) add further impetus to the claim that there can be a connection between ritual, memory, and the body, and their writing extends the argument that widespread soul loss can lead to a breakdown of a social order. In *How Societies Remember*, Connerton (1989: 3) observes, "It is an implicit rule that participants in any social order must presuppose a shared memory." It is this connection to a common past that serves to "legitimate a present social order." Connerton goes on to argue that in the case of serious injury, there can be a "narrative discontinuity" triggered by the loss of "personal memory," "cognitive memory," or "patterns of behavior" (id at 24, 26).

What I will suggest is that the massive onset of race and ethnic diversity at Del Rey University disturbed the narrative continuity of the Western Eurocentric curriculum and its whiteness-based behavior system; subsequent to this, the onset of intercultural storytelling filled that vacuum with a sharing of *multiple* memories, polyphonically. What was shared in this intercultural space, however, was not one universalizing memory (Eurocentric or Chicano-centric or male based) but the process of telling. In place of soul loss occasioned by the end of Eurocentrism or Catholic-centric or heterosexist discourse, there was the hope that a new social order might just lie around the corner. So while no one history bound this group together, a new space was established where individual soul and community could both be created—by sharing stories.

In *Time and the Other*, Fabian (1983: 30) extends this thinking to the dimension of time. In intersubjectivity, Fabian contends, participants occupy the same moment in time. They are "coeval, i.e. share the same Time." What I will suggest here is that the space of an intercultural storytelling simultaneously allows each storyteller to occupy her or his own place in history (through one's geo-ethnic family history) while also sharing that time with others who are themselves active listeners and storytellers. In other words, an intercultural storytelling enables participants to occupy a common space *and time* even though each story tells of a different distant place and accesses a wholly different family history. This is a critical development for the diverse urban campus as it implies that the breakdown of one universalizing history (a Eurocentric one, for instance) can be addressed in a constructive way by invoking multiple histories that in their telling, offer some chance of achieving harmony across difference. As the U.S. reconsiders the harm caused to the ethnic traditions of a diverse world by the monolithic trajectory of its own capitalist behavior, an intercultural pedagogy may constitute a far more constructive alternative.

"What would happen to the West," Fabian queries (1983: 35), "if its temporal forces were suddenly invaded by the Time of the Other?" Asked twenty years ago, this inquiry takes on added significance as the U.S. enters deep into the global century and comes to understand that the de-particularizing effects of its democracy and capitalism can hardly be expected to stave off future soul loss for its own people. So while the harsh effects of objectification and soul loss might be effectively reversed through intercultural storytelling at a college or university campus, one now has this larger sense that the wider social order administered by the U.S. democracy, capitalism, arts and media must *also* be modified in ways that make soul creation possible.

Another result of the complementarity encountered at Del Rey University is that it is now possible to reach a fresh interpretation of the negative impact of social fraternities and sororities on the outcomes for white students reported in chapter 3. In the face of mounting racial and ethnic diversity on those campuses, a retreat to homogeneous white enclaves while in college arguably left those students in the status of "unfulfilled souls," a social location that later in life could lead to a profound ambiguity and even prefigure the collapse of the social order these individuals would one day govern. Not unlike the superficiality of enhanced feelings of community (and declines in other social measures) found in the regression analyses of responses of Greek college students, some of the leaders of the twenty-first century U.S. indeed seem "drawn together" before the encroaching heterogeneity of a diverse global society.

In contrast to this, the two-part nature of an intercultural storytelling at staff and student intercultural workshops manifests a clear example of what is *not* a flight to safety of one's own group. In moving to alternative stories, intercultural participants set in motion a courageous, shared group approach to human development based in complementarity with formerly "oppressed" and formerly "privileged" members learning together. Storytelling on this campus became the primary mechanism through which race fears were removed and complementarity was achieved. Stated differently, *it was through storytelling that the negative effects of objectification and soul loss were reversed*. In essence, the onset of alternative stories became a counter discourse to the language use pattern of a subject/object split. Here, new "central values" could be explored based in mutuality, interdependence, and soul creation rather than any one universal history to which all must subscribe. "I am me, through you" was indeed the feeling that resulted from a sharing of dreams of new social spaces where oppressions and fears are removed—and dreams by others are heard.

At the same time, it should be emphasized that it did not work for training sessions to leap directly to the second stage and skip over or minimize the significance of stories of pain, fear, or uncertainty. In effect, both forms of storytelling were critical to this process of becoming personally "rooted" to past and place. What I will suggest is that as storytellers completed their journeys through (a) stories of pain and (b) dreams of a new place, they were *"mutually in immanence with"* each other; they were growing together.

Taken together, the two steps of storytelling about past pain and dreaming about a different future thus enacted a kind of interconnectiveness between human beings and a rootedness to past and place not possible from *either* the space of binary oppositionality to power *or* the progressives' attempt to grant "equity and access" to an otherwise hierarchical university structure. In providing a pedagogical alternative to objectification and soul loss, the intercultural project surfaced a third way to conceive of power as neither force applied against others nor resistance to that force, but instead, a form of interconnectiveness through storytelling.

Culture and Power Transcended

At an intercultural campus, "story" and "storytelling" thus supercede culture and power as principal mediums defining positionality. Through story, earlier norms of individualism and competition become less important and storytelling becomes the means by which the sharing power is operationalized. At an intercultural campus, the "power" that occurs is accessed and cultivated by each individual internally but in "mutual immanence with" others who are finding personal power in much the same way. In other words, the onset of complementarity and mutual immanence makes possible a transition away from binary, fixed notions of culture and self formerly produced through unequal power relations (e.g., Ong, 1996) to new uses of culture, power, and subjectification that are not so dichotomous or essentialized (Toyota, 2001; Tanaka, 2002a). Imbricated in a mutual immanence of personalities, the intercultural breaks the pattern of resistance and resistance back. In fact, once non-binary, non-category-based identity constructions are launched, even the pastiche attached to the recent analytics of whiteness begins to lose its luster and relevance.

Applying a sociocultural analysis to Del Rey University, it was the sharing of this journey by formerly dominant and formerly oppressed members that enabled all involved to throw off the practice of "objectifying" the other (as demon, as oppressor, as inferior object) and move to a place that offers new connections between memory, ritual, and the body—for each individual. The important event here was that dominant and oppressed members began this journey of soul creation together. In this way, complementarity and mutual immanence represent inviting alternatives to the self-perpetuating violence of binary oppositionalities, impermeable enclaves and resistance. Stated differently, *it is when a college admits a diverse class—and offers intercultural experiences that elide objectification and binary language use patterns—that the limits of culture and power are transcended.*

From the above, I will develop a further hunch that when an individual grows in mutual immanence with others, it not only changes how we teach diversity, it makes possible an even larger shift at the "macro" level of the wider society. I will argue below that the trajectory of progressive work is fundamentally altered when the intercultural interactions of students at a U.S. college or university prefigure the transformation of a society.

Macro Social Change

While not anticipated, the non-binary and non-oppositional qualities of an intercultural pedagogy at Del Rey University surfaced yet another useful tool for those who work in the rich fields of social change. This was the notion that a "parallel system" can exist within a larger hierarchical campus environment that otherwise remains male, Catholic, white, heterosexual, and upper- and upper-middle-class. In the smaller spaces of intercultural workshops within the larger Del Rey campus hierarchy, there was no need for oppressed parties to waste energy pointing fingers at dominant groups or protesting against the administration. In safe spaces for dialogue and storytelling, individuals were free to dream of actually changed classrooms or offices or academic departments and link their own personal growth to that process. With the intercultural nature of these spaces, individuals possessing different identities and shifting subjectivities worked together to nurture their interdependence, complementarity and interconnectiveness, *because of* their difference.

The Concept of "Parallel Systems"

In other words, it was the onset of parallel, intercultural spaces that made release from soul loss—and arrival at complementarity—possible for members of both formerly dominant *and* formerly oppressed groups. In fact, this co-immanence of former oppressor and formerly oppressed may well adumbrate an advanced stage of human development for transnational social spaces not possible under dichotomous, resistance-based strategies for social justice. For future projects to benefit from the lessons of an intercultural campus, planners may want to consider creating spaces within a larger system where energy is not wasted attempting to correct or push back the larger violence of an entrenched hierarchy but positive change is nonetheless pursued.

There are antecedents for parallel systems. In *Los hombres verdaderos*, Carlos Lenkersdorf (1996) writes a sociolinguistic ethnography of the Maya-Tojolabal of Chiapas, Mexico, a people who in his estimation are beyond the need for resistance. Representing thirty years of research, Lenkersdorf's study reveals a close connection between the subject-to-subject language use patterns of the Tojolabal and their self-governing communities that exist in parallel with a national Mexican government that carries out the very U.S. free market policies they oppose. In this case, local communities in over 1,000 villages and small cities have created and collaboratively manage their own schools, women's rights programs, job training, health centers, and local civic governance (see also Flores, Tanaka & McLaren, 2001). Founded on the daily practices of intersubjectivity, these "autonomous communities" may reasonably be seen to foreshadow the intercultural project at Del Rey University.

Arriving at a similar conclusion, Michel de Certeau (1986) employed mythology, travelogue, and odyssey in his own study of Central American Indians and traced how the cultural specificity of these local populations *destabilized* the Western writer's treatment of them as an "object" (id. at 228). "(R)ather than conforming to our model in self-defense against it" (id. at 230), de Certeau adds, the Indians created their own schools, their own governance system, their own reconnection to earth that ultimately sustained a self-managed democracy. In other words, both de Certeau and Lenkersdorf underscore the notion that there can be a close link between intersubjectivity and the tangible steps a people will take to create and sustain their own self-governed civil society—where a whole society can exist outside the operation of objectification. In an even more astonishing conclusion, it was the success of this alternative to the U.S. representative democracy that led de Certeau (id. at 231) to conclude that in the participatory democracy of Central America, "the idea and effectiveness of Western democracy are everywhere undermined."

What is exceedingly interesting is that this movement to create autonomous communities has now reached the United States and in a formal sense. In a Mexican-American subcommunity in San Bernadino, California, residents have initiated the "Calpulli Project," replicating in novel ways the participatory democracy movement of southern Mexico. Reviewed ethnographically by Mariangela Rodriguez (1998), the Calpulli Project is conceivably the first attempt to create a newly "autonomous community" in the United States. In *Mito, identidad y rito: mexicanos y chicanos en california*, Rodriguez describes this local Latino community's decision to cast off impoverished local conditions that were perpetually left unaddressed by the world Catholic Church and build their own parish community. Tracking the Chiapas experience, this parish community—featuring its own economy, governance, social welfare system, schooling, job training, and catechism—operates "in parallel with" the global Catholic Church. Like the autonomous communities in Chiapas, the Calpulli Project in California is self-reliant and does not deplete its energy "protesting" against hierarchy or demanding outside aid. The next challenge would be to apply the Chiapas and Calpulli models to more heterogeneous communities in the U.S., a task that would seem to require having intercultural skills.

Not far from San Bernadino, another autonomous community is emerging in East Los Angeles through the work of a group of young Latino artists and musicians. Called "the Eastside Café," this autonomous community is not so much a physical place or government agency as "a state of mind" that moves from one locale to another addressing the needs that the local city government and businesses are failing to acknowledge (Eastside Café, 2002; Flores, 2003).

Still under development, this "youth led social change project" (Cruz, 2003) may one day turn into a self-governance system for a major sub-community of Los Angeles, modeled after the autonomous communities of Chiapas.

Not unlike the nascent Eastside Café, researchers in New York report that Vietnamese-American students have established their own separate spaces at a high school in Buffalo, where they can explore "contradictory impulses" (Weis & Centrie, 2002). With more "free spaces" observed at venues like the MollyOlga project in New York (Fine, Weis, Centrie & Roberts, 2000), the rise of parallel systems across the United States signals a growing public interest in autonomous communities and suggests the need for deeper study of the phenomenon. At the MollyOlga community arts project, for instance, the self-governance process is already being conducted in racially mixed groups—a development that has large implications for a diverse society seeking to find new ways to self-govern interculturally. It is interesting that the practices of all these communities recapitulate the characteristics of participation-based Native American democracies not only in Chiapas, Mexico, but New England, where the Iroquois have practiced participatory democracy for centuries through the longhouse (see e.g., Grinde & Johansen, 1991). What this suggests is that the U.S. has in some ways come "full circle" in acknowledging that in some communities, the best features of its own democracy are indigenous-based.

A collective reading of Lenkersdorf, de Certeau, Rodriguez, Flores, Weis, and Centrie, Fine et. al., and Grinde and Johansen will suggest that while "resistance" may initially be necessary to push back the harsh effects of an oppressive regime, the onset of "parallel systems" that operate in audacious independence of that regime may constitute a more viable long-term alternative to strategies based in binary oppositionality. Indeed, a larger shift in progressive U.S. scholarship may already be taking place toward construction of parallel, self-governing demo-cratic communities that do not waste resources fighting against the interests of Eurocentrists, heterosexists, wealthy capitalists, or male-dominant viewpoints. If so, it would be interesting to pose this process itself as a larger form of "alternative storytelling" after the fashion of narrative therapists, feminist theorists, and critical race theorists—but this time performed in an ongoing way *by a whole community*. With individuals no longer having to spend time in resistance to oppression, citizens can also make their community building and dreaming part of a personal process of becoming "citizen subjects" (e.g., Sandoval, 2000: 183) who have voice and participate with others who are also becoming subjects. In this way, the "micro" practices of complementarity and "macro" practice of parallel systems appear to go hand-in-hand.

Simply put, the onset of intercultural learning enables individuals to extend their dual stories of pain and dreaming by adding the next step of constructing actual, parallel spaces where they can safely experiment with some of those hopes and dreams. In a highly practical way, then, the idea of creating a parallel system—in concert with intercultural storytelling—might one day help a diverse population move beyond the limits of culture and power and make possible a new society sustained by binding and reunifying social institutions.

In a larger sense, the successful testing of each new parallel system that invites direct participation by diverse members of an intercultural campus may mark a critical turning point in social change work in the twenty-first century—by providing a model in the form of one organizational change that can be replicated in a larger effort to create a more "participatory" alternative to the U.S. "representative" democracy. In other words, a parallel system-based strategy for diversity in the twenty-first century could well turn diversity work into part of a larger project to change the democracy.

The Intercultural as Precursor to a New Democracy

If racial fragmentation on college campuses reflects in any way the racial tensions within diverse U.S. and global societies—and it appears it does—it stands to reason that new models tested on college and university campuses might one day be templates for positive change in the wider society. While still evolving, the experiment to create intercultural, non-binary spaces at Del Rey University brings fresh hope for a new democracy defined by something *other than* homeland insecurity or notions of "a declining West."

Here I want to pause and draw attention to some of the macro economic forces that are gaining significance in American daily life. While conservative think tanks have arguably capitalized on the fear and uncertainty that some white Americans have experienced in the face of rising U.S. diversity (see e.g.,

Cokorinos, 2003), the same think tanks have also been vehicles for a larger social thrust of "free market capitalism" (see e.g., Cockburn, et. al., 2001; *Monthly Review,* 2002) driving a neoliberal strategy of global economic domination. Indeed, it would be timely to formally study the connection between race fear (at home and directed at Afghans, Iraqis, Iranians, Koreans, Columbians, Chinese, and others) and a Neoliberal Project that is removed from public debate.

In other words, at a time when some U.S. diversity practices were unintentionally "blaming the white person," the neoliberal think tanks were finding it that much easier to pander to the race fears of white Americans as a smokescreen while diverting the machinery of U.S. civil society (its media, it public education, its representative democracy) to war applications that had the purpose of advancing their own economic interests. In a nation still looking for positive interpretations of diversity, U.S. progressives may well have been trumped; the question now is whether it is too late to take up in a formal sense the onset of this neoliberal democracy (e.g., Klees, 1999) and actively explore and test "alternative democracies" that engage all members of a society collaboratively rather than out of dichotomous dialectics and tired race divisions.

While not possible to address fully here, it should be emphasized that a neoliberal, free market ideology is, at its heart, antithetical to the notion of complementarity among world nations. The "us-against-them" mentality intrinsic to a free market model of deregulation and competition is diametrically opposed to a model of collaboration and interdependence. Yet each time U.S. oil policies and free market tactics trigger resentment and violence back on to the U.S., it should be increasingly clear that the security of the U.S. might be better served by a wholly different global personality based in interdependence across national and ethnic difference instead of a predatory vision of taking.

What does this suggest for future research? I argue education must not only be viewed in relation to economic and political institutions, it must become a prime contributor to a movement to remake the economy and democracy. It would do no good to address diversity needs like affirmative action and neglect to respond to the larger economic forces that hem those interests in. To extend this out, the most encouraging conclusion from these eight years of research is that subjectivity, intersubjectivity, and parallel systems collectively constitute a powerful and proactive alternative to the binary, predatory, and homogenizing practices of free market capitalism and its globalization. At Del Rey University, these characteristics sustained local notions of *autonomy* and collective *sense of belonging* that seem wholly lacking under a neoliberal model of fungibility, individual competition, and erasure of local culture (e.g., Guano, 2001).

Overlooked in the press of these macro developments and cultivated race fears is the shocking outcome that the U.S. public is becoming increasingly disengaged from its own democracy. While investigations into the disenfranchising of the U.S. public linked to free market capitalism and race pandering will need to be conducted elsewhere (e.g., Klein, 2001, 2003; Tanaka, 2002c; Atwood, 2003; Vidal, 2003), I will argue in the interest of inviting new model building that the elements of a better, more cohesive, and diverse democracy might one day be constructed by testing some of the characteristics of autonomy and participation employed with great success in Chiapas, at MollyOlga, and in the Del Rey intercultural project.

Specifically, a more *participatory democracy* would appear to have several emergent traits worth considering as an increasingly diverse U.S. seeks to bind itself together: re-engagement of the individual with civic life, learned interdependence with others, and a linking of one's own life trajectory to citizenship and positive social change (see also, Fine et. al., 2000; Flores, Tanaka & McLaren, 2001; Guinier & Torres, 2002: 297–299; Polletta, 2002; Kelly, 2003: 127; Markowitz, Helman & Shir-Vertesh, 2003: 308–309; Tanaka & Flores, in press). In this regard, it is worth noting that just as the daily communicative practices of intersubjectivity, interdependence, and complementarity proved so critical to the Del Rey University experiment, the autonomous and participatory communities of southern Mexico have long featured a sociolinguistic pattern in which each person's public voice is dependent upon helping others to have voice and agency (see also Evans & Boyte, 1986: 16).

In a more participatory democracy, Sirianni and Friedland (2001) conclude:

(C)itizens become more knowledgeable about the political system, develop a greater sense of their own efficacy, and widen their horizons beyond their own narrow self-interest to consider a broader public good...Participation engenders a sense of ownership and responsibility for improving local conditions.

Stated in a different way, reconstructing education for a diverse U.S. democracy will likely mean producing graduates "who are more informed, engaged, and socially responsible citizens in our interdependent but still unequal democracy" (Musil & Wathington, 2002). In other words, the pull to interdependence between individuals will likely grow even stronger in the years to come.

In light of the above, it is encouraging to see the recent surge of interest in local community building that envisions the United States as a more participatory civil society (e.g., Boyte & Kari, 1996; Barber, 1998; Anderson, 1998: 586; Sandoval, 2000; Sirianni & Friedland, 2001; Klein, 2001: 89; Warren, 2001; Alperovitz, Imbroscio & Williamson, 2002; Anzaldua & Keating, 2002; Gong, 2003; Isaac, 2003). While these approaches could well serve as local models for larger structural change in the democracy, the next challenge will be for other researchers to test these models in highly diverse, non-binary contexts.

In a diverse society, it now seems obvious Americans will want to possess intercultural skills if they are to engage each other in meaningful dialogues to improve their local communities. Subjectivity, complementarity, interdependence, storytelling, and parallel system building are all practices that would aid in creating local precursors for a more "participatory" democracy in the United States. Given the diverse nature of the American public, any new democracy grounded in direct participation will need to be, by definition, intercultural.

In summary, while limitations in binary thinking about diversity have been reported in recent years (e.g., Powell, 1999: 3; Tharp, Estrada, Dalton & Yamauchi, 2000: 58; Nozaki, 2000: 375; J. E. Davis, 2002), it is hoped this book will convince readers it is now possible to do something about this—by dreaming of and building parallel systems that engage all members of a diverse community in a shared, non-binary human experience where all citizens are "subjects." One further possibility is that the transition to a greater sense of interconnectiveness on college and university campuses will lead future U.S. leaders to be more compassionate and strategic by placing America in a position of interdependence and harmony with other nations in a diverse global society.

CONCLUSION

We have come a long way from the three misconceptions raised at the beginning of this book: (1) that white Americans do not want to learn about diversity, (2) that there are no alternatives to Western Eurocentrism and multiculturalism, and (3) that it is not possible to build community out of a diverse group of people. We now know that Americans do not have to choose from a limited menu of Eurocentrism or ethnic separatism and can instead envision a third place where members of a diverse society will learn and share across difference and no culture dominates. What I have learned from these studies is that it is also possible to look into the source of a particular social fragmentation and address it through storytelling and model building in anticipation of a better human society.

What I will reiterate with a degree of urgency is that the intercultural model occasioned by racial fragmentation at one U.S. university can be a template for social change on a broader scale that addresses the growing racial fissures in U.S. and world political and economic systems. Extending far beyond multiculturalism, the *non*-dichotomous nature of "the intercultural"—locating each individual in a meaningful place and time—constitutes a radical departure from formulations in education that direct themselves to categories of difference or that place oppressed groups "in binary opposition to" dominant white, male, heterosexual, or capitalist discourses.

Though important to the early success of diversity programs, both category-based and resistance-based approaches have now arguably been appropriated in ways that make impossible the original aims. Indeed, the shrinking nature of the world evidenced in the current U.S. racial demographic shift argues in favor of a national diversity strategy that departs from fixed categories—essentialized through binary notions of culture and power—and investigates instead the relational nature of each individual's association with others as "subjects." Stated differently, researchers will need to ask in future projects, *what will be the nature of the self in a diverse world society and how will we teach this individual more effective "transnational" norms and duties?*

Human Development and Social Change

The eight years of research presented here suggest that during times of systemic social stress like the demographic shift impacting Del Rey University, there is a heightened connection between individual human development and social change. Put in different terms, the breakdown of mediating systems creates an opportunity for *individuals* to remake their own environments in ways that turn the negative effects of *macro* forces into positive social outcomes while advancing their own personal growth.

Human Development and Social Change Interconnected

As the United States enters an era where the average citizen can no longer afford to ignore such "macro" developments as transcontinental demographic shifts, global capitalism, and an increasingly apparent U.S. penchant for war, educators will want to know how to account for this in their daily work. Simply put, these macro social forces directly impact U.S. children and their families. Absent any action to improve the larger social context within which one's own children and family exist, the result would be to continue to be pounded by such forces—that is, to be an "object" of such forces.

What this means is that more research is needed to explore how to incorporate into educational practices the growing connection, during a systemic collapse, between individual human development and the actions an individual takes to evoke positive change in larger U.S. social systems like the democracy, the economy, the arts, education, and the media. This line of thinking holds that in a transnational urban space, each individual will enhance her/his own personal growth by actively engaging in projects that make social relations in an organization egalitarian, participatory, and anticipatory of larger change in society. By the same token, this individual might not be so successful at evoking actual social change until s/he also comes to better know her or himself.

While clearly a notion that demands more field based testing, this connection is not without support among sociocultural and education theorists. In a pivotal piece examining the possibilities for progressive work beyond resistance, Sherry B. Ortner (1996: 296) states:

> *The importance of subjects (whether individual actors or social entities) lies not so much in who they are and how they are put together as in the projects that they construct and enact.* For it is in the formulation and enactment of those projects that they both become and transform who they are, and sustain or transform their social and cultural universe. (Emphasis added.)

In the same vein, Demerath (2003: 137) reports how the Manus in Papua New Guinea engage simultaneously in social change and personal growth via an "emerging personal subjectivity that privileges direct experience and perception as well as freely entered social relationships." Echoing the earlier conclusions of Barbara Christian and Edward Said, Demerath (id at 144) encounters a clear "epistemological shift away from inherited or collective knowledge and toward knowledge generated by direct experiences or firsthand observation."

Popkewitz (1998b: 12, 14) lends further weight to the claim that individual human development and social change are interconnected when he hypothesizes that action research methods can be vehicles that engage students and teachers in participatory methods that remake the soul. What I argue is that the creation of an intercultural campus—particularly where initiated through intercultural storytelling—puts into play the kind of social change conceptualized by Ortner, Demerath, and Popkewitz, where work to make a new community bears a direct relationship to one's own personal growth. In the parallel spaces of intercultural workshops and classrooms, individuals act out the importance of personal experience and story—and begin to fashion new central values through practices of complementarity and interdependence.

Indeed, once a 1990s over-reliance on "mid-range" analysis of mediating systems of culture and power is set aside, a closer examination can be launched into storytelling as a point of intersection between individual agency and the macro social forces that impact the individual. Restated for the transnational educator, *storytelling constitutes a site where individual human development and macro social change intersect.* At the same time, the Del Rey project demonstrates that storytelling alone is not enough. In impacted transnational social spaces, it is exceedingly important for participants to extend the benefits of their dual storytelling (after the fashion of narrative therapy) by adding an action component where the storytelling sets in motion specific change in an organization that "models" future change in the wider society.

In other words, a "narrative therapy" inspired approach to human development in transnational spaces can be amended to have an action component that reflects actual movement toward social change. This approach can encompass: (1) stories of pain, fear, or oppression, (2) analysis of current or historical asymmetry, (3) alternative stories or dreams of actually changed social spaces, *and now* (4) steps taken by the individual to create parallel systems or spaces where those dreams can be carried out. In education contexts, a fifth step might also be added: (5) self-assessments performed by teachers tracking their own personal growth from teaching others how to do this. With further testing, these five steps could outline a "social change pedagogy" where teachers and researchers evaluate in more formal terms the relationship between individual human development and the steps a person takes to make a society better.

As more and more U.S. colleges and universities translate the dual importance of human development and social change into student programming, courses, and scholarly research, the aims of the diversity movement envisioned in the 1960s can come to fruition in the form of a level playing field defined not by resistance but by storytelling, interdependence and actual social change. In other words, as soon as the diversity movement lets go of rigid categories of race identity–and redefines the nature of the self through new norms of interdependence, complementarity, and personal connection to past and place—it lays a foundation for even larger change at the macro level of the economy and democracy. At base, it intones an overall world view that is both non-binary *and* participatory.

Techniques for Social Change

Abstracted further, one might hypothesize a list of social change techniques for diverse, transnational societies. Such a list would include intercultural storytelling and performance, dreaming, narrative therapy, model building, parallel systems construction, autonomous community building, new norms of complementarity and interdependence, and anticipatory action research (Ctibor et. al. 2002; Aaen et. al., 2002; Aaen et al, 2003). These are all approaches that worked well in the research reported in this book.

At the same time, social change researchers will want to closely examine the methods and practices of women's movements around the world as they have been successfully tested, in many cases, over a long period of time. These include forming "a second economy" (Matynia, 1995: 392), repositioning women's relation to the state (Lamas, Martinez, Tarres & Tunon, 1995: 329), collabora-tions with "dominant" group members (Anzaldua & Keating, 2002), cross-subjective alliances across generations and gender (Jean-Klein, 2000; Klein, 2003), counter-publics linked to schools (Kelly, 2003: 127), the writing of stories by schoolchildren (Orellana, 1999: 66-69), and the creation of a civil society (Basu, 1995: 9). While my work has been heavily informed by feminist anthropologists who emphasize the importance of creating alternative regimes (e.g., Martin, 1987; Kondo, 1990a; Gailey, 1998; Mendoza-Denton, 1999), the work of the above scholars to report actual change efforts linked to personal growth adds a heightened sense of purpose into my future research.

In addition to intercultural and feminist approaches, the work of educational activism (e.g., Gitlin, 1994; Fine et. al., 2000) lends further impetus to the particular idea that educational venues can be effective vehicles for positive social change. One of those projects presents a self-directed, teacher-based approach for African Americans who have been historically oppressed (Foster, 1994) and this is a strategy that reflects the spirit of autonomy and parallel systems reported here. At the same time, the conceptual tools advanced in this book—intersubjectivity, a storytelling pedagogy, complementarity, model building, and parallel systems building, among others—suggest another quantum shift may be in the offing. With the success of the techniques reported here, it appears that "social change" will itself need to be recast, so that it is less a reform of existing social institutions and more nearly an act of creating wholly new institutions that better engage a diverse U.S. public.

Taken together, the contributions of global women's movements, educational activism, and now intercultural applications of action research lend a degree of momentum to future work in social change. From this momentum comes a deeper wish to re-examine the nature and trajectory of America.

The Idea of America

In concluding this book, the three studies presented here underscore that alternatives are possible to the kind of race fear, loss of meaning, and "End of the West" emotionality that have come to define American life in the wake of the horrible September 11 bombings. In a crashing geo-political context where race diversity injects a steady undercurrent of uncertainty, it is interesting to see that white college students want to learn about diversity and U.S. leaders seem to know so little about how to collaborate across difference.

American citizens already see the irony in the fact that while they have been learning to interact in harmony across race and ethnic difference inside U.S. borders, they are forced to be on the receiving end of a fear-based form of capitalism that triggers "blowback" on them from resentful, angry people of color around the world. Stated in more positive terms, while students in many U.S. colleges and universities are benefitting from diversity programs that expose them to the histories of people of color, we are at a point where future U.S. leaders must be taught the *inter*cultural skills and perspectives they will need to work collaboratively with others in a diverse *global* sphere. One might even suggest the time for possessing those assets is now overdue.

What these eight years of research tell me is that there is now a note of optimism for the prospect of peace and harmony in a diverse world society. But to achieve peace on a global scale, it also seems clear that the hard work must begin at home—where being intercultural means more than just putting diverse groups of students together on one campus. In an increasingly diverse U.S., being intercultural will mean taking the time and effort to acquire new habits of storytelling, interdependence, and model building that will likely redefine "the idea" of America.

REFERENCES

Aaen, L., Andersson, A., Arduini, S., Baghdassarian, R., Collins, T., Franker, M., Garlock, E. Herrera, D., Hinson, B., Hunter-McGrath, P., Knight, J., Inverno, C., Middlebrooks, N., Moreno, M., Pittman, C., Saghari, E., Tugnoli, A., Zargarian, T., & Zwicky, B. (2003, January–May). Discussions about human development and social change, Pacific Oaks College, Pasadena, CA.

Aaen, L., Andersson, A., Arduini, S., Certo, D., Franker, M., Garlock, E., Herrada, M., Hinson, B., Hunter-McGrath, P., Knight, J., Olson, A., Tugnoli, A., Watson, D.L., West, J., Zee, G., & Zwicky, B. (2002, September–December). Discussions about participatory action research and social change, Pacific Oaks College, Pasadena, CA.

Aaen, L., Parker-Hayes, P., Adams, K., Chaney, A., Clark, M., Cosby, J., Higgins, S., Hunkins, M., Jornensen, F., Mitchell, L., Peralt, M., Williams, C., & Young, M.H. (2000). *Parallel lives, parallel process.* Unpublished manuscript, Pacific Oaks College, Pasadena, CA.

Aguilar-San Juan, K. (1994). *The state of Asian America: Activism and resistance in the 1990's.* Boston: South End Press.

Alfaro, L. (1999). Everybody has a story: Who's listening? *Unity & Difference*, 1(1), 1–6.

———, Coleman, W., & McLaren, P. (1999, December 5). An intersubjective storytelling at the opening of *Unity & Difference* journal. Self-Help Graphics, Los Angeles, California.

Alperovitz, G., Imbroscio, D., & Williamson, T. (2002). *Making a place for community: Local democracy in a global era.* New York: Routledge.

Allport, G. (1954). *The nature of prejudice.* Reading, MA: Addison-Wellesley.

Altbach, P.G. & Lomotey, K., eds. (1991). *The racial crisis in American higher education.* New York: State University of New York Press.

Anderson, G.L. (1998). Toward authentic participation: Deconstructing the discourses of participatory reforms in education. *American Educational Research Journal, 35*(4), 571–603.

Anzaldua, G. (1987). *Borderlands/la frontera: The new mestiza.* San Francisco: aunt lute books.

Anzaldua, G. & Keating, A., eds. (2002). *This bridge we call home: Radical visions for transformation.* New York: Routledge.

Apple, M. W. (1990). *Ideology and curriculum.* 2nd ed. New York: Routledge.

Apple, M. W. & Christian-Smith, L. K. (1991). *The politics of the textbook.* New York: Routledge.

Arextega, B. (1997). *Shattering silence: Women, nationalism, and political subjectivity in Northern Ireland.* Princeton, NJ: Princeton University Press.

Aronowitz, S. & Giroux, H. A. (1991). *Postmodern education: Politics, culture, & social criticism.* Minneapolis: University of Minnesota Press.

Arratia, M. (1997). Daring to change: The potential of intercultural education in Aymara communities in Chile. *Anthropology & Education Quarterly,* 28(2), 229–250.

Association of American Colleges & Universities (2002, November 15). Seminar on civic engagement in a diverse democracy, University of Southern California, Los Angeles, CA.

Astin, A. W. (1977). *Four critical years.* San Francisco: Jossey-Bass Publishers.

———— (1975). *Preventing students from dropping out,* San Francisco: Jossey-Bass Publishers.

———— (1984). Student involvement: A developmental theory for higher education," *Journal of college student personnel,* 24(4), 297–308.

———— (1991). *Assessment for excellence.* New York: Macmillan, Inc.

———— (1993a). Diversity and multiculturalism on campus: How are students affected? *Change,* 25(2), 44–49.

———— (1993b). *What matters in college: Four critical years revisited.* San Francisco: Jossey-Bass Publishers.

———— (1995). Discussion about writing and musical polyphony, UCLA, Los Angeles, CA.

———— (1996). *Celebrating individualism and collaboration: A musical metaphor.* Unpublished manuscript, Los Angeles: UCLA.

Astin, A.W. & Dey, E.L. (1996). *Causal analytical modeling via blocked regression analysis (CAMBRA): An introduction with examples.* Unpublished manuscript, Los Angeles: UCLA.

Astin, A.W., Wingard, T.L., & Trevino, J.G. (1991). *The UCLA campus climate for diversity.* Los Angeles: Higher Education Research Institute, UCLA.

Atkinson, P. (1991). *The ethnographic imagination: Textual constructions of reality.* London: Routledge.

Atwood, M. (2003, March 28). A letter to America. *The Globe and Mail.*

Bakhtin, M.M. (1990/1919–1924). *Art and answerability.* Austin, Texas: University of Texas Press.

———— (1981/1930s). *The dialogic imagination.* Austin, Texas: University of Texas Press.

———— (1984/1929). *Problems of Dostoevsky's poetics.* Minneapolis: University of Minnesota Press.

———— (1984/1965). *Rabelais and his world.* Bloomington: Indiana University Press.

———— (1993/1924). *Toward a philosophy of the act.* Austin, Texas: University of Texas Press.

Barber, B.R. (1998). *A place for us: How to make society civil and democracy strong.* New York: Hill and Wang.

Barrett, R. (1999). Indexing polyphonous identity in the speech of African American drag queens. In Bucholtz, M., Liang, A.C., & Sutton, L.A., eds. *Reinventing identities*. New York: Oxford University Press.

Basso, K. H. (1979). *Portraits of a whiteman: Linguistic play and cultural symbols among the Western Apache*. London: Cambridge University Press.

Basu, A., ed (1995). *The challenge of local feminisms: Women's movements in global perspective*. Boulder, CO: Westview Press.

Bauman, R. & Briggs, C. L. (1990). Poetics and performance as critical perspectives on language and social life. *Annual Review of Anthropology*, 19, 59–99.

——— (2000). Language philosophy as language ideology: In Kroskrity, P. V., ed., *Regimes of language*. Santa Fe: School of American Research.

Behar, R. & Gordon, D. A., eds (1995). *Women writing culture*. Berkeley, CA: University of California Press.

Bell, D. (1992). *Faces at the bottom of the well: The permanence of racism*. New York: Basic Books.

Bennett, J. W. (1996). Applied and action anthropology. *Current Anthropology*, 36, 23–53.

Bennett, W.J. (1988). *Our children & our country: Improving America's schools and affirming the common culture*. New York: Simon & Schuster.

——— (1992). *The de-valuing of America*. New York: Summit Books.

Berger, P.L. & Luckman, T. (1967). *The social construction of reality*. Garden City, New York: Anchor Books.

Bhabha, H. (1994). *The location of culture*. London: Routledge.

Bloom, A. (1987). *The closing of the American mind: How higher education has failed democracy and impoverished the souls of today's students*. New York: Simon and Schuster.

Bourdieu, P. (1980). *The Logic of Practice*. Stanford: Stanford University Press.

——— (1984). *Homo academicus*. Stanford: Stanford University Press.

Bourdieu, P. & Passeron, J. C. (1977). *Reproduction in education, society and culture*, 2nd ed. London: Sage Publications.

Boyte, H. & Kari, N. (1996). *Building America: The democratic promise of public work*. Philadelphia: Temple University Press.

Bratich, J. Z., Packer, J., & McCarthy, C., eds. (2003). *Foucault, cultural studies, and governmentality*. Albany, NY: SUNY Press.

Briggs, C. A. (1996). The politics of discursive authority in research on the "invention of tradition." *Cultural Anthropology*,11(4), 435–469.

Brodkin, K. (1994). How did Jews become white folks? In Gregory, S. & Sanjek, R., eds., *Race*. New Brunswick, NJ: Rutgers University Press.

Brown v. Board of Education of Topeka, Kansas, 345 U.S. 483 (1954).

Bruner, J. (1986). *Actual minds, possible worlds*. Cambridge, MA: Harvard University Press.

Bucholtz, M. (1999). Bad examples: Transgression and progress in language and gender studies. In Bucholtz, M., Liang, A. C., & Sutton, L. A., eds., *Reinventing identities: The gendered self in discourse*. New York: Oxford University Press.

Bucholtz, M., Liang, A.C., & Sutton, L.A., eds. (1999). *Reinventing identities.* New York: Oxford University Press.

Burbeles, N. & Rice, S. (1991). Dialogue across difference: Continuing the conversation. *Harvard Educational Review,* 61(4), 393–416.

Butler, J. (1990). *Gender trouble: Feminism and the subversion of identity.* New York: Routledge.

————— (1993). *Bodies that matter: On the discursive limits of "sex."* New York: Routledge.

California Postsecondary Commision (2000). Oakland, CA.

Capps, L. (1999). Constructing the irrational woman: Narrative interaction and agoraphobic identity. In Bucholtz, M., Liang, A.C., & Sutton, L.A., eds., *Reinventing identities.* New York: Oxford University Press.

Carnegie Foundation for the Advancement of Teaching (1990). *Campus life: In search of community.* Boyer, E. L., Foreword. Princeton, New Jersey: Carnegie Foundation.

Change (1991, September/October). Diversity: The quest for community, 23(5).

Change (1992, January/February). The curriculum & multiculturalism, 24(1).

Chatterjee, P. (1989). Colonialism, nationalism, and colonized women: The contest in India, *American Ethnologist,* 16(4), 622–633.

Cheney, L. (1989). *Fifty hours: A core curriculum for college students.* Washington, D.C.: National Endowment for the Humanities.

Cherryholmes, C. (1988). *Power and criticism: Poststructural investigations in education.* New York: Teachers College Press.

Chesler, M.A. (1995, December). *Strategic planning for multicultural organizational change in higher education.* Unpublished manuscript. Los Angeles: UCLA Ombuds Office.

————— (1996, January). *Resistance to the multicultural agenda in higher education.* Unpublished manuscript. Los Angeles: UCLA Ombuds Office.

Chickering, A.W. & Reisser, L. (1993). *Education and identity.* San Francisco: Jossey-Bass Publishers.

Christian, B. (1987). The race for theory. *Cultural Critique,* 6, 51–63.

Chronicle of Higher Education (2003, February 14). Prime Numbers. P. A9.

Chun, A. (2000). From text to context: How anthropology makes its subject. *Cultural Anthropology,* 15(4), 570–595.

Clandinin, J.D. & Connelly, F.M. (1994). Personal experience methods. In Denzin, N.K. & Lincoln, Y.S., eds., *Handbook of qualitative research.* Thousand Oaks, CA: Sage Publications.

Clayton-Pederson, A. (2001). Closing remarks at seminar on the future of diversity, The James Irvine Foundation, Claremont Graduate University, Claremont, CA.

Clifford, J. (1986). Introduction: Partial truths. In Clifford, J. & Marcus, G., eds., *Writing culture: The poetics and politics of ethnography.* Berkeley, CA: University of California Press.

————— (1988). *The predicament of culture: Twentieth century ethnography, literature, and art.* Cambridge, Massachusetts: Harvard University Press.

———— (1992). Traveling cultures. In Grossberg, L., Nelson, C., & Treishler, P., eds., *Cultural Studies*. London: Routledge.

Clifford, J. & Marcus, G.E., eds. (1986). *Writing culture: The poetics and politics of ethnography*. Berkeley: University of California Press.

Coates, J. (1999). Changing feminities: The talk of teenage girls. In Bucholtz, M., Liang, A. C., & Sutton, L. A., eds., *Reinventing identities: The gendered self in discourse*. New York: Oxford University Press.

Cockburn, A., St. Clari, J., & Sekula, A. (2001). *5 days that shook the world: Seattle and beyond*. London: Verso.

Cocks, J. (1991). Augustine, Nietzsche, and contemporary body politics. *Differences: A Journal of Feminist Cultural Studies*, 3(1), 144–158.

Cohen, L. (2003, 3 January). The politics of mass consumption in America. *Chronicle of Higher Education*. B9.

Cokorinos, L. (2003). *The assault on diversity: An organized challenge to racial and gender justice*. New York: Rowman and Littlefield.

Collins, P. H. (1986). Learning from the outsider within: The sociological significance of black feminist thought. *Social Problems*, 33, S14–S32.

Connerton, P. (1989). *How societies remember*. Cambridge: Cambridge University Press.

Cooperative Institutional Research Program (1995). Higher Education Research Institute. UCLA. Los Angeles, CA.

Cornwell, G. H. & Stoddard, E. W. (1994). Things fall together: A critique of multicultural curricular reform. *Liberal Education*, fall, 1994.

Costantino, T.E. & Greene, J.C. (2003). Reflections on the use of narrative in evaluation. *American Journal of Evaluation*, 24(1): 35–49.

Crane, D. (1982). Cultural differentiation, cultural integration, and social control. In Gibbs, J.P., ed., *Social control: Views from the social sciences*. Beverly Hills: Sage Publications.

Crapanzano, V. (1992). *Hermes' dilemma & Hamlet's desire: On the epistemology of interpretation*. Cambridge, MA: Harvard University Press.

———— (2000). *Serving the word: Literalism in American from the pulpit to the bench*. New York: New Press.

Cross, W.E., Jr. (1991). *Shades of black: Diversity in African-American identity*. Philadelphia: Temple University Press.

Crossley, N. (1996). *Intersubjectivity: The fabric of social being*. Thousand Oaks, CA: Sage Publications.

Cruz, C. (2001). Toward an epistemology of a brown body. *International Journal of Qualitative Studies in Education*, 14(5), 637–669.

———— (2003). Testimonial narratives and queer street youth: Toward an epistemology of the brown body. Dissertation in progress, University of California, Los Angeles, CA.

Cruz, C. & McLaren, P. (2003). Queer bodies and configurations: Toward a critical pedagogy of the body. In Shapiro, S. & Shapiro, S., eds., *Body movements: Pedagogy, politics, and social change*. Creskill, NY: Hampton Press.

Ctibor, B., Garlock, E., Jasiukunis, K., Lukas, D., McAllister, M., Navarro, N., Olson, A., Romo, G., Sevareid, M., Shafer, J., Shaheen, C., & Watson, D.L. (2002, January). Dialogue about human development and social change, Pacific Oaks College, Pasadena, CA.

Daniel, G.R. (1992). Beyond black and white: The new multiracial consciousness. In Root, M.P.P., ed., *Racially mixed people in America*. Newbury Park: Sage Publications.

———(1999). Assimilation or transculturation? The dynamics of ethnic relations reconsidered. *Unity & Difference*, 1(1), 43–48.

Darder, A. (1991). *Culture and power in the classroom: A critical foundation for bicultural education*. New York: Bergin & Garvey.

Davis, J. E. (2002, May). Race, gender, and sexuality: (Un)doing identity categories in educational research. Book review of *Bad boys: Public schools in the making of black masculinity*, by A. A. Ferguson and *Subject to identity: Knowledge, sexuality, and academic practices in higher education*, by S. Talburt. *Educational Researcher*, 31(4), 29–32.

Davis, M. (1990). *City of quartz: Excavating the future in Los Angeles*. New York: Vintage Books.

Davis, N.Z. (1965). *Society and culture in early modern France*. Stanford, CA: Stanford University Press.

de Certeau, M. (1986). *Heterologies: Discourse on the other*. Minneapolis: University of Minnesota Press.

Deleuze, G. (1986). *Foucault*. Minneapolis: University of Minnesota Press.

Delgado, R., ed. (1995). *Critical race theory: The cutting edge*. Philadelphia: Temple University Press.

Delgado, R. & Stefancic, J., eds. (1997). *Critical white studies: Looking behind the mirror*. Philadelphia: Temple University Press.

Deloria, V. (1969). *Custer died for your sins*. New York: MacMillan.

Demerath, P. (2003). Negotiating individualist and collectivist futures: Emerging subjectivities and social forms in Papua New Guinean high schools. *Anthropology & Education Quarterly*, 34(2), 136–157.

Diaz, D. (1995). Public space and culture: A critical response to conventional and postmodern visions of city life. In Darder, A., ed., *Culture and difference*. Westport, CN: Bergin & Garvey.

Dreyfus, H.L. & Rabinow, P. (1983). *Michel Foucault: Beyond poststructuralism and hermeneutics*. Chicago: University of Chicago Press.

D'Souza, D. (1991). *Illiberal education: The politics of race and sex on campus*. New York: The Free Press.

Duster, T., ed. (1991). *The diversity project*. Berkeley, CA: Institute for the Study of Social Change, University of California at Berkeley.

——— (1993). The diversity of California at Berkeley: An emerging reformulation of "competence" in an increasingly multicultural world. In Thompson, B. & Tyagi, S., eds., *Beyond a dream deferred: Multicultural education and the politics of excellence*. Minneapolis: University of Minnesota Press.

Eastside Café (2002, May). Dialogues in preparation for creation of an autonomous community in El Sereno, Los Angeles, California. Eastsidecafe_2000@yahoo.com.

Elden, M. & Chisholm, R. F. (1993). Emerging varieties of action research: Introduction to the special issue. *Human Relations*, 46(2), 121–141.

Erikson, E. (1959). *Identity and the life cycle.* New York: W.W. Norton & Company.

Evans, S.M. & Boyte, H. C. (1986). *Free spaces: The sources of democratic change in America.* Chicago: University of Chicago Press.

Fabian, J. (1983). *Time and the other: How anthropology makes its object.* New York: Columbia University Press.

Fanger, D. (1965). *Dostoevsky and romantic realism: A study of Dostoevsky in relation to Balzac, Dickens, and Gogol.* Chicago: University of Chicago Press.

Fanon, F. (1967). *Black skin, white masks.* New York: Grove Weidenfeld.

Ferguson, A. A. (2000). *Bad boys: Public schools in the making of black masculinity.* Ann Arbor, MI: University of Michigan Press.

Fersen, N. (1968–1969). Conversations about pochva, Dostoyevsky and writing, Williams College, Williamstown, MA.

Fine, M., Weis, L., Powell, L.C., & Wong, L.M., eds. (1997). *Off white: Readings on race, power, and society.* New York: Routledge.

Fine, M., Weis, L., Centrie, C., & Roberts, R. (2000). Educating beyond the borders of schooling. *Anthropology & Education Quarterly*, 31(2), 131–151.

Flores, R. (2003, May). Interview on autonomous community building and the failure of representative democracy in the United States. KPFK, Los Angeles, CA.

Flores, R., Tanaka, G., & McLaren, P. (2001). Autonomy and participatory democracy: An ongoing discussion on the application of the Zapatista method in the United States. *International Journal of Education Reform,* 10(2), 130–144.

Foster, M. (1990). The politics of race: Through the eyes of African-American teachers. *Journal of Education*, 172(3), 123–141.

——— (1994). The power to know one thing is never the power to know all things: Methodological notes on two studies of Black American teachers. In Gitlin, A., ed., *Power and method: Political activism and educational research.* New York: Routledge.

——— (1997, June 21). Insider research: What counts as critical. Keynote speech presented at Reclaiming Voice Conference, University of Southern California School of Education.

Foucault, M. (1971). *The archaeology of knowledge & the discourse on language.* New York: Pantheon Books.

——— (1972). *Power/knowledge: Selected interviews & other writings.* New York: Pantheon Books.

——— (1975). *Discipline & punish: The birth of the prison.* New York: Vintage Books.

——— (1976). *The history of sexuality: An introduction.* Vol. 1. New York: Vintage Books.

——— (1983). Afterword: The subject and power. In Dreyfus, H. L. & Rabinow, P., *Michel Foucault: Beyond structuralism and hermeneutics.* Chicago: University of Chicago Press.

——— (1984). *The history of sexuality: The use of pleasure.* Vol. 2. New York: Vintage Books.

Frankenberg, R. (1993). *The social construction of whiteness: White women, race matters,* Minneapolis: University of Minnesota Press.

———— (1995). When we are capable of stopping, we begin to see: Being white, seeing whiteness. In Thompson, B. & Tyagi, S., eds., *Names we call home: Autobiography on racial identity.* New York: Routledge.

Freire, P. (1990). *Pedagogy of the oppressed.* New York: Continuum.

Gailey, C. (1998, May 8). Introduction: Conference on culture and systemic collapse. Annual meeting of the American Ethnological Society, Toronto, CN.

Gardiner, M. (1992). *The dialogics of critique: M.M. Bakhtin & the theory of ideology.* New York: Routledge.

Gates, H.L. Jr. (1992). *Loose canons: Notes on the culture wars.* New York: Oxford University Press.

Geertz, C. (1973). *The interpretation of cultures.* New York: Basic Books.

Gilligan, C. (1982). *In a different voice: Psychological theory and women's development.* Cambridge, Mass: Harvard University Press.

Giroux, H. (1992). *Border crossings: Cultural workers and the politics of education.* New York: Routledge.

Giroux, H.A. & McLaren, P., eds. (1989). *Critical pedagogy, the state, and cultural struggle.* Albany, NY: SUNY Press.

———— (1994). *Between borders: Pedagogy and the politics of cultural studies.* New York: Routledge.

Gitlin, A., ed. (1994). *Power and method: Political activism and educational research.* New York: Routledge.

Gomez-Pena, G. (1992). Border brujo. Performance at Highways Performance Space, Santa Monica, CA.

Gong, J. (2003). Realizing power: A critical realist's view of participatory policymaking in educational reform. Dissertation in education, UCLA, Los Angeles, CA.

Goodwin, M. H. (1990). *He-said-she-said: Talk as social organization among black children.* Bloomington, IN: Indiana University Press.

———— (1999). Constructing opposition within girls' games. In Bucholtz, M., Liang, A.C., & Sutton, L.A., eds., *Reinventing identities.* New York: Oxford University Press.

Gramsci, A. (1971). *Selections from the prison notebooks of Antonio Gramsci.* New York: International Publishers.

Gratz v. Bollinger (2003), United States Supreme Court No. 02-516.

Grinde, D. A. & Johansen, B.E. (1991). *Exemplar of Liberty: Native America and the evolution of democracy.* Los Angeles: American Indian Studies Center, UCLA.

Grutter v. Bollinger (2003). United States Supreme Court No. 02-241.

Guano, E. (2002). Spectacles of modernity: Transnational imagination and local hegemonies in neoliberal Buenos Aires. *Cultural Anthropology, 17*(2), 181–209.

Guha, R. & Spivak, G. C. ed (1988). *Selected subaltern studies.* New York: Oxford University Press.

Guinier, L. & Torres, G. (2002). *The miner's canary: Enlisting race, resisting power, transforming democracy.* Cambridge: Harvard University Press.

Gumperz, J. (1982). *Discourse strategies.* London: Cambridge University Press.

Gutierrez, R. (2002). Beyond essentialism: The complexity of language in teaching mathematics to Latina/o students. *American Educational Research Journal,* 39(4), 1047–1088.

Gwaltney, J.L. (1993). *Drylongso: A self-portrait of black America.* New York: The New Press.

Habermas, J. (1991). *The structural transformation of the public sphere: An inquiry into a category of bourgeois society.* Cambridge, Massachusetts: MIT Press.

Hand, S. (1988). Translating theory, or the difference between Deleuze and Foucault. In Deleuze, G., *Foucault.* Minneapolis: University of Minnesota Press.

Harris, F. (1997). Paper presentation by an undergraduate student at Del Rey University student of color research symposium on how to improve the institution.

Hebdige, D. (1988). *Hiding in the light.* New York: Routledge.

Hemmings, A. (2000). Lona's links: Postoppositional identity work of urban youths. *Anthropology & Education Quarterly,* 31(2), 152–172.

Hernandez, G. (1995). Multiple subjectivities and strategic positionality: Zora Neale Hurston's experimental ethnographies. In Behar, R. & Gordon, D.A., eds., *Women writing culture.* Berkeley: University of California Press.

Herrnstein, R.J. & Murray, C. (1994). *The bell curve: Intelligence and class structure in American life.* New York: The Free Press.

Holquist, M. (1990). Introduction: The architectonics of answerability. In Bakhtin, M.M. (1990). *Art and answerability.* Autsin, TX: University of Texas.

hooks, b. (1992). Representing whiteness in the black imagination. In Grossberg, L., Nelson, C., & Teichler, P., eds., *Cultural Studies.* New York: Routledge.

hooks, b. & West, C. (1991). *Breaking bread: Insurgent black intellectual life.* Boston: South End Press.

Howe, A. C. (2001). Queer pilgrimage: The San Francisco homeland and identity tourism. *Cultural Anthropology,* 16, 35–61.

Hu, N.B. (2000). Higher education demographics summarized, Los Angeles, CA.

Hu, N.B. & Tanaka, G. (2001, June). Does interculturalism affect campus values for a favorable learning and teaching environment? Paper presented at Association for Institutional Research, Long Beach, CA.

Hughes, R. (1993). *Culture of complaint: The fraying of America.* New York: Oxford University Press.

Hungry Mind Review (1998, spring). Whiteness: what is it? 45. St. Paul, MN: The National Book Magazine.

Hunt, D. M. (1997). *Screening the Los Angeles riots: Race, seeing, and resistance.* Cambridge: Cambridge University Press.

Hunt, L., ed. (1989). *The new cultural history.* Berkeley: University of California Press.

Hurston, Z. N. (1935). *Mules and men.* New York: Harper Perennial.

Hurtado, S. (1992). The campus racial climate: Contexts of conflict. *Journal of Higher Education*, 63(5), 539–569.

Hwang, D. H. (1994). Facing the mirror. In Aguilar-San Juan, K., ed., *The state of Asian America: Activism and resistance in the 1990s*. Boston: South End Press.

Ignatiev, N. & Garvey, J., ed. (1996). *Race traitor*. New York: Routledge.

Isaac, J.C. (2003, April 11). The state of civil society. *The Chronicle of Higher Education*, B12–B13.

Jackson, M. (1998). *Minima ethnographica: Intersubjectivity and the anthropological project.* Chicago: University of Chicago Press.

Jean-Klein, I. (2000). Mothercraft, statecraft, and subjectivity in the Palestinian intifada. *American Ethnologist,* 27(1), 100–127.

——— (2001). Nationalism and resistance: The two faces of everyday activism in Palestine during the intifada. *Cultural Anthropology*, 16(1), 83–126.

Jeffries, L. (1990–1993). Various speeches given on the east coast of the United States. *Journal of Linguistic Anthropology*, 11(1), June, 2001.

Kaplan, C. (1997, February 21). The romance of distance and the comforts of home: Demystifying spatial metaphors in an era of globalization. Paper delivered at conference "Hybrid Cultures and Transnational Identities," UCLA Faculty Center, Los Angeles, California.

Kelly, D.M. (2003). Practicing democracy in the margins of school: The teenage parents program as feminist counterpublic. *American Educational Research Journal,* 40(1), 123–146.

Kimball, R. (1990). *Tenured radicals: How politics has corrupted our higher education.* New York: Harper & Row.

King, L. (2003). Subjectivity as identity: Gender through the lens of Foucault. In Bratich, J.Z., Packer, J., & McCarthy, C., eds., *Foucault, cultural studies, and governmentality.* Albany, NY: SUNY Press.

Kjetsaa, G. (1987). *Fyodor Dostoyevsky: A writer's life,* New York: Viking.

Klees, S.J. (1999). Privatization and Neo-Liberalism: Ideology and evidence in rhetorical reforms. *Current Issues in Comparative Education*, 1(2), 1–7.

Klein, N. (2001, May–June). Reclaiming the commons. *New Left Review*, 9, 81–89.

——— (2003). Demonstrated ideals. Book review of Gitlin, T. (2003), *Letters to a young activist,* New York: Basic Books. In Los Angeles Times Book Review, April 20, 2003. R10–R11.

Kondo, D. (1990a). *Crafting selves: Power, gender, and discourses of identity in a Japanese workplace.* Chicago: University of Chicago Press.

——— (1990b). M. Butterfly: Orientalism, gender and a critique of essentialist identity. *Cultural Critique*, 16, 5–29.

——— (1995). Bad girls: Theater, women of color, and the politics of representation. In Behar, R. & Gordon, D. A., eds., *Women writing cultures.* Berkeley, CA: University of California Press.

Kristol, I. (1991). The tragedy of multiculturalism. *The Wall Street Journal*, July 31, 1991.

Kroskrity, P. V. (2000). Identity. *Journal of Linguistic Anthropology*, 9(1), 107–110.

Laclau, E. & Mouffe, C. (1985). *Hegemony and socialist strategy: Towards a radical democratic politics*. London: Verso.

Lamas, M., Martinez, A., Tarres, M. L., & Tunon, E. (1995). Building bridges: The growth of popular feminism in Mexico. In Basu, A., ed., *Women's movements in global perspective*. Boulder, CO: Westview Press.

Land, I. (2003). What happens when social constructivist therapy is applied to the residential treatment of chemically dependent men? MA thesis proposal, Pacific Oaks College, Pasadena, CA.

Lather, P.(1991). *Getting smart: Feminist research and pedagogy with/in the postmodern*. New York: Routledge.

Leiris, M. (1946). *L'age d'homme*. Paris: Gallimard. Trans. Richard Howard as *Manhood*. Berkeley: North Point Press (1985).

Lenkersdorf, C. (1996). *Los hombres verdaderos: Voces y testimonios tojolabales*. Mexico City: Siglo Ventiuno Editores.

Lett, J. (1987). *The human enterprise: A critical introduction to anthropological theory*. Boulder, Colorado: Westview.

Levi-Strauss, C. (1966). *The savage mind*. Chicago: University of Chicago Press.

Lippard, L.R. (1990). *Mixed blessings: New art in a multicultural America*. New York: Pantheon Books.

Lipsitz, G. (1998). *The possessive investment in whiteness: How white people profit from identity politics*. Philadelphia: Temple University Press.

Lodge, D. (1990). *Bakhtin: Essays on fiction and criticism*. London: Routledge.

Lorde, A. (1979). The master's tools will never dismantle the master's house. In Moraga, C. & Anzaldua, G., eds. (1983), *This bridge called my back: Writings by radical women of color*. New York: Kitchen Table Women of Color Press.

Malaguzzi, L. (1993). History, ideas, and basic philosophy. In Edwards, C., Gandini, L., & Foreman, G., eds., *The hundred languages of children: The Reggio Emilia approach to early childhood education*. Norwood, NJ: Ablex Publishing.

Marcos, S. (2001). *Our word is our weapon: Selected writings*. New York: Seven Stories Press.

Marcus, G.E. & Fischer, M.M.J. (1986). *Anthropology as cultural critique: An experimental moment in the human sciences*. Chicago: University of Chicago Press.

Markowitz, F., Helman, S., & Shir-Vertesh, D. (2003). Soul Citizenship: The black Hebrews and the state of Israel. *American Anthropologist*, 150(2): 302–312.

Marranca, B. & Dasgupta, G., eds. (1991). *Interculturalism & performance*. New York: PAJ Publications.

Martin, E. (1987). *The woman in the body: A cultural analysis of reproduction*. Boston: Beacon Press.

Maslach, C., ed. (1991). *Promoting student success at Berkeley: Guidelines for the future.* Report of the Commission on Responses to a Changing Student Body. Berkeley: University of California.

Matthieson, P. (1962). *Under the mountain wall: A chronicle of two seasons in stone age New Guinea.* New York: Penguin Books.

Matynia, E. (1995). Finding a voice: Women in postcommunist central Europe. In Basu, A., ed., *The challenge of local feminisms: Women's movements in global perspective.* Boulder, CO: Westview Press.

Mauss, M. (1954). *The gift.* London: Cohen and West.

McCarthy, C. & Apple, M. W (1988). Race, class and gender in American educational research: Towards a nonsynchronous parallelist position. *Perspectives in education,* 4(2), 67–89.

McCarthy, C. & Crichlow, W., ed. (1993). *Race, identity and representation in education.* New York: Routledge.

McIntosh, P. (1988). White privilege and male privilege: A personal account of coming to see correspondences through work in women's studies. Working Paper No. 189, Center for Research on Women, Wellesley College, Wellesley, Massachusetts.

—— (1989). White privilege: Unpacking the invisible knapsack. *Peace and Freedom,* July/August, 202–204.

McLaren, P. (1994a). White terror and oppositional agency: Towards a critical multiculturalism. *Strategies,* 7, 98–131.

—— (1994b). Multiculturalism and the postmodern critique: Toward a pedagogy of resistance and transformation. In Giroux, H.A. & McLaren, P., ed. (1994). *Between borders: Pedagogy and the politics of cultural studies.* New York: Routledge.

—— (1997). The ethnographer as postmodern flaneur: Critical reflexivity and posthybridity as narrative engagement. In Tierney, W. G. & Lincoln, Y. S., eds., *Representation and the text: Reframing the narrative voice.* Albany, NY: SUNY Press.

McLaren, P. & Leonardo, Z. (1997). Jean Baudrillard's chamber of horrors: From Marxism to terrorist pedagogy. In McLaren, P., ed., *Revolutionary multiculturalism: Pedagogies of dissent for the new millenium.* Boulder, CO: Westview Press.

Mendoza-Denton, N. (1999). Turn-initial *no*: Collaborative opposition among Latina adolescents. In Bucholtz, M., Liang, A. C., & Sutton, L. A., eds., *Reinventing identities,* New York: Oxford University Press.

Mercer, J.R. (1990). *Campus climate for women graduate students at UCR 1989–1990.* Riverside, CA: University of California Riverside Affirmative Action Committee.

Mills, C.W. (1990). *The sociological imagination.* London: Oxford University Press.

Mohanty, C.T. (1988). Under western eyes: Feminist scholarship and colonial discourses. *Feminist review,* 30, 65–88.

—— (1993). On race and voice: Challenges for liberal education in the 1990s. In Thompson, B. W. & Tyagi, S., eds., *Beyond a dream deferred: Multicultural education and the politics of excellence.* Minneapolis: University of Minnesota Press.

Monthly Review (2002, April). The new face of capitalism: slow growth, excess capital, and a mountain of debt. 53, 1–14.

Morrison, T. (1992). *Playing in the dark: Whiteness and the literary imagination.* Cambridge, MA: Harvard University Press.

Musil, C.M. & Wathington, , H.D. (2002, December 17). Correspondence regarding AAC&U working forum on civic engagement in a diverse democracy. Washington, D.C.: Association of American Colleges & Universities.

Myrdal, G. (1944). *American dilemma.* New York: Harper & Brothers.

Nancy, J.-L. (1991). *The inoperative community.* Minneapolis: University of Minnesota Press.

Narayan, K. (1993). How native is the 'native' anthropologist? *American Anthropologist, 95,* 671–686.

National Center for Educational Statistics (2000). Washington, D.C.

Nietzsche, F. (1967). *On the genealogy of morals.* New York: Vintage Books.

Noddings, N. (1984). *Caring: A feminine approach to ethics and moral education.* Berkeley: University of California Press.

———— (1991). Stories in dialogue: Caring and interpersonal reasoning. In Witherell, C. & Noddings, N., eds., *Stories lives tell: Narrative and dialogue in education.* New York: Teachers College Press.

Nordstrom, C. & Martin, J., ed. (1992). *The paths to domination, resistance and terror.* Berkeley: University of California Press.

Nozaki, Y. (2000). Essentializing dilemma and multiculturalist pedagogy: An ethnographic study of Japanese children in a U.S. school. *Anthropology & Education Quarterly, 31(3),* 355–380.

Oakes, J. (1992). Can tracking research inform practice? Technical, normative and political considerations. *Education Researcher,* May, 12–21.

Ochs, E. & Capps, L. (1996). Narrating the self. *Annual Review of Anthropology, 25,* 19–43.

Ong, A. (1987). *Spirits of resistance and capitalist discipline: Factory workers in Malaysia.* Albany, NY: SUNY Press.

———— (1996). Cultural citizenship as subject making: Immigrants' negative racial and cultural boundaries in the United States. *Current Anthropology, 37(5),* 737–762.

Orellana, M. F. (1999). Good guys and "bad" girls: Identity construction by Latina and Latino student writers. In Bucholtz, M., Liang, A.C., & Sutton, L.A., eds., *Reinventing identities.* New York: Oxford University Press.

Ortiz, F. (1947/1940). *Cuban counterpoint.* New York: Alfred A. Knopf.

Ortner, S. B. (1996). Resistance and the problem of ethnographic refusal. In McDonald, T. J., ed., *The historic turn in the social sciences.* Ann Arbor, MI: University of Michigan Press.

Palmer, P.J. (1997). *A place called community.* Lebanon, Pennsylvania: Pendle Hill.

Park, K. (1993). Public ethnographer: In pursuit of intercessory ethnography. *Anthropology UCLA, 20,* 1–26.

Pascarella, E.T. & Terenzini, P.T. (1991). *How college affects students.* San Francisco: Jossey-Bass Publishers.

Paulin, D.R. (1997). De-essentializing interracial representations: Black and white border crossings in Spike Lee's "Jungle Fever" and Octavia Butler's "Kindred." *Cultural Critique*, 36, 165–193.

Polletta, F. (2002). *Freedom is an endless meeting: Democracy in America's social movements.* Chicago: University of Chicago Press.

Popkewitz, T. (1997). A changing terrain of knowledge and power: A social epistemology of educational research. *Educational Researcher*, 26(9), 18–29.

———— (1998a). Dewey, Vygotsky, and the social administration of the individual: Constructivist pedagogy as systems of ideas in historical spaces. *American Educational Research Journal*, 35(4), 535–578.

———— (1998b). The culture of redemption and the administration of freedom as research. *Review of Educational Research*, 68(1): 1–34.

Powell, T.B., ed. (1999). *Beyond the binary: Reconstructing cultural identity in a multicultural context.* New Brunswick, NJ: Rutgers University Press.

Pratt, M. L. (1995). Arts of the contact zone. In Bartholome, D. & Petrosky, A., eds., *Reading the lives of others.* New York: St. Martin's Press.

Prus, R. (1997). *Subcultural mosaics and intersubjective realities: An ethnographic research agenda for pragmatizing the social sciences.* Albany, NY: SUNY Press.

Rabinow, P. (2002). Midst anthropology's problems. *Cultural Anthropology*, 17(2), 135–149.

Radhakrishnan, R. (1996). *Diasporic mediations: Between home and location.* Minneapolis, MN: University of Minnesota Press.

Ramirez, M. & Castaneda, A. (1974). *Cultural democracy: Biocognitive development and education.* New York: Academic Press.

Regents of the University of California v. Bakke, 438 U.S. 265 (1978).

Rodriguez, M. (1998). *Mito, identidad y rito: Mexicanos y chicanos en california.* Mexico City: Ciesas, Miguel Angel Porruba Grupo Editorial.

Roediger, D. R. (1991). *The wages of whiteness: Race and the making of the American working class.* London: Verso.

Rosaldo, R. (1988). Ideology, place and people without culture. *Cultural Anthropology*, 3(1), 77–87.

———— (1989). *Culture & truth: The remaking of social analysis.* Boston: Beacon Press.

Roth, J. (1992). Of what help is he? A review of Foucault and education. *American Educational Research Journal*, 29(4), 683–694.

Sacco, E. F. (1999). ADOBE LA's cultural explainers: Locating a post-uprising project. *Unity & Difference*, 1(1), 95–104.

Sacks, K. B. (1989). Toward a unified theory of class, race and gender. *American Ethnologist*, 16(3), 534–550.

Said, E. W. (1979). *Orientalism.* New York: Vintage Books.

———— (2000). *Reflections on exile and other essays.* Cambridge, MA: Harvard University Press.

Sandoval, C. (1990). Feminism and racism: A report on the 1981 National Women's Studies Conference. In Anzaldua, G., ed., *Making face, making soul–haciendo caras: Creative and critical perspectives by feminists of color*. San Francisco: aunt lute books.

——— (2000). *Methodology of the oppressed*. Minneapolis, MN: University of Minnesota Press.

Schama, S. (1991). *Dead certainties (unwarranted speculations)*. New York: Alfred A. Knopf.

Scheurich, J. J. (1993). Toward a white discourse on white racism. *Education Researcher*, 22(8), 5–16.

Schieffelin, B. (2000). Introducing Kaluli literacy: A chronology of influences. In Kroskrity, P. V., ed., *Regimes of language*, Santa Fe: SAR.

Schlesinger, A.M. Jr. (1991). *The disuniting of America: Reflections on a multicultural society*. Knoxville, TN: Whittle Direct Books.

Schutz, A. (2000). Teaching freedom? Postmodern perspectives. *Review of Educational Research*, 70(2), 215–251.

Scott, J. C. (1985). *Weapons of the weak: Everyday forms of peasant resistance*. New Haven, CN: Yale University Press.

——— (1990). *Domination and the arts of resistance: Hidden transcripts*. New Haven, CN: Yale University Press.

——— (1992). Domination, acting, and fantasy. In Nordstrom, C. & Martin, J., eds., *The paths to domination, resistance, and terror*. Berkeley, California: University of California Press.

Scott, J. W. (1991). The evidence of experience. *Cultural Inquiry*, 17, 773–797.

Shohat, E. (1997, February 21). Nationalism, multiculturalism, feminism. Paper delivered at conference Hybrid Cultures and Transnational Identities, UCLA Faculty Center, Los Angeles, California.

Shohat, E. & Stam, R. (1994). *Unthinking Eurocentrism: Multiculturalism and the media*. London: Routledge.

Sirianni, C. & Friedland, L. (2001). *Civic innovation in America: Community empowerment, public policy, and the movement for civic renewal*. Berkeley, CA: University of California Press.

Sleeter, C.E., ed. (1991). *Empowerment through multicultural education*. Albany, NY: SUNY Press.

Smith, D.G. (1989). *The challenge of diversity: Involvement or alienation in the academy*. Washington, D.C.: The George Washington University Press.

Solorzano, Daniel G. (1992). An exploratory analysis of the effects of race, class, and gender on student and parent mobility aspirations. *The Journal of Negro Education*, 61(1), 30–44.

Spivak, G. (1988). Can the subaltern speak? In Nelson, C. & Grossberg, L., eds., *Marxism and the interpretations of culture*, Urbana, IL: University of Illinois Press.

——— (1994). Can the subaltern speak? In Williams, P. & Chrisman, L., ed., *Colonial discourse and post-colonial theory*. New York: Columbia University Press.

Springer, L., Terenzini, P. L., Pascarella, E. T., & Nora, A. (1995). Do white students perceive racism toward minority students on predominantly white campuses? Paper delivered at American Educational Research Association, April, 1995.

Stoler, A.L. (1991, May). Sexual affronts and racial frontiers. Paper presented at TNI conference, Amsterdam, Holland.

Strathern, A. J. (1996). *Body thoughts.* Ann Arbor: University of Michigan Press.

Strauss, A. & Corbin, J. (1994). Grounded theory methodology: and overview. In Denzin, N.K. & Lincoln, Y.S., eds., *Handbook of qualitative research.* Thousand Oaks, CA: Sage Publications.

Talburt, S. (2000). *Subject to identity: Knowledge, sexuality, and academic practices in higher education.* Albany, NY: SUNY Press.

Tamanoi, M. A. (1998). *Under the shadow of nationalism: Politics and poetics of rural Japanese women.* Honolulu, HI: University of Hawaii Press.

Tanaka, G. (1992). Campus community: Why professors have a duty to include race and gender diversity in their courses and research. Unpublished manuscript, UCLA, Los Angeles, CA.

——— (1993). Book review of *Multicultural teaching in the university* by Schoem, D., Frankel, L., Zuniga, X., & Lewis, E., *Amerasia Journal,* 19(3), 38–47.

——— (1994). Toward unity and difference: The traveling art of cultural explainers. In LeClerc, G. & Moctezuma, A., eds., *Cultural explainers: Portals, bridges and gateways.* Venice, CA: Social and Public Art Resource Center.

——— (1995, spring). Deconstructing Christmas. *Taboo: The Journal of Culture and Education,* 1, 38–47.

——— (1996). Dysgenesis and white culture. In Kincheloe, J., Steinberg, S., & Gressen, A., eds., *Measured lies: The bell curve examined.* New York: St. Martin's Press.

——— (1996–1997). Where is Mkhan'yasi? *Anthropology UCLA,* 22, 10–43.

——— (1997). Pico college. In Tierney, W. G. & Lincoln, Y. S., eds., *Representation and the text.* Albany, NY: SUNY Press.

——— (1999). Ressentiment. *Anthropology and Humanism,* 24(1), 75–77.

——— (2002a). Higher education's self-reflexive turn: Toward an intercultural theory of student development. *Journal of Higher Education,* 73(2), 263–296.

——— (2002b). Remaking the subject for anthropological discourse. Dissertation in anthropology, filed at University of California, Los Angeles, CA.

——— (2002c, April 27). When the anti-capitalism movement takes to the streets: Public protest as public ethnography. Paper presented at "The Color of Money, A Conference on Visuality and Economics," University of California, Irvine, CA.

Tanaka, G., Bonous-Hammarth, M., & Astin, A. (1998). An admissions process for a multiethnic society. In Orfield, G. & Miller, E., eds., *Chilling admissions: The affirmative action crisis and the search for alternatives.* Cambridge, MA: Harvard Education Publishing Group.

Tanaka, G. & Cruz, C. (1998). The locker room: Eroticism and exoticism in a polyphonic text. *International Journal of Qualitative Studies in Education,* 11(1), 137–153.

Tanaka, G., Cruz, C., & McLaren, P. (2000, May). Intercultural performing tours as a vehicle for building intersubjective schools. Grant proposal to the University of California Institute for Research in the Arts, funded May 23, 2000.

Tanaka, G. & Flores, R. (in press). Caminando juntos: On intersubjectivity and the promise of participatory democracy. In Herrera, J. F., ed. (in press), *Chili con karma: Investigations on the new borderlands and other questions*. Philadelphia: Temple University Press.

Tate, W. (1997). Critical race theory and education: History, theory and implications. *Review of Research in Education*, 22, 195–247.

Taussig, M. (1987). *Shamanism, colonialism, and the wild man: A study in terror and healing.* Chicago: University of Chicago Press.

Taylor, D. (1991). Transculturating transculturation. In Marranca, B. & Dasgupta, G., eds., *Interculturalism & performance*, New York: PAJ Publications.

Tax, S. (1958). The Fox project. *Human Organization*, 17, 17–19.

———— (1975). Action anthropology. *Current Anthropology*, 116(4), 514–517.

Tedlock, B. (1984). The beautiful and the dangerous: Zuni ritual and cosmology as an aesthetic system. *Conjuctions*, 6, 246–265.

Tharp, R. G., Estrada, P., Dalton, S. S., & Yamauchi, L. (2000). *Teaching transformed: Achieving excellence, fairness, inclusion, and harmony.* Boulder, CO: Westview Press.

Therborn, G. (1980). *The ideology of power and the power of ideology*. London: Editions and NLB.

Thompson, B. (1995). Time traveling and border crossing: Reflections on white identity. In Thompson, B. & Tyagi, S. *Names we call home: Autobiography on racial identity*. New York: Routledge.

Toyota, T. (2001, November 7). Transnational Asia America: Reconfiguring the borders of political activism. Paper presented at UCLA Anthropology Department, Haines Hall, Angeles, California.

Transition, An International Review. The white issue, 73, Durham, NC: Duke University Press.

Trevino, J. & Ewing, K. (2002). Tackling campus intergroup relations: The intergroup relations center at Arizona State University. *Diversity Digest*, summer, 02, 6–7, 11.

Trinh T. M. (1990). Not you/Like you: Post-colonial women and the interlocking questions of identity and difference. In Anzaldua, G. ed., *Making face, making soul–haciendo caras: Creative and critical perspectives by feminists of color*. San Francisco: aunt lute books.

———— (1991). *When the moon waxes red: Representation, gender and cultural politics*. New York: Routledge.

Tsing, A. L. (1993). *In the realm of the diamond queen: Marginality in an out-of-the-way place.* Princeton, NJ: Princeton University Press.

Tyler, S.A. (1986). Post-modern ethnography: From document of the occult to occult document. In Clifford, J. & Marcus, G., eds., *Writing cultures*. Berkeley, CA: University of California Press.

———— (1987). *The unspeakable: Discourse, dialogue and rhetoric in the postmodern world.* Madison, WI: University of Wisconsin Press.

United States v. Carolene Products Co., 304 U.S. 144 (1938).

Unity & Difference (1999, fall). 1(1).

University of California (1993). A declaration of community: Report of the universitywide campus community task force, Berkeley, CA.

Vidal, G. (2003, February 15). Speech on democracy and despotism. Hollywood, CA.

Vigil, J. D. & Roseman, C. (1998). Ethnicity and place: Combining anthropological and geographical perspectives on ethnicity in America. Paper presented at the annual meeting of the American Anthropological Association, Philadelphia, PA.

Visweswaran, K. (1994). *Fictions of feminist ethnography.* Minneapolis: University of Minnesota Press.

Voloshinov, V. N. (1973/1929). *Marxism and the philosophy of language.* Cambridge, MA: Harvard University Press.

Wagner, R. (1975). *The invention of culture.* Chicago: University of Chicago Press.

———— (2001). *An anthropology of the subject.* Berkeley: University of California Press.

Wai Young, L. (1982). Inscrutability revisited. In Gumperz, J., ed., *Language and social identity.* London: Cambridge University Press.

Warren, M. R. (2001). *Dry bones rattling: Community building to revitalize American democracy.* Princeton, N.J.: Princeton University Press.

Weis, L. & Centrie, C. (2002). On the power of separate spaces: Teachers and students writing (righting) selves and future. *American Educational Research Journal,* 39(1), 7–36.

West, C. (1993). *Race Matters.* Boston: Beacon Press.

White, M. & Epston, D. (1990). *Narrative means to therapeutic ends.* New York: W.W. Norton & Company.

Williams, P.J. (1991). *The alchemy of race and rights: Diary of a law professor.* Cambridge, MA: Harvard University Press.

Willis, P. (1977). *Learning to labor: How working class kids get working class jobs.* New York: Columbia University Press.

———— (1990). *Common culture.* Boulder, Colorado: Westview Press.

Witherell, C. & Noddings, N., eds. (1991). *Stories lives tell: Narrative and dialogue in education.* New York: Teachers College Press.

Wood, D. R. (2000). Narrating professional development: Teachers' stories as texts for improving practice. *Anthropology & Education Quarterly,* 31(4), 426–448.

Woolard, K. A. & Schieffelin, B. B. (1994). Language ideology. *Annual Review of Anthropology,* 23, 55–82.

Young, R. J. C. (1990). *White mythologies: Writing history and the West.* London: Routledge.

———— (1995). *Colonial desire: Hybridity in theory, culture and race.* New York: Routledge.

Zinsser, W. (1988). *On writing well: An informal guide to writing nonfiction.* New York: Harper & Row.

INDEX

Studies in the Postmodern Theory of Education

General Editors
Joe L. Kincheloe & Shirley R. Steinberg

Counterpoints publishes the most compelling and imaginative books being written in education today. Grounded on the theoretical advances in criticalism, feminism, and postmodernism in the last two decades of the twentieth century, Counterpoints engages the meaning of these innovations in various forms of educational expression. Committed to the proposition that theoretical literature should be accessible to a variety of audiences, the series insists that its authors avoid esoteric and jargonistic languages that transform educational scholarship into an elite discourse for the initiated. Scholarly work matters only to the degree it affects consciousness and practice at multiple sites. Counterpoints' editorial policy is based on these principles and the ability of scholars to break new ground, to open new conversations, to go where educators have never gone before.

For additional information about this series or for the submission of manuscripts, please contact:

> Joe L. Kincheloe & Shirley R. Steinberg
> c/o Peter Lang Publishing, Inc.
> 275 Seventh Avenue, 28th floor
> New York, New York 10001

To order other books in this series, please contact our Customer Service Department:

> (800) 770-LANG (within the U.S.)
> (212) 647-7706 (outside the U.S.)
> (212) 647-7707 FAX

Or browse online by series:
> www.peterlangusa.com